CW00677772

Total War

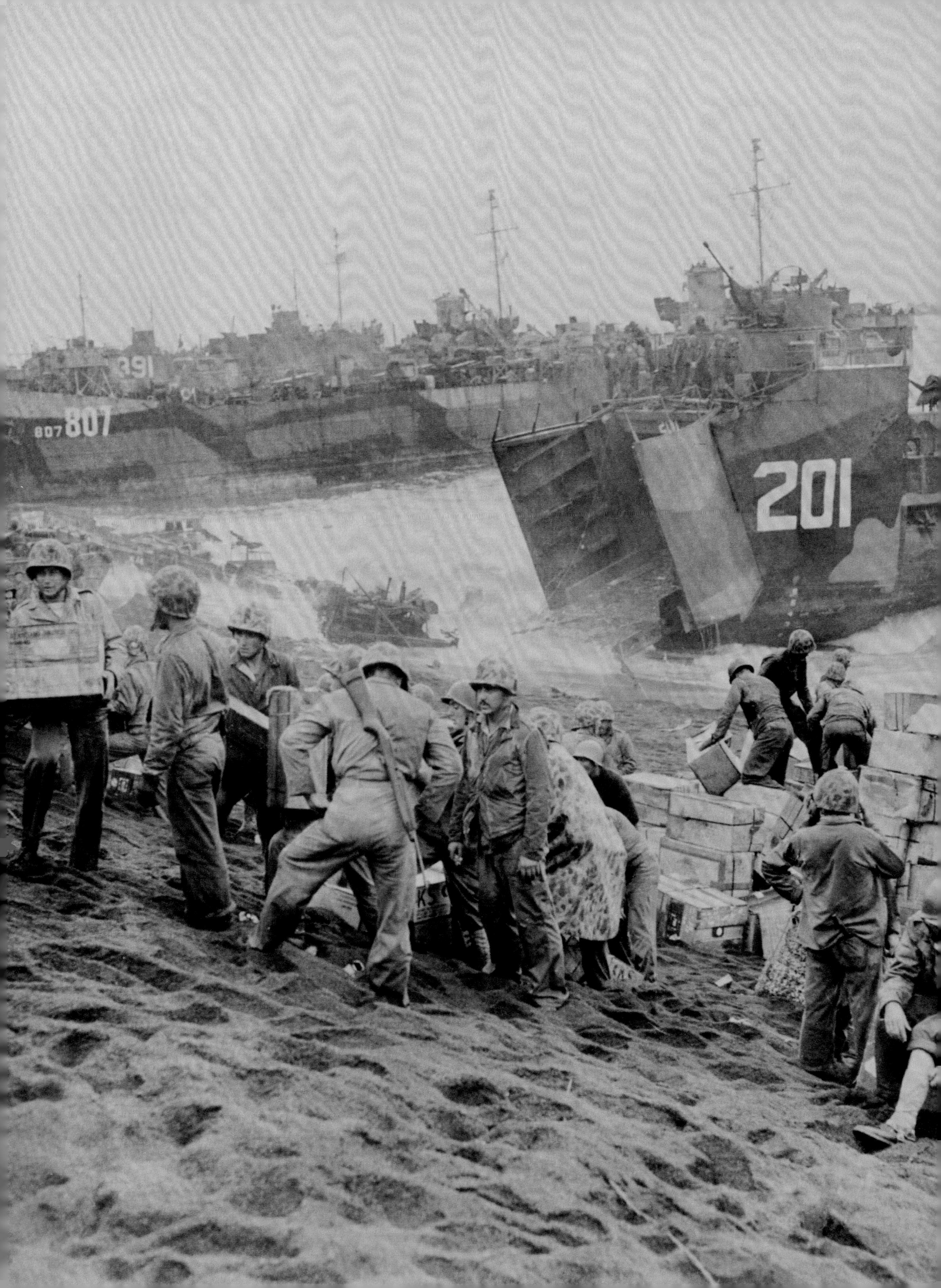
391
807
807
201

Total War

A People's History of the Second World War

Kate Clements, Paul Cornish and Vikki Hawkins

Foreword by Margaret MacMillan

With 390 illustrations

FOREWORD

MARGARET MACMILLAN

INTRODUCTION

PEACE LOST

WAR ENGULFS EUROPE

BRITAIN'S WAR

GLOBAL WAR

VICTORY IN THE BALANCE

THE END AND AFTER

Foreword   Margaret MacMillan

The Second World War was a total and a global war. Millions of men and women were mobilized, and vast numbers moved about the world. Economies worked at full tilt to churn out the hundreds of thousands of trucks, armoured vehicles, aeroplanes, ships and countless other goods, from ammunition to socks, that the war effort needed. Governments harnessed science and technology to produce new devices, medicines and weaponry: the jet engine, radar, penicillin, the atomic bomb. There was fighting around the globe – in the Arctic and the African deserts, on mountains, plains and in jungles, and on land, sea and in the air.

The war was even more far-reaching in its scale and scope than the First, and we still live with its consequences. It remains, too, in our imaginations and memories. We may have read some of the hundreds of histories and memoirs, looked at the photographs and films, listened to the music from the time, or visited the great war memorials or museums. We may even have memorabilia, an old uniform or gun brought home by a family member. Yet there will always be more to learn and understand.

The story of the Second World War is one not only of grand strategy and epic battles, but also of the countless individuals whose lives were destroyed or altered forever. The conflict was fought across peaceful fields and through cities and towns. It was waged by brute force and by brains. It could not have been won for the Allies without the heroic Soviet soldiers of Stalingrad or the codebreakers at Bletchley. It was fought with great bravery and great cruelty. We remember the millions of deaths and the atrocities. We remember the big battles – the Normandy landings, El Alamein, Iwo Jima – but so many more are now half-forgotten, like those of the Burma campaign or in the Balkans.

Those of us who have known only peace wonder how people endured and survived, whether it was the privations, the innumerable nights sleeping in makeshift shelters, the destruction of their cities, or the weary months and years of rebuilding. Patriotism helped to mobilize the British when they stood against Germany, and the Russians resisted the German invasion out of love of Mother Russia. Ideologies – of race, religion and ethnic nationalism – also played their part, helping to turn many fronts into bloodlands where international conventions no longer held, and the enemy was seen as less than human. The Japanese prison guards treated their Western captives brutally because they despised them. The Nazis worked their Slavic forced labourers to death and set out to exterminate the Jews.

The old distinction between the home and the battle front largely vanished. Civilians were no longer seen as non-combatants but as part of the war machine, and so they became targets too. Even in the First World War, destroying the enemy's morale and capacity to fight had been an important strategy, but by the Second the means to do so were much greater. All sides used propaganda, delivered by dropping leaflets or via radio broadcasts, to urge the enemy to give up. With the advent of more advanced weapons, from increasingly powerful bombers to the bombs they carried, it was now possible to destroy the enemy's factories, railways, dams, houses – and people. Older siege-and-starvation tactics were also used. Leningrad (now St Petersburg again) endured for almost nine hundred days with a terrible loss of life. Hitler's submarines tried to sever the crucial link across the Atlantic that fed the British and their war effort.

The war had so many faces and was experienced in so many ways. Those who lived in countries under occupation endured the humiliation of defeat, the commandeering of essentials such as food, and the imposition of forced labour to keep their conquerors fully supplied. The occupied lived always with the fear of reprisals – mass executions and villages destroyed – yet many still found ways of resisting. In unoccupied Britain the threat of German invasion may have waned by 1941, but the death and destruction fell from the skies until the end. The war's impact was also felt in the government's increasing control over society and its resources. Rationing and strict controls on imports helped to ensure that the British people had enough to eat and that supplies for the war effort kept pouring across the Atlantic. As they had done in the First World War, women stepped into men's jobs, often bearing the extra burden of still caring for their families.

In the course of the war, two separate conflicts – one in Europe and the other in Asia – had merged into a global one, with dozens of countries and their peoples drawn in. From the Americas to the Pacific, Europe to the Far East, the Middle East to Africa, the war had upended governments, shattered communities, and left a vast trail of death and devastation. Few parts of the world, and few people, had not been touched by it, either directly or indirectly. As this book shows so vividly, this was a total war: total in the aims of many of its belligerents, total in the demands it placed on societies, and total in its impact. After six long years of struggle, the global death toll was 60 million; much of the world lay in ruins; and millions of desperate refugees were seeking safety.

The aftermath of the war also forms part of the story told here. The Allies undertook to hold the leaders of the defeated nations to account in a series of war-crimes trials. The Nuremburg and Tokyo trials have been much criticized since, but they established the principle that leaders could be tried for genocide and crimes against humanity. The end of the war brought hope as well: that the lessons of the past could be learned, and a better and fairer world created. Many of those hopes of 1945 came to fruition, from greater European cooperation to the founding of the United Nations. Others, however, did not, as a new form of conflict with a new name came to divide the world. Among the many legacies of the Second World War was the Cold War between the United States and the Soviet Union, which grew out of the tensions in the wartime alliance against the Axis and out of competing goals and values. Now that the Cold War too has ended, we have the necessary distance to think again about the Second World War, and about what it meant – and continues to mean – to us all. This book will help us do just that.

Introduction

What is total war? There is no simple dictionary definition, but today we would probably characterize it as a form of war that reaches beyond the battlefield, and which requires the mobilization of the economies and societies of the combatants. It is a form of war in which civilians play as vital a role as servicemen and -women, and in which they are likely to be targeted by their country's enemies. It is a form of war where little respect is paid to international laws and conventions, and where the line between lawful killing and murder is blurred. We can apply this definition so readily because we have in our minds the not-so-distant example of the Second World War – a conflict in which 60 million people died, the majority of whom were not in uniform. It was, and remains, the archetype of total war.

The phrase 'total war', or *guerre totale* in French and *totale Krieg* in German, was freely used in the period between the First and Second World Wars. Theorists and politicians sought to influence military strategy or public policy by sharing their visions of it. Meanwhile, popular novelists generated apocalyptic imaginings of the impact of such a war. At the time, public fears and government preparations concentrated largely on the threat of aerial bombardment. And they did not focus merely on defence. The oft-quoted statement by the British interwar prime minister Stanley Baldwin that 'the bomber will always get through' is seldom coupled with his further assertion that 'the only defence is in offence, which means that you have to kill more women and children more quickly than the enemy if you want to save yourselves'. Across the world many civilians were already being targeted from the air, and many more were able to see the effects as they watched newsreels covering fighting in China, Ethiopia and Spain. It could be argued that, when the global conflict finally arrived, the effects of aerial bombing struggled to live up to their pre-war billing – or, to be specific, that the anticipated number of casualties per ton of high explosives had been overestimated. Equally, however, it can be claimed that, in almost every other aspect, the strains and the horrors of total war far exceeded people's worst imaginings.

Central to the writing of this book, from the outset, was a desire to place Britain's war in a global context. We do not offer a starting date for the war. In the UK, the focus has always fallen on 3 September 1939, when Britain and France declared war on Germany. But for Poland, this was already day three of more than five years of national martyrdom. And what of the people of Ethiopia, who had been living under a brutal Italian occupation since their country succumbed to invasion in 1935–36, or of the vast population of China, facing a third year of war against the invading Japanese? For millions, therefore, the war had begun before 1939; and for a similar portion of the world's population, the death, destruction and dislocation of war did not simply come to a halt in 1945.

We also take the view that the Holocaust was a central element of the war, and that it was the war that provided both the milieu and the impetus for this terrible crime against humanity. Consequently, in this book, the Holocaust is treated as an integral part of the narrative. Although for many people – either as perpetrators or victims – the Second World War was a racial war, this was not something that featured in people's pre-war fears of total war; nor has it been a strong feature of traditional anglophone public memories of the conflict. It is a deficiency that we hoped to address.

We were aware too that in Britain, as well as in most other countries, public understanding of the Second World War has a tendency to be nationalistic, even parochial. In creating a new representation of the war for the twenty-first century, we therefore sought to offer a more global and diverse

Soldiers of the Norwegian Army during Germany's invasion of their country in 1940.

9

picture. From a British perspective, one of the essential steps was to put the national experience of the war, as well as our own, individual experience of it, into a global context. To give just one example, it is surprising, given the centrality of the Blitz to British visualizations of the war, that relatively few people in the UK are aware of the massively greater destructive impact of the Allied Combined Bomber Offensive against Germany and its allies, let alone the analogous experience of people in such Asian cities as Chongqing or Tokyo. In recent decades there has been an increasing awareness of the immense contribution of the Soviet Union to winning the war on land against Nazi Germany, but the war in Asia and the Pacific still occupies a subsidiary place in most Western perceptions of the war. We wanted to give due prominence both to the immense and awful struggle faced by the people of China, and to Japan's extraordinary attempt to establish hegemony over huge swathes of the Eastern hemisphere.

The role and nature of imperialism also needed to be addressed. For a British audience this meant encouraging a step back from traditional engagements with 'Empire'. We wanted to look beyond the comfortable image of the various sons of the Empire marching to war 'Together', as the famous wartime poster sought to show. Fundamentally, it was the Empire, and Britain's control of the sea lanes that linked it together, that allowed the UK to fight the war as it did. Even in the dark days of 1940, Britain did not stand alone. It could exploit its imperial possessions and its loyal Dominions for money and natural resources. It could also ship its imperial manpower around the world to fight for it – Punjabis to Egypt and Italy, Nigerians to Burma, Canadians to France, to name but a few. Consequently, the people who fought or worked for the war effort were far more diverse in their origins than is generally remembered today. For instance, British soldiers in the Fourteenth Army in Burma were outnumbered four-to-one by Indian and African soldiers. Again, at the outbreak of war, a quarter of Britain's merchant seamen were so-called Lascars, recruited from India and around the shores of the Indian Ocean. Of the 103 army divisions mobilized by Britain during the war, 54 were from the Empire and Dominions, which also provided 40 per cent of RAF Bomber Command's aircrew. However, this imperial effort was never entirely voluntary and, while the war shook up the racist precepts on which much of the Empire was governed, such attitudes still prevailed. The response, or lack of it, to the Bengal famine of 1943 is just the starkest example of such a mindset.

Empire also looms large in another context. In the interwar period, the empires of Britain and France, victors of the First World War, stood at their greatest extent. We should not be surprised that they were looked upon enviously by other powers – not only Germany, which had been stripped of its imperial possessions in 1919, but also by two powers that felt they had not gained sufficient reward for being on the *winning* side in the First World War: Japan and Italy. Their desire to follow the example given by Britain and France and make themselves 'Great Powers' through imperial conquest was denounced at the time, and we still use it to apportion 'blame' for the war now. However, in their own contemporary opinion, their frustration was justified; as the Japanese foreign minister Yosuke Matsuoka put it, 'the Western powers had taught the Japanese the game of poker ... but after acquiring most of the chips, they pronounced the game immoral and took up contract bridge.'

As we now know, of course, the Second World War precipitated the end of imperialism as it then existed. While this outcome was an actual war aim of the United States, few ordinary people at the time would have predicted

Across the world, millions of civilians had to flee the fighting between Allied and Axis forces. These Belgians are leaving their homes during the Battle of the Bulge.

such world-changing consequences. Which brings us to another central precept that was applied to the writing of this book: contemporaneity. That is to say, we have represented the war as people would have seen and understood it at the time, without applying hindsight. This has allowed us not only to maintain the focus on personal experiences of the conflict, but also to avoid clogging our narrative with attempts to debunk the many myths and misconceptions that have grown up around the war since 1945. We hope, therefore, that this book will harness the immediacy and poignancy of personal stories and the multivocal eloquence of objects to stimulate a fresh way of looking at a familiar story – essentially by making it *less* familiar. We hope that you will be taken beyond cinematic representations or Internet memes and into the real war. You will find extraordinary examples of ordinary people responding to the challenges and dangers of war, together with objects – both humble and remarkable, small and large – that speak to us across the years of an even wider, shared experience of the conflict. What we cannot claim is that this will be a comfortable read. Not when our subject is an unparalleled example of the immense suffering caused by total war.

Papuan civilians carry supplies during the fighting near Wau in New Guinea in 1943. The Australian forces owed much to these men, who kept the forward troops supplied and helped to evacuate the wounded.

CHAPTER 1

PEACE LOST

INTERWAR UNREST
1938

■ Countries wishing to revise the Great War peace settlements

■ Countries wishing to maintain the settlements

▢ Democratic countries

▢ Authoritarian countries

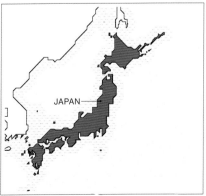

Disturbers of the Peace: Japan, Italy and Germany

Chiang Kai-shek had become the leader of China's nationalist party, the Guomindang, in 1926, following the death of its founder, Sun Yat-sen. As commander-in-chief of the National Revolutionary Army, he led a military campaign to unify China under his leadership. At the same time, he ordered the massacre of thousands of communists who had previously cooperated with his party. His attempts to unify and modernize his country attracted the sympathy of many across the world – particularly in the United States. The gentle, scholarly pose he adopts in this photograph was probably aimed at such supporters.

On 18 September 1931 a small charge of dynamite caused minor damage to a railway line near the city of Mukden (now Shenyang) in the north-eastern Chinese province of Manchuria. It had been detonated by an officer of the Japanese Army with the intention that Chinese dissidents should be blamed. Japan maintained a garrison in the region – ostensibly to protect its interests in the Japanese-controlled South Manchuria Railway. Now, using the Mukden explosion as a pretext, these troops began to expand Japanese rule over the whole of Manchuria. Within six months, the Chinese warlord-ruler of the province had been driven out and, in his place, Japan had created the puppet state of Manchukuo.

⊕ Japan's destiny?

Passionate patriotism dominated Japanese culture in the 1930s. Japan's people honoured their emperor, Hirohito, as a living god. Many took pride in the aggressive actions of their armed forces in China. Even children's clothing, such as this *chanchanko* (sleeveless jacket), could reflect militaristic sentiments. Anyone who did not sign up to this nationalist vision faced intimidation and violence.

The conquest of Manchuria did not stem from Japanese government policy. It was instigated by two army colonels who held ultra-nationalist political beliefs. Like many in the Imperial Japanese Army, they felt that Japan must expand its empire in order to gain access to the resources it needed to be a 'Great Power'. During the 1930s this military faction was able to force its aggressive policies through. They proclaimed their loyalty to Japan's ruler, Emperor Hirohito, but simultaneously distanced him from politics by stressing his semi-divine status. Politicians who opposed these 'super-patriots' were threatened with violence. Some were assassinated. As one politician put it, 'the military are like an untamed horse left to run wild. If you try head-on to stop it, you'll get kicked to death.' In imposing its vision of Japan's imperial destiny, the army enjoyed strong support from rural Japan. Most soldiers were recruited from the countryside, where their relatives were suffering great hardship due to the worldwide economic slump of the 1930s.

The creation of Manchukuo was a threat to the world order that had been established by the peace settlements agreed in the wake of the Great War of 1914–18. The League of Nations, created to resolve international disputes, refused to recognize the new state and ruled that Japan had acted unlawfully. Japan had felt slighted by the Versailles peace conference of 1919, from which it had not received the territorial gains it expected as one of the victorious Allies. Moreover, the Japanese felt insulted by the conference's refusal to apply the principle of racial equality to its decision-making. Now, according to Sadao Araki, minister of war, it was time for Japan to make its own destiny: 'the Whites have made the countries of Asia mere objects of oppression and imperial Japan should no longer let their impudence go unpunished.' It withdrew from the League of Nations, which proved powerless to enforce its ruling on Manchuria. But the Japanese super-patriots were not satisfied. With the mineral wealth of Manchuria secured, they sought to extend Japanese military control south into China.

China was recovering from a century of Western economic exploitation and a period of fragmentation in which power had been divided among regional warlords. In the mid-1920s a nationalist movement, the

China and Japan

JAPAN'S DESIRE TO EXPAND ITS EMPIRE LEADS TO WAR WITH CHINA

Japan's creation of the puppet state of Manchukuo following its invasion of Manchuria in 1931 marked the beginning of its expansion into China. Six years later, the two countries were at war.

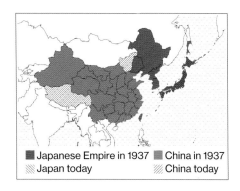

Japanese Empire in 1937 ■ China in 1937
Japan today ■ China today

REPUBLIC OF CHINA

In the mid-1920s, the nationalist Guomindang movement had begun to reunify a fragmented nation. The movement's leader, Chiang Kai-shek, claimed to govern the whole country.

TERRITORY
9.8 million km²

POPULATION
412 million

ARMY
1.7 million

EMPIRE OF JAPAN

Japan wanted to expand its empire to gain access to the resources it needed to be a 'Great Power'. Once the mineral wealth of Manchuria had been secured, it looked to extend its control into the rest of China.

TERRITORY
1.98 million km²

POPULATION
132 million

ARMY
800,000

Figures refer to China and Japan in 1937

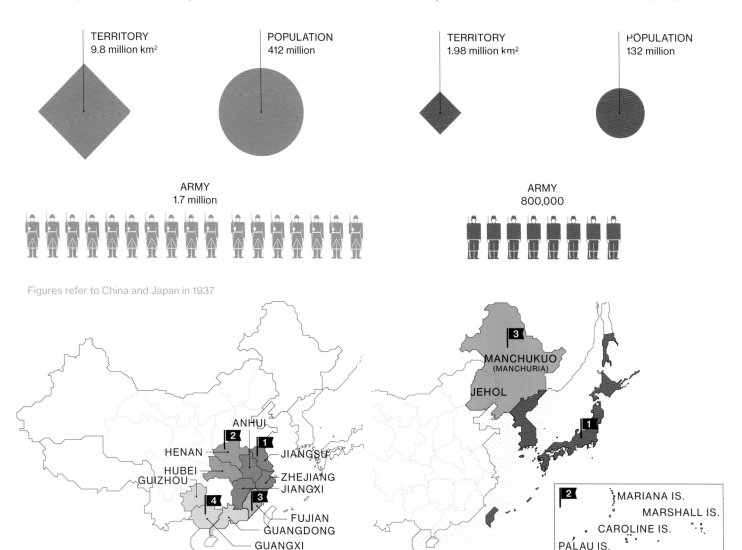

TERRITORIES UNDER CHINESE NATIONALIST CONTROL

1. ■ 1928: Anhui, Zhejiang, Jiangxi, Jiangsu
2. ■ 1929–30: Henan, Hubei
3. ■ 1934: Fujian
4. ■ 1936: Guangdong, Guangxi, Guizhou

TERRITORIES UNDER JAPANESE EMPIRE

1. ■ 1870–1910: Japanese Empire
2. ■ 1920: Mariana Is., Marshall Is., Palau Is., Caroline Is.
3. ■ 1931–32: Manchukuo, Jehol

JAPAN'S INVASION OF CHINA

Following the outbreak of war between Japan and China in 1937, Japanese troops quickly pushed south. By 1939, the conflict had become deadlocked.

JAPANESE-HELD TERRITORIES

■ Up to 1932 ■ 1937–38

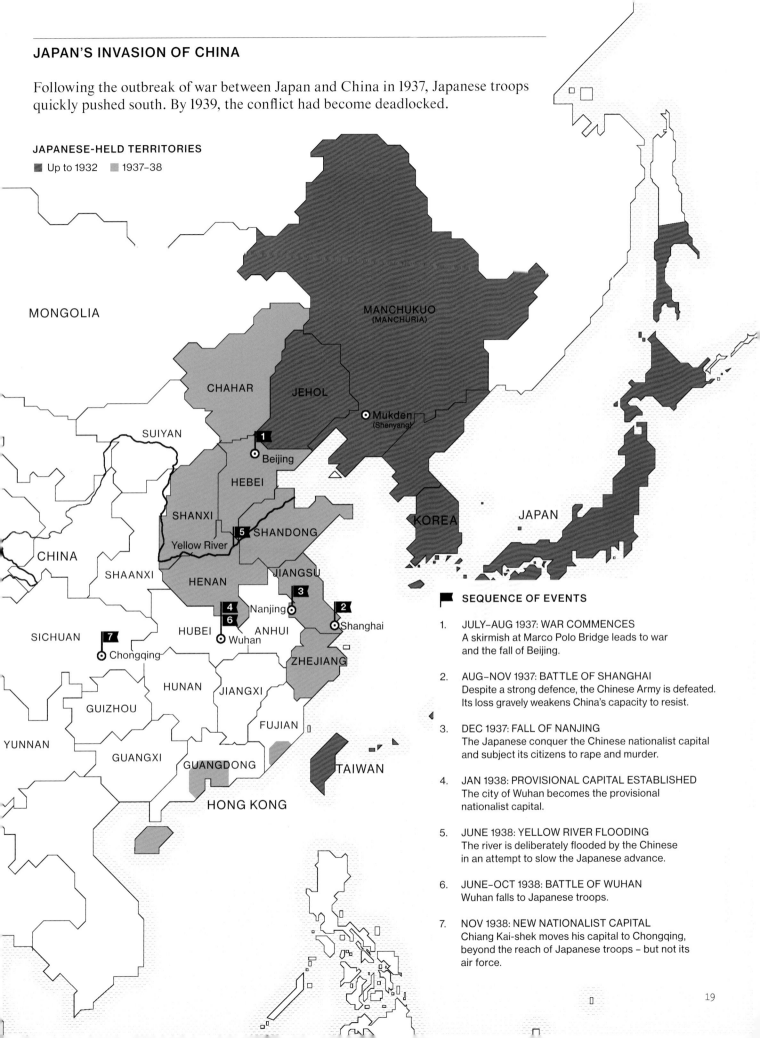

MONGOLIA

MANCHUKUO
(MANCHURIA)

CHAHAR

JEHOL

⊙ Mukden
(Shenyang)

SUIYAN

1 ⊙ Beijing

HEBEI

SHANXI

5 SHANDONG

Yellow River

CHINA

SHAANXI

HENAN

JIANGSU

3

4 ⊙ Nanjing

2

6

⊙ Shanghai

HUBEI

ANHUI

SICHUAN **7**

⊙ Chongqing

⊙ Wuhan

ZHEJIANG

HUNAN

JIANGXI

FUJIAN

GUIZHOU

YUNNAN

GUANGXI

GUANGDONG

TAIWAN

HONG KONG

KOREA

JAPAN

SEQUENCE OF EVENTS

1. JULY–AUG 1937: WAR COMMENCES
A skirmish at Marco Polo Bridge leads to war and the fall of Beijing.

2. AUG–NOV 1937: BATTLE OF SHANGHAI
Despite a strong defence, the Chinese Army is defeated. Its loss gravely weakens China's capacity to resist.

3. DEC 1937: FALL OF NANJING
The Japanese conquer the Chinese nationalist capital and subject its citizens to rape and murder.

4. JAN 1938: PROVISIONAL CAPITAL ESTABLISHED
The city of Wuhan becomes the provisional nationalist capital.

5. JUNE 1938: YELLOW RIVER FLOODING
The river is deliberately flooded by the Chinese in an attempt to slow the Japanese advance.

6. JUNE–OCT 1938: BATTLE OF WUHAN
Wuhan falls to Japanese troops.

7. NOV 1938: NEW NATIONALIST CAPITAL
Chiang Kai-shek moves his capital to Chongqing, beyond the reach of Japanese troops – but not its air force.

Guomindang, had begun to reunify China. Under its leader, Chiang Kai-shek, it now claimed to govern the whole country. In reality, Chiang was forced to make deals with local warlords and faced armed opposition from communist guerrillas. But the biggest threat to China came from Japan, which was exploiting lingering Chinese political divisions to extend its control in the north. In July 1937 a clash between Japanese and Chinese troops at the Marco Polo Bridge, north of Beijing, led to full-scale war. Neither side was willing to rein in its soldiers. While most of Japan's leaders thought that the time was ripe to exploit the riches of China, many Chinese, especially in the cities where Guomindang support was at its strongest, believed that now was the moment to make a stand against Japanese aggression.

Beijing swiftly fell to the Japanese Army, which continued a southward advance that largely followed China's railways. Meanwhile, a major battle erupted at Shanghai, where Japanese troops had landed. Shanghai, with its large International Settlement, was China's chief window to the West. Knowing that the eyes of the world were upon it, Chiang Kai-shek committed his best troops to its defence. But after a hard struggle they were defeated, with their loss gravely weakening China's capacity to resist. By the end of 1937 the Japanese had conquered the nationalist capital, Nanjing. The world looked on horrified as tens of thousands of the city's residents were subjected to mass rape and murder by the victorious Japanese soldiers. In the following summer the Japanese advanced on the industrial centre of Wuhan. Desperate to delay them long enough to evacuate his factories and government, Chiang ordered the breaking of dykes on the Yangtze River. Hundreds of thousands of the local inhabitants drowned and millions became refugees. Chiang now moved his capital south-west to Chongqing, in mountainous Sichuan province. The city lay beyond the reach of Japan's troops, although not the bombs of its air force. Chiang's aim was to refuse to negotiate with the invaders and to try to wear them out through dogged resistance. This policy began to work, with the vastness of China, and its limited transport infrastructure, frustrating Japanese ambitions. Japan sent ever more men to bolster its army but, by 1939, the war had become deadlocked – a quagmire from which Japan could not extricate itself without appearing to have been defeated. For those Chinese people enduring hunger, displacement, the forced recruitment of their sons into the army (regarded as a virtual death sentence) or Japanese occupation, the suffering appeared to have no end.

ABOVE Japanese troops prepare to scale the walls of the Chinese city of Kaifeng. The Japanese Army doubled in size during the 1930s.

OPPOSITE This Japanese air-dropped propaganda sheet shows much of China allegedly happy under Japanese control, while the Chinese nationalist leader, Chiang Kai-shek, cowers in the south-west. The English annotations were made by the British person who picked up the sheet in the port of Shantou in 1938. By 1939, Japan had conquered China's north and east, and had largely cut it off from the world by capturing its ports. China could now import goods only across its southern borders with Burma and French Indochina.

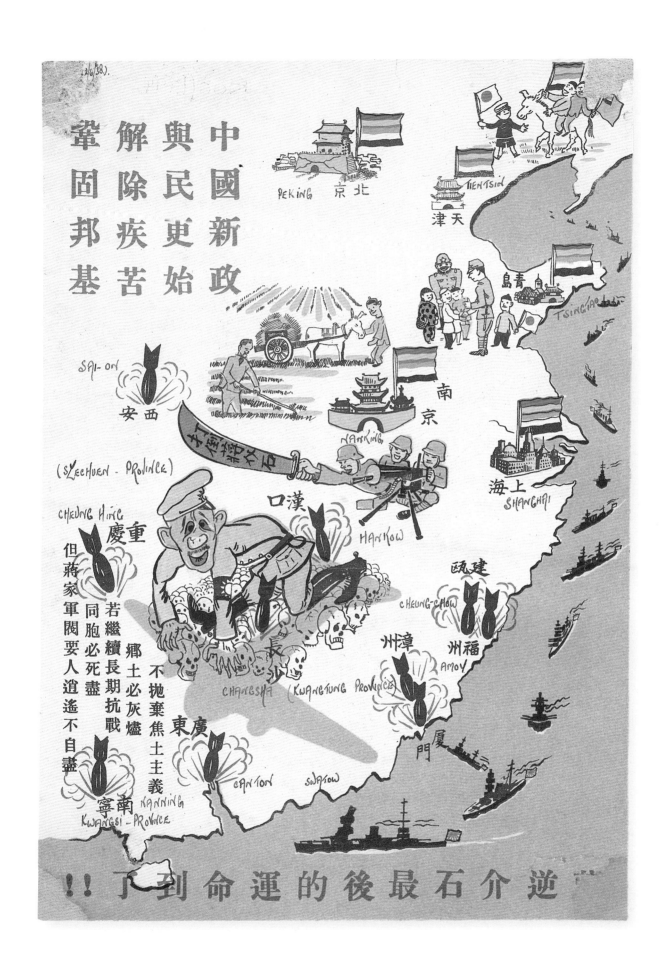

⊕ A new Roman Empire?

ABOVE Mussolini's rise to power was aided by his thuggish paramilitary supporters, the *Squadristi*, also known as the Blackshirts. By the 1930s, they had become a key part of the fascist state, as the MVSN. The uniforms and insignia of this fascist militia echoed those of the Arditi – the Italian special forces of the Great War – who, for the fascists, offered an ideal of Italian manhood. This MVSN black fez was adapted from similar headgear worn by the Arditi.

BELOW Mussolini presents a banner to the Alpine Battalion of the Blackshirts.

In Europe another dissatisfied victor of the Great War set about challenging the post-war world order. In the wake of its costly participation in the conflict, Italy had descended into political turmoil. Exploiting fears of communism and drawing on nationalist sentiment, Benito Mussolini had manoeuvred his Fascist Party into power. Fascism grew out of a right-wing reaction to the rising power of socialism. *Fasci* (named after the ancient Roman symbol of authority) were loosely connected groups of men – many of them war veterans – who were prepared to use violence against the Left. Mussolini became their figurehead and eventually welded them into a single party. He was able to do this because of his own credentials as a wounded veteran, his editorship of a newspaper that served as his mouthpiece, and his willingness to suppress his ideological excesses when necessary, in order to attract the financial and political support of the establishment. Under his leadership, fascism came to be characterized by a combination of anti-communism, nationalism, militarism and a lust for imperial expansion. In 1922, taking advantage of the desperation for political stability on the part of Italy's king and its parliament, Mussolini engineered his own appointment as prime minister. Once in control he subverted democracy and changed the constitution. By 1926 Italy had become the world's first fascist state, with Mussolini, or Il Duce, as its dictator. Opponents faced violence at the hands of Mussolini's black-shirted thugs, the *Squadristi*. Once fascism was established, the latter were transformed into a national militia, which Mussolini hoped would lead the way in creating a virile and martial 'race'. But although Italy had the outward appearance of a totalitarian state, Mussolini still had to reach accords with the king, the army and the Roman Catholic Church in order to sustain his grip on the country. The fascist regime's loudly trumpeted programmes for addressing Italy's economic problems, such as 'The Battle of the Lira' and 'The Battle for Grain', proved to be shams – although this did little to dispel growing public belief in Mussolini's personal infallibility.

Many Italians had been dismayed at the 'mutilated victory' of 1918, when Italy had not received all that had been promised by France and Britain to induce it to enter the war on their side. This grievance was exploited by Mussolini, who offered the vision of a new 'Roman Empire' in Africa and the Mediterranean basin. Italy had maintained a precarious grip on Libya since 1912, and the fascist regime was happy to resort to brutal methods to establish firm control there. Mussolini's gaze then turned to the Ethiopian Empire. He sought to avenge a humiliating defeat suffered by Italy during the previous century, when attempting to invade this independent state. In 1935, ignoring international opposition and half-hearted sanctions imposed by the League of Nations, he ordered the invasion of Ethiopia. In a bitter war, in which each side accused the other of atrocities, and in which the

This painting on antelope hide by an Ethiopian artist shows Ethiopians (left) resisting the Italian invaders (right). Among the latter are Italian colonial troops, recruited in Libya and Italian Somaliland. They are supported by aircraft. Emperor Haile Selassie of Ethiopia, in an address to the League of Nations, denounced the use of air-dropped mustard gas against his people: 'Women, children, cattle, rivers, lakes and fields were constantly drenched with this deadly rain '

Royal Italian Air Force sprayed mustard gas on Ethiopian soldiers and civilians, Ethiopia was defeated. Its emperor, Haile Selassie, was forced into exile, while the Italians established control by doing deals with local leaders and conducting vicious reprisals against any resistance. Mussolini authorized a policy of 'terror and extermination against the rebels and the accomplice population' with 'tenfold retaliation'. Meanwhile, his popularity among Italians soared to new heights.

Mussolini made another bold move by sending a large expeditionary force to aid the Nationalist rebels in the civil war that broke out in Spain in 1936. The Nationalists, who included the indigenous Spanish fascist movement, were also supported by Germany, while the left-wing government forces received aid from the Soviet Union. Europe's democracies, led by Britain and France, followed a policy of non-intervention, with their distaste for the Spanish government's politics outweighing their desire to stop the advance of fascism. By early 1939 the Nationalists had triumphed, establishing an authoritarian state under the dictatorship of General Francisco Franco. By this time many in the democratic world were beginning to reflect belatedly on the words of Haile Selassie at the League of Nations in 1936: 'it is us today, it will be you tomorrow.'

⊕ The death of German democracy

Defeat in the Great War had brought revolution to the streets of German cities and, in its wake, a weak democracy. The politicians of the so-called Weimar Republic proved unable to form stable or long-lasting administrations. Nor was the government ever able to eliminate the uniformed paramilitary organizations, representing rival political factions, that brought intimidation and violence to German streets. The republic struggled to find the money to offer the financial support that the public demanded for war-wounded men and war widows. It was also required to

ABOVE Italian SM79 bombers in Spanish Nationalist insignia, during the Spanish Civil War.

BELOW Despite displaying a nostalgia for the ancient Roman Empire, fascist Italy embraced modernism – particularly in art and architecture. This sculpture, by Renato Bertelli, is entitled *Profilo continuo di Mussolini* (Continuous Profile of Mussolini). From whatever direction it is viewed, the sculpture offers a silhouette-like profile of Il Duce, very much in the way he liked to be portrayed, with a firm, jutting jaw.

pay 'reparations' for wartime damage, imposed on it by the 1919 Versailles peace treaty, although it found ways to avoid doing so. When it defaulted in 1922, France reacted by occupying Germany's chief industrial region, the Ruhr. When workers there went on strike in protest, the German government printed money to support them, starting a period of hyper-inflation that further weakened public belief in the republic. During the second half of the 1920s the statesmanship of Gustav Stresemann began to return calm and economic stability to Germany, and also to re-establish it as an equal partner in world affairs. But in 1930 the global economic slump, which had originated in the Wall Street Crash of the previous year, hit Germany hard.

With many threatened with ruin for the third time in fifteen years (first by wartime inflation, then by the hyper-inflation of the 1920s, now by worldwide economic depression), German people increasingly looked for a radical answer to their economic suffering. They found it in the National Socialist Party, led by Adolf Hitler. Hitler was an avowed enemy of democratic government, but after failing to overthrow the Weimar Republic by means of a coup in 1923, he had resolved to take an electoral route to power. This did not mean that he had renounced violence, as he could still call on the thuggery of his paramilitary supporters, the *Sturmabteilung* (SA), known in English as the Brownshirts. His political progress was also assisted by the fact that he was a spellbinding public speaker. By 1932 he had become the single most persuasive voice in German politics. Two elections in that year established Hitler's 'Nazis' as the largest party in parliament. With no one else able to form a stable government, Germany's president, the war hero Field Marshal Hindenburg, appointed Hitler chancellor on 30 January 1933. Within weeks he was able to use the burning-down of the parliament building, following an arson attack, as a pretext for subverting the constitution. The Communist Party was suppressed, the Social Democrats intimidated, and other parties cajoled into passing an 'enabling act' that gave Hitler what amounted to dictatorial powers. These moves were backed by violence, or the threat of violence, from the Brownshirts. In the summer of 1934, however, Hitler brought the SA under tighter control by shooting the most unruly of its leaders. He took the opportunity to murder some old political enemies at the same time. Germans – inured to political violence – generally applauded this brutal imposition of 'order'. In August 1934, following the death of the aged Hindenburg, Hitler put the finishing touches to his seizure of power, combining the offices of chancellor and president in the role of Führer, and obliging the German Army to swear an unconditional oath of loyalty to him.

⊕ Nazi Germany

This portrait of Adolf Hitler, *Der Führer* (1937) by Heinrich Knirr, hung in the waiting room of the German embassy in London. While Hitler was extreme in his politics, he was notably conservative in his artistic tastes. He evidently approved of Knirr's strictly academic style, as Knirr was the only artist to be accorded the privilege of painting Hitler from life.

Austrian-born Adolf Hitler's political beliefs were influenced by the antisemitic politics that he was exposed to as a youthful drifter in Vienna, the comradeship he found during his wartime service with the German Army, and the collapse of Germany into revolution in 1918. Extreme racism was fundamental to Hitler's mentality. In his world vision, different 'races' were competing in a struggle for survival. He was determined that the German 'race', or *Volk*, would win this struggle and dominate the world. His dream was to create an empire in Eastern Europe into which the German *Volk* could expand. Hitler had a particular hatred for Jews. He created for himself a dark fantasy, which cast them as racial enemies and an insidious destructive force within Germany itself – despite the fact that only around 400,000 of Germany's 67 million citizens considered themselves to be Jewish. Almost immediately after becoming chancellor, Hitler began to make his warped vision of Germany's future a reality.

While there was widespread awareness of the racial underpinning to Hitler's politics, most Germans were persuaded to focus their attention elsewhere. There was nothing new about antisemitism in itself. By adopting unorthodox economic policies and creating a labour corps, the Nazis achieved significant success in combatting unemployment. The Nazi state also fostered a spirit of German community, or *Volksgemeinschaft*, which, at least superficially, created a society based on a community spirit that was seen as uniquely German. The Nazi Party absorbed or took over virtually every civil organization and all aspects of welfare and community activity, from the police services to the Red Cross. Scouting movements were replaced by Nazi youth organizations. Indoctrination of the young was viewed as the key to securing a Nazi future. Boys were tomorrow's soldiers, while girls would grow up to bear the many children that an expanding, warlike Germany would require. A proliferation of uniforms began to clothe an ever wider number of people, a development that, Hitler claimed, enabled Germans to 'walk together arm in arm, without regard to their station in life'. People could swagger in these uniforms at dramatically choreographed party rallies or at Germany's many traditional local festivals, which were themselves Nazified.

The counterpart to the *Volksgemeinschaft* was the persecution of those not considered to merit inclusion in it. Political enemies of Nazism were swiftly dealt with. Some fled into exile, some were murdered. Thousands were rounded up and forced to endure hard labour and brutal discipline in one of the new 'concentration camps' created to incarcerate opponents of the regime. Unsurprisingly, many people found it expedient to put aside political beliefs that contradicted Nazi philosophy. Political prisoners were soon joined in the concentration camps by others judged unworthy to

ABOVE AND RIGHT The Nazis won support by promoting a German sense of community. These lapel badges celebrate participation in trips arranged by the Nazi *Kraft durch Freude* (KdF, 'Strength through Joy') organization. By the late 1930s, the KdF was the world's largest tour operator, even owning a small fleet of passenger ships.

play a part in Nazi society – people from the Roma community, Jehovah's Witnesses, gay men and those branded as 'asocial', 'work-shy' or habitual petty criminals.

A more gradual but even more sinister programme of persecution was instituted against Germany's Jews, or, more precisely, those *defined* as Jews by Nazi race laws. These people were progressively deprived of their rights and livelihoods. As early as April 1933 Jews were expelled from the civil service and the judiciary. Subsequent laws barred them from being lawyers, teachers or university students. Jewish-owned businesses were seized and taken into state 'trusteeship'. Further indignities heaped upon Germans of Jewish descent included being banned from public swimming pools, being required to adopt the additional forenames 'Israel' or 'Sara', and even being forbidden from keeping pets. In November 1938 a night of violence, covertly encouraged by the Nazi Party, saw Jewish businesses and synagogues attacked, and Jews themselves beaten, killed or arbitrarily detained in concentration camps. This shocked the world and outraged many Germans.

One thing that had united Germans even before Hitler's rise to power was a hatred of the terms of the Treaty of Versailles. In this they could have had no more energetic champion than the Führer. Ignoring restrictions that had been placed on Germany by the peace treaty, Hitler gave orders to

expand and re-equip the army and to create an air force. The precarious early economic success of the Nazi regime was very largely the result of this massively increased military spending. In March 1936 Hitler took the highly symbolic step of ordering troops into the Rhineland – the region west of the Rhine that had been demilitarized under the terms of the peace treaty. This was a huge gamble, but it paid handsomely when the world saw that Britain and France lacked the will to enforce the treaty. By 1938, with Germany gathering strength militarily, Hitler decided on an even bolder attack on the status quo. According to the terms of the 1919 peace settlements, any union of the two German-speaking nations of Germany and Austria was expressly forbidden. Hitler, exploiting calls by Austrian Nazis for

unification with Germany, and tempted by the thought of using Austrian industry and resources to bolster his now struggling economic programme, sent his troops into Austria. This takeover, swiftly ratified by a plebiscite, passed off without bloodshed and, once again, Britain and France did nothing to reverse it. Austria became a province of the German Reich, while its currency reserves more than wiped out the huge deficit that the German economy had racked up since 1933. Hitler had launched his takeover of Austria only after he had received confirmation that neighbouring Italy would raise no objections. By 1937 he had won over his fellow dictator Mussolini – a man who had once dismissed him as a 'garrulous monk' – and now became the dominant partner in their relationship. In November of that year, Italy had joined Germany and Japan as a signatory of the Anti-Comintern Pact – ostensibly aimed at their mutual enemy, the Soviet Union, but also, as the Italian foreign minister put it, 'unmistakably anti-British'.

ABOVE German Heinkel He 111E bombers. Germany exaggerated the power of its rapidly growing air force to intimidate its rivals.

RIGHT Hitler sought to overthrow the restrictions placed on Germany by the 1919 Versailles peace settlement. One of these restrictions prohibited the union of Germany with its German-speaking neighbour, Austria. In March 1938 Hitler ordered his troops to march into Austria, an action that was not only unopposed but also welcomed by the majority of Austrians. This poster is from the referendum – rigged to guarantee a massive 'yes' vote – held to rubber-stamp the *Anschluss*, or the 'joining' of Germany and Austria.

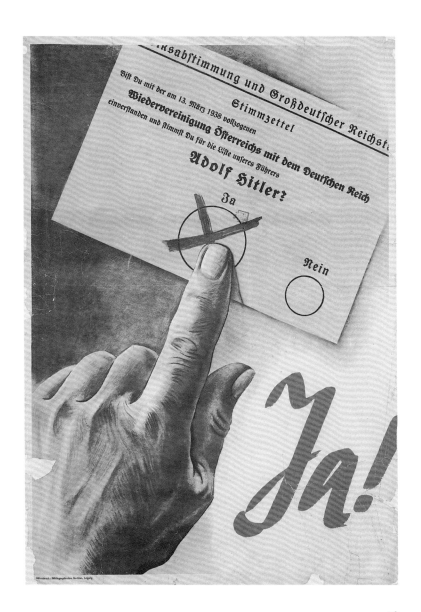

The World of the 1930s and Fear of Total War

⊕ Democracy under threat

The gigantic upheaval of the Great War had overthrown the accepted international order, smashed four empires, and created new states. The peacemakers hoped that national 'self-determination' and democratic structures would create a more stable world. But, for many, the war did not end in 1918. Revolutions and civil wars undermined hopes of democratic co-existence. Few countries were satisfied with the outcome of the war. The political turmoil of the post-war years saw some countries turn away from democracy, in favour of authoritarian rule. Above all, the world's first communist state, the Soviet Union, rose from the ashes of Imperial Russia. To many across the world, its existence was an inspiration; to others, it was a threat. Fascism was the most uncompromising response to the 'red menace'. Indeed, its origins lay in a time of social unrest that Italians called the *biennio rosso* (two red years) of 1919–20. But despite the existence of fascist movements in many countries, only in Italy and Germany did such extremists take power. In western Europe and Scandinavia (with the exception of Portugal and, eventually, Spain) democracy survived. In many other countries, the populist radicalism of fascism was kept in check – with force where necessary – by socially conservative authoritarian governments.

A further blow was dealt to democracy by the Great Depression. With its origins in the US stock market crash of 1929, this unprecedented economic crisis spread inexorably across the world. In the United States itself, unemployment and business failures rocketed. Farmers, already struggling with low crop prices, were forced from their land when banks foreclosed loans. The US government imposed high tariffs on imports, hoping to help American producers, but this merely hastened the spread of the slump to the wider world and prompted other nations to abandon free trade in favour of protectionism. American banks also called in loans that had been made abroad, notably to Germany, ensuring that the Depression struck particularly hard there. Eventually, almost the entire world – from Japanese rice farmers and British shipbuilders to Caribbean banana exporters – was stricken, as trade, agricultural prices and manufacturing slumped. As jobs became scarce, women's rights suffered, with women being increasingly forced out of the workplace. Welfare services were overwhelmed by the numbers of jobless people, and, across the world, people went hungry. Not surprisingly, many looked to politically extreme solutions to this disaster. The rise to power of the Nazis was just the most notable example of a further movement away from democracy that took place during the 1930s.

One major power appeared to be immune to the Depression: the Soviet Union. Many on the political left celebrated this as proof of the superiority of communism over capitalism. But life for the people of this 'Workers' Paradise' was every bit as grim as it was for those suffering from the slump. Soviet communism was based on the precepts of Karl Marx, but had undergone many contortions as its first leader, Lenin, had struggled to establish his regime during the chaos of the Russian Civil War (1917–22). Marx had anticipated communist revolution occurring in highly industrialized

Western Europe; Lenin, however, had tried to carry it out in a far less advanced country. From a power struggle within the Soviet leadership that followed Lenin's death in 1924, Joseph Stalin had emerged triumphant. By the 1930s he had effectively established himself as dictator of the world's most totalitarian state. He exerted a level of control that exceeded even that of the fascist dictators. Nobody, whether in the Communist Party, the armed forces or in society at large, dared to oppose him. All lived in fear of imprisonment or violent death if identified by Stalin or his henchmen as politically unreliable. This state of terror reached a climax between 1936 and 1938, when hundreds of thousands of people were executed or sent to labour camps, largely on evidence either fabricated or gathered under torture. The victims of this purge included senior political figures and army officers, as well as two chiefs of the very organization that carried it out: the NKVD, Stalin's security service.

Stalin's paranoia extended – with more reason, perhaps – to foreign powers, which, he was convinced, were ever ready to destroy the Soviet Union. In order to thwart them, he looked to transform the Soviet Union into a leading industrial and military power. He viewed the situation starkly, saying, 'we are fifty or a hundred years behind the most advanced countries. We must make good this distance in ten years. Either we do it or we shall be crushed.' He therefore instituted two successive 'five-year plans' of industrialization. By 1939 these had achieved astonishing results. To give just two examples, steel production was quadrupled, and electricity generation was increased almost tenfold. But for the Soviet people, this progress was made at great personal cost. Many in the cities faced inadequate housing, with multiple families and individuals obliged to share overcrowded communal apartments. Consumer goods were in short supply, as their production was a low priority. Worse, during the early 1930s, when Stalin ordered the rapid collectivization of agriculture to secure food for the growing urban and industrial centres, millions died of starvation in the countryside of southern Russia and, particularly, in Ukraine.

⊕ Democracy and imperialism

The presidency of the charismatic Franklin D. Roosevelt, beginning in 1933, brought new hope and confidence to the people of the United States, although the 'New Deal' he offered did not magically end the Depression. This economic nightmare would continue to haunt America for the remainder of the decade, and one of its effects was to turn the US in upon itself. Americans were already wary of the outside world, having been persuaded that their intervention in the First World War had been a costly waste of time. During the mid-1930s public opinion forced Roosevelt to sign the Neutrality Acts, aimed at keeping the United States out of foreign wars. As one senator put it, 'to Hell with Europe and with the rest of those nations.' Americans relied on their strong navy to keep them safe; the US Army was the nineteenth largest in the world, no bigger than Portugal's. An exception to this isolationism was the American public's support for China, which many regarded as a fledgling democracy deserving US protection. With America thus preoccupied, leadership of the democratic world should have fallen on the shoulders of Europe's chief democracies, Britain and

France. However, as successive failures to oppose aggression by Japan, Italy and Germany showed, they too felt unable to take on such a role.

Each had its own internal problems. France was bitterly divided politically between Left and Right. But this was seldom reflected by its governments, which were an ever changing mosaic of ministries formed from the same old faces, and which faced frequent accusations of corruption. Disdainful citizens dismissed the whole system as the 'Republic of Pals'. In 1934 violent demonstrations by extreme right-wing groups in Paris threatened to bring down the government. Within two years, however, in a startling swing of the political pendulum, a left-wing coalition was elected, which attempted to introduce radical social reforms. Its efforts were undermined by the Depression and the continuing deep political schism in France. But French democracy had survived – although only after a fashion, as women still did not have the vote.

In Britain the political extremes made even less headway against British parliamentary tradition. The noisy posturing of Sir Oswald Mosley and his British Union of Fascists may have made the headlines, but it never seriously threatened democracy. The Depression struck Britain selectively. Old industries like shipbuilding, mining and the textile business – largely based in the north – suffered badly. When shipyards and mills closed, there was seldom another local source of employment for people to turn to. The result for many was a life of poverty and hopelessness. Meanwhile, however, a new type of consumer-based industry was enjoying rapid expansion in the Midlands and the south, feeding a growing market for such commodities as radios, vacuum cleaners and even cars. House building, including state-backed schemes to replace slums with council housing, also began to help Britain out of the slump. And despite appearing to be in danger of becoming two nations in one, the British still displayed a remarkable ability to unite over national events. They shared in the trauma of the abdication of King Edward VIII, and, when his successor George VI was crowned, the festivities went on for most of May 1937.

Despite their domestic democratic traditions, Britain and France both had empires. Already huge in 1914, these empires had been augmented when the victorious Allies had carved up the former German and Ottoman empires between them in 1919. They dwarfed the colonial possessions still held by the Netherlands, Portugal and Belgium, and acted as aspirational examples for the now-expanding empires of Italy and Japan. The French Empire was largely focused on north and west Africa, although France also ruled Syria, Lebanon and modern Vietnam, Laos and Cambodia. For many French people, this empire was a symbol that France remained a great power. It was also regarded as a potential reservoir of manpower in time of war. This was especially welcome, as France was painfully aware that its low birth rate meant that it could never field as many soldiers as its rival Germany.

The British Empire was divided on racial lines. Australians, Canadians, New Zealanders and white South Africans enjoyed self-government, by virtue of living in a Dominion. Many in Britain thought that India too should be given Dominion status, but they were met with strong opposition, and Indians were accorded only very limited democratic rights. Elsewhere, particularly in Britain's African and Caribbean colonies, the inhabitants had no political voice at all. The failure to extend sufficient democratic rights to Indians encouraged the growth of a powerful Indian independence movement. This was based on non-violent protest, as advocated by the movement's most charismatic leader, Mohandas Karamchand Gandhi. In the Middle East, however, Britain was faced with rebellion. Having put down costly revolts in Egypt and Iraq in the wake of the Great War, Britain had been relieved to give them self-rule while maintaining a military presence in this strategically important region. But in Palestine, which Britain governed under a League of Nations mandate, there was a violent uprising by Arabs opposed to growing Jewish immigration. Even more worryingly for Britain, the Dominions followed increasingly independent paths – as indeed they had been permitted to do under the Statute of Westminster 1931. Britain could still claim sovereignty over a quarter of the world's people, but it could no longer count on their unquestioning submission to its leadership.

Hitler's March to War

⊕ Europe's last year of peace

Hitler had re-armed and expanded Germany with minimal opposition from Europe's other powers. But he had never envisaged that German dominance would be established peacefully. He was fully prepared to go to war – eager, even, as he harboured fears that he might die before he could lead Germany to greatness. Having absorbed Austria, he set his mind on the destruction of neighbouring Czechoslovakia. Hitler regarded this democratic state as a 'lie', created by the hated 1919 peace settlement. Significantly, it also possessed valuable natural resources and highly developed industry. As an excuse for military action, he used the presence in Czechoslovakia of a large minority of German speakers, the so-called Sudeten-Germans. They lived chiefly in regions bordering the German Reich. Hitler, backed by Sudeten-German Nazis, claimed that this minority was oppressed. He hoped to stir up so much unrest in Czechoslovakia (where tensions also existed between Czechs and Slovaks) that he could invade it on the pretext of restoring order.

Britain and France were increasingly aware of the threat posed by a resurgent Germany, although their leaders had only a limited understanding of both the nature of the Nazi regime and Hitler's megalomaniac and racist world view. Czechoslovakia was an ally of France, but France felt itself too weak to confront Germany alone. It needed to act in concert with Britain, with the result that French foreign policy increasingly took its lead from Britain's. Both countries made it clear to Hitler that they would not stand aside if he used violence against Czechoslovakia. As Hitler's threats against the Czechs mounted, the British prime minister, Neville Chamberlain, took the dramatic step of flying to Germany to speak to Hitler in person. Chamberlain found little to admire about the Führer, describing him as 'the commonest little dog' he had ever met. But in common with the great majority of British people, he wanted to preserve peace at almost any cost. The two leaders discussed the possibility of Czechoslovakia ceding to Germany the areas where German-speakers formed a majority. Hitler still threatened war but hesitated when he realized that, without a pretext for launching an invasion, he would be diplomatically isolated.

ABOVE Neville Chamberlain's efforts to avoid war by finding a compromise with Hitler made the British prime minister a hero, as this commemorative plate shows. He was even cheered by Germans when he arrived for the Munich Conference, at which Germany's annexation of the Czech territory of Sudetenland was agreed. Many in Britain believed that he had 'saved civilization'. As time passed, however, the Munich Conference came to be seen as a 'betrayal', since Czechoslovakia itself had been given no say. Forced to hand over territory, it was left almost defenceless.

RIGHT In Munich, Chamberlain asked Hitler to join him in signing this document declaring the 'desire of our two peoples never to go to war with one another again'. On his return to Britain, Chamberlain announced that it represented 'peace for our time'. But within hours he began to regret this claim, which he realized had been prompted by euphoria stimulated by the cheering crowds that greeted his return.

OPPOSITE This handkerchief celebrates the twentieth anniversary of the foundation of Czechoslovakia. The only democratic state in central Europe, Czechoslovakia was ethnically diverse, and some of its people resented the political power of its Czech majority. Discontent among Czechoslovakia's large German minority was exploited by Hitler. He ordered the local Nazi Party to make impossible demands on the Czech government, hoping to create a situation in which the German Army could invade to 'restore order'.

Prompted by Britain, Mussolini offered to broker a settlement. This led to the Italian chairing a conference between Britain, France and Germany in Munich on 29 September 1938. Here it was agreed that the Sudeten-German lands would be ceded to Germany. The Czech government was given no voice at the conference, but was persuaded by Britain and France to accept its outcome. Significantly, the regions handed over to Germany held not only most of Czechoslovakia's German-speakers, but also most of its strong border defences. The Munich agreement was welcomed with relief by many people across Europe, who had feared a war. But there was revulsion too, at the way in which Britain and France had been complicit in the bullying of a small democratic state. More than one British commentator used the expression 'peace without honour'. Hitler himself was furious at having been 'cheated' out of a military campaign. In March 1939, ignoring the Munich agreement, he ordered his troops into Czechoslovakia, which, with its defences already undermined, succumbed without a fight. The Czech lands became a protectorate of the Reich; Slovakia became a puppet state of Germany.

> We, the German Führer and Chancellor and the British Prime Minister, have had a further meeting today and are agreed in recognising that the question of Anglo-German relations is of the first importance for the two countries and for Europe.
>
> We regard the agreement signed last night and the Anglo-German Naval Agreement as symbolic of the desire of our two peoples never to go to war with one another again.
>
> We are resolved that the method of consultation shall be the method adopted to deal with any other questions that may concern our two countries, and we are determined to continue our efforts to remove possible sources of difference and thus to contribute to assure the peace of Europe.

Neville Chamberlain

September 30, 1938.

This scarf celebrates Germany's expansion between 1935 and 1939. It shows Austria incorporated into the Reich as 'Ostmark'; the Czech lands as the *Reichsprotektorat* of Bohemia and Moravia; and Slovakia as a puppet state. Also shown is Memelland, a slice of territory lost to Germany after the First World War that Hitler forced Lithuania to hand over in March 1939.

The next barrier to Hitler's empire-building was Poland. Once again, he disguised his designs for outright conquest by focusing on issues that he claimed were of vital interest to Germany. The Treaty of Versailles had separated East Prussia from the rest of Germany to create a coastline for Poland, and its major port, Danzig, had been made a 'free city' under the protection of the League of Nations. Hitler demanded the return of Danzig to German rule. Britain and France, outraged at Hitler's treatment of the Czechs, decided that the time had come to make a stand. They guaranteed Poland against German attack. This was ironic: having ignored the plight of democratic Czechoslovakia, Britain and France were now pledging to go to war to preserve authoritarian Poland – a country that had been pleased to snap up a juicy titbit of Czech territory when Germany had dismembered Czechoslovakia.

The outcome of the Czechoslovakian crisis had persuaded Britain and France that war with Germany was very likely to occur in the not-too-distant future. Their people, for whom the slaughter of the Great War was still a vivid memory, had long lived with the fear that war would return, and that this time it would be a 'total war', in which civilians would suffer as much as fighting men. Chief among the terrors that people imagined such a war would bring was aerial bombardment. Popular culture reflected this fear. A deadly, unprovoked bombing attack on Britain featured in the 1936 science-fiction film *Things to Come* (based on a 1933 H. G. Wells novel), while in *The Menace of the Clouds*, written in 1937, Lionel Charlton insisted that 'the very heart of a country now lies open to a peculiarly horrible form of attack which neither science nor invention can prevent'. Newsreels reinforced public concern by showing the bombing of Chinese towns by Japan and, later, the bombing of Madrid and Barcelona by German and Italian aircraft

ABOVE This doll, Trixie, was brought to Britain by Inga Pollak, a twelve-year-old Jewish refugee from Vienna. In late 1938 British campaigners had persuaded the government to accept unaccompanied Jewish child refugees. Eventually, 10,000 children were admitted to Britain under the *Kindertransport* (children's transport) scheme. Each child travelled with a single small suitcase, leaving their loved ones behind to an uncertain future.

RIGHT This die-cast model Hurricane, part of the Dinky Toys range, reflects the rapid improvements made to Britain's air defences in the late 1930s. Two new monoplane fighters, the Hawker Hurricane and the Supermarine Spitfire, were among the best in the world. New anti-aircraft guns went into production, and a technologically advanced electronic early warning system – radar – was developed.

during the Spanish Civil War. The destruction of the small Basque town of Guernica by German bombers made a powerful impact. German rearmament and the Nazis' eagerness to trumpet the alleged might of Germany's new air force, the Luftwaffe, brought fears of attack even closer to home. Strong pacifist sentiment existed in both Britain and France, and was prominently promoted in the former from 1934 onwards by the Peace Pledge Union. However, there was widespread public support when the obvious menace posed by Nazi Germany induced both governments to hasten the rearmament of their countries. Defence industries were brought under closer government control and new factories were built to enable the further expansion of production if war came. Britain in particular poured resources into improving its air defences. Gas masks were issued to civilians, who were also encouraged to volunteer their services to new air-raid precaution organizations. In a highly symbolic act, which brought back memories of the Great War, Britain introduced a limited measure of conscription in April 1939. The Military Training Act meant that, once again, British men would be obliged by law to take up arms.

Nazi Germany's unrelenting persecution of Jews and political opponents drove many of them to seek safe havens abroad. The November Pogrom of 1938 gave a powerful impetus to German Jews to leave if they could. The imposition of Nazi rule in Austria and the Czech lands brought persecution to new and substantial Jewish communities. While emigration was still possible for these people, the Nazi state ensured that they could take little with them in the way of money or possessions. The resulting penniless refugees found that much of the world was unwilling to take them in. Britain, with some reluctance, admitted around 50,000 Jewish refugees. There was considerable public criticism of this decision, with fears being stoked of refugees 'stealing' British jobs. Adult refugees were generally allowed into the UK only if they could prove that they had financial support, or had an offer of employment in the types of work that struggled to fill vacancies, such as domestic service or agricultural labour.

CELIA HORWITZ

In December 1938, Celia 'Cilly' Horwitz, a twelve-year-old Jewish girl, left Hamburg in Germany under the *Kindertransport* scheme. While living with a foster family in London, Cilly received this letter from her father, Walter. In it, he encourages her to reply in English.

Cilly's foster family did not get on with her and sent her to a refugee hostel. When the British wartime evacuation of children began, Cilly had to move yet again – this time along with her schoolmates to rural Norfolk.

Cilly's mother survived the war, but her father was deported to his death at Maly Trostenets, a Nazi extermination camp just outside Minsk, in late 1941.

Walter Horwitz   Hamburg 13.d.24.6.39.
                                   Dillstr.16 .

My dear sweet Cilly .

            How happy have you made me with your photo .
            Dearling, you look very fine and I am very
prond of such a big daughter.

            Be very brave to your foster- parents .
            I am very happy to know that you are
happy and healthy . Mutti will be satisfeid to hear so many good
things from you .

            Please write many English letters to me
that is a useful exercise for me .

            With thousand kisses for you I am ,
                 yours loving
                      Papi.

KATE WOHL

Fearing for her future as a Jew in Germany, nineteen-year-old Kate Wohl sought refuge in Britain. Under UK law she was considered an adult and was not permitted to enter the country unless she had a guarantee of work.

Like many other Jewish refugees, Kate was forced to accept the kind of menial job for which there was a shortage of British applicants. In 1939 she began working as a cook for a British family. She used this recipe book that she had brought with her from Germany, adding English recipes as she went along.

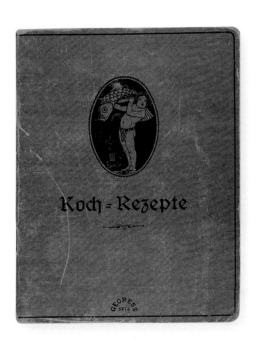

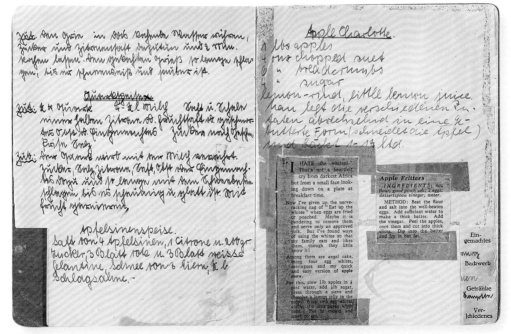

VIRGINIA COWLES

As a young US journalist, Virginia Cowles made a name for herself reporting the Spanish Civil War. She continued to report from across Europe as a wider war threatened. Well-connected socially, she met leading figures on both sides of Europe's political divide.

In April 1939 she wrote this report after visiting Eastern Europe. It offers a penetrating analysis of Stalin's cautious foreign policy, which 'shelved' the Soviet Union's 'ideological crusade' so that 'today its allegiance is bound to the Soviet Fatherland and its energies tuned to the cry of self-defence'.

Virginia's portrait was taken by the British society photographer Angus McBean.

```
N-A-N-A---39. COWLES NO. 1.
        RELEASE PM PAPERS WITH NO SUNDAY EDITION, SATURDAY, APRIL 8.
            AM PAPERS                            SUNDAY,   APRIL 9.
MANAGING EDITOR:
                THIS IS THE FIRST OF TWO ARTICLES ON SOVIET RUSSIA'S
MILITARY STRENGTH. THE SECOND WILL BE FOR RELEASE MONDAY, APRIL 10,
BUT IT MAY BE COMBINED WITH THE FIRST ARTICLE IF YOU CHOOSE.

            SOVIET ARMY WEAKENED
              BY PURGE OF OFFICERS


PRECEDE:
        SOVIET RUSSIA'S MILITARY POWER AND THE EFFECTS OF
    THE "PURGE" ON THE RED ARMY ARE EXAMINED HERE IN THE
    FIRST OF TWO ARTICLES BY A CORRESPONDENT OF THE LONDON
    TIMES WHO RECENTLY RETURNED TO ENGLAND AFTER A VISIT TO
    MOSCOW AND OTHER PARTS OF RUSSIA.

                            END PRECEDE


    BY VIRGINIA COWLES
    COPYRIGHT,1939, BY THE LONDON TIMES AND THE NORTH AMERICAN NEWSPAPER
            ALLIANCE, INC.    WORLD COPYRIGHT RESERVED.


    LONDON, APRIL 8.---DURING THE LAST TWENTY YEARS THE FOREIGN POLICY
OF THE SOVIET UNION HAS SWUNG LIKE A PENDULUM FROM AN AGGRESSIVE
POLICY OF WORLD REVOLUTION TO A NEGATIVE POLICY OF SELF-DEFENSE.
THIS "BOULEVERSEMENT" IS DUE LESS TO A CHANGE IN SOVIET PHILOSOPHY
THAN TO THE INTERNAL DIFFICULTIES WITH WHICH THE REGIME IS BESET.
    PEACE IS ESSENTIAL TO STALIN'S PROGRAM OF INDUSTRIALIZATION,
AND, WITH THE NATION'S FRONTIERS MENACED BY A GROWING THREAT
IN BOTH THE EAST AND THE WEST, THE SOVIET UNION HAS THROWN ITS
DIPLOMATIC WEIGHT ON THE SCALES OF THE NON-AGGRESSIVE POWERS.  IT
HAS TEMPORARILY SHELVED ITS IDEOLOGICAL CRUSADE AND DISCARDED
ITS OATH TO THE INTERNATIONAL WORLD PROLETARIAT; TODAY ITS
ALLEGIANCE IS BOUND TO THE SOVIET FATHERLAND AND ITS ENERGIES
TUNED TO THE CRY OF SELF-DEFENSE.
    THE EFFECTIVENESS OF RUSSIAN ARMAMENTS AND THE STRIKING POWER OF
THE RED ARMY HAVE BEEN A MATTER OF CONSIDERABLE SPECULATION.  THE RED
ARMY IS NUMBERED AT OVER 2,000,000, WHILE IT IS ESTIMATED THAT IN THE
EVENT OF A GENERAL MOBILIZATION 12,000,000 MEN COULD BE PLACED IN
THE FIELD.
        (MORE)
```

⊕ Outbreak

When Hitler heard of the Anglo-French guarantee to protect Polish sovereignty, he exploded: 'I will cook them a stew that they will choke on!' Few at the time would have anticipated his subsequent course of action. Any attack on Poland would have to take into consideration the stance of the Soviet Union. Poised directly to the east of Poland, the huge Soviet Army might intervene. Britain and France made a tentative attempt to secure an agreement with Stalin to this effect, although centuries of hatred and suspicion of Russia meant that Poland would never willingly request such assistance. But Hitler moved more decisively. Putting aside the ideological war he had always fought against communism, he proposed a cynical pact with Stalin that would see Germany and the Soviet Union divide up Eastern Europe between them. Stalin was also willing to put political principle aside in the interests of shoring up the Soviet Union's western defences. On 23 August 1939, a German–Soviet non-aggression pact was signed in Moscow. This ideological somersault amazed the whole world, not least the citizens of both signatories. As Stalin said to the German foreign minister, Joachim von Ribbentrop, 'we have been pouring buckets of shit over each other's heads for years now ... are we to make our peoples believe all is forgotten and forgiven?' Safe in the knowledge that Stalin would assist, rather than hinder, him, Hitler gave the order for the invasion of Poland. The German armed forces attacked on 1 September 1939. With the previous year's Czechoslovakia crisis still fresh in his mind, Hitler refused to believe that the British and French would intervene. When he was given the news that they intended to stand by their pledge to Poland and declare war on Germany, the Führer turned to Ribbentrop with a 'savage look' and asked, 'What now?'

A beaming Joseph Stalin at the signing of the Nazi–Soviet non-aggression pact in Moscow on 23 August 1939. Germany's foreign minister, Joachim von Ribbentrop, is on the far left of the photograph; his Soviet counterpart, Vyacheslav Molotov, stands on the far right.

WAR ENGULFS EUROPE

EUROPE
SEPT 1939–JUNE 1940

- German Reich
- German-occupied territories
- Soviet Union
- Soviet annexations

INVADED TERRITORIES

1. Poland: 1 Sept 1939
2. Finland: 30 Nov 1939
3. Denmark, Norway: 9 Apr 1940
4. Low Countries: 10 May 1940
5. France: 12 May 1940
6. Baltic states: 15 June 1940
7. Romania: 28 June 1940

INVASION ROUTES

→ German Reich
→ Soviet Union

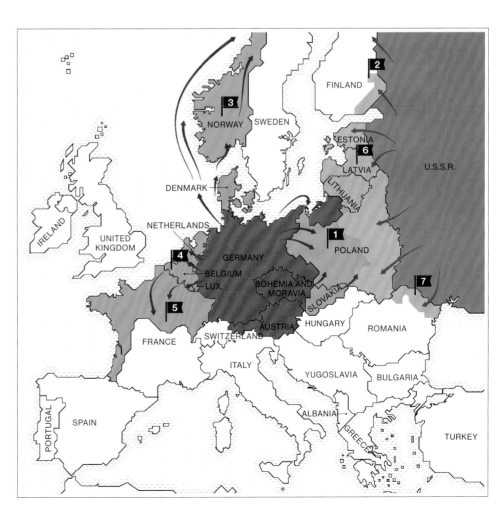

The Destruction of Poland and the 'Bore War'

🌐 Poland invaded

In the early hours of 1 September 1939, an elderly German battleship, the *Schleswig-Holstein*, ostensibly on a 'courtesy' visit to the port of Danzig, opened fire on the Westerplatte peninsula, the site of a Polish military depot. The first salvo of huge, 28-centimetre shells signalled the start of the Second World War in Europe. At the same time, German troops, supported by overwhelming air power, crossed the Polish border. Poland's unhelpful geographical position meant that it had to face invasion from three different directions. Its army was large, but made the fatal error of attempting to defend Poland's borders against all these attacks at once. From the outset the invaders acted with brutality, bombing undefended towns and shooting civilians. Many more civilians than soldiers were killed in the fighting. In little more than a week, German troops had reached the outskirts of Poland's capital, Warsaw, signalling the start of a three-week battle for the city. On 17 September Poland was dealt a further deadly blow, when the Soviet Union – under a secret agreement associated with its pact with Germany – invaded from the east. By 6 October Poland had been overwhelmed. The fighting was over, but the real agony for Poland's people was only just beginning, as Hitler and Stalin divided the country between them and subjected it to a ruthless occupation.

Following the German–Soviet conquest of Poland in 1939, the victors quickly established a brutal overlordship. Poland ceased to exist. Most of its territory was incorporated into either Germany or the Soviet Union. The Germans drove Poles from their property and replaced them with *Volksdeutsche* (ethnic Germans brought from other Eastern European countries). They murdered leading members of Polish society as well as Polish psychiatric patients, and forced the country's 3 million Jews to live in overcrowded ghettos. Stalin, similarly, ordered the deportation of thousands of Poles and arrested members of Poland's intelligentsia. The remaining rump of Poland, the German-controlled *Generalgouvernement*, became a racial 'dumping ground' – the destination for displaced Poles and, soon, Jews and Roma deported from the Reich. This photograph shows members of the Roma community held at a camp at Radom in the *Generalgouvernement*.

To German dismay, Britain and France fulfilled their pledge to go to war in defence of Poland. Germany was sent an ultimatum demanding that it cease its invasion by 11 am on Sunday, 3 September. In London, with no response having been received, Prime Minister Chamberlain made a radio broadcast from 10 Downing Street announcing Britain's declaration of war on Germany. His weary voice asked his audience to 'imagine what a bitter blow it is to me that all my long struggle to win peace has failed'. One listener wrote that she held her 'chin high and kept back the tears at the thought of all the slaughter ahead. When *God Save the King* played, we stood.' At 11.28 am, an air-raid warning sounded in London. It was a false alarm.

Poland Torn Apart

IN A MATTER OF WEEKS THE COUNTRY CEASED TO EXIST

Poland emerged from the First World War as an independent state after more than 200 years of subjugation. However, it took just a few weeks for Germany and the Soviet Union to crush the country.

■ Poland in 1939
▨ Poland today

TIMELINE

SEPT 1939

1 SEPT 1939

GERMANY INVADES POLAND

German troops, supported by overwhelming air-power, cross the Polish border from three different directions: north, west and south.

DANZIG

LODZ

KRAKOW

17 SEPT 1939

SOVIET UNION INVADES POLAND

Soviet troops invade Poland on two fronts: the Western Belorussian and Western Ukrainian.

WILNO

KOCK

LVOV

OCT 1939

27 SEPT 1939

POLISH FORCES CAPITULATE

Under attack from all sides, Warsaw surrenders to the Germans.

1 OCT 1939

FIGHTING CEASES, POLAND IS DIVIDED

The last organized resistance by the Polish Army ends at Kock.

Between 8 and 12 October, northern and western Poland are annexed to the German Reich. The remaining German-occupied area becomes the *Generalgouvernement* (General Government), administered from Krakow. Eastern Poland is incorporated into the Belorussian Soviet Socialist Republic (SSR) and the Ukrainian SSR.

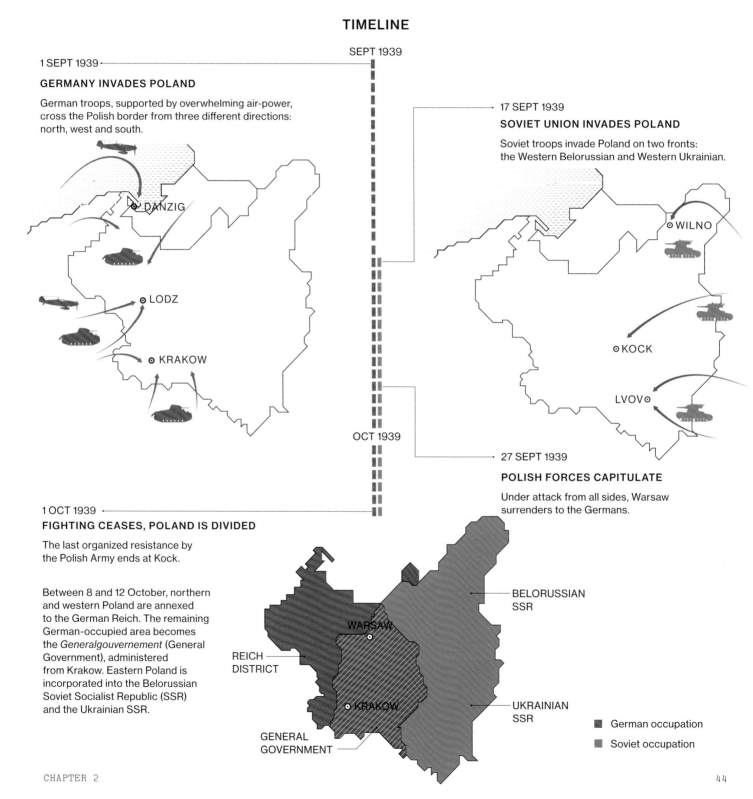

BELORUSSIAN SSR

WARSAW

REICH DISTRICT

UKRAINIAN SSR

KRAKOW

GENERAL GOVERNMENT

■ German occupation
■ Soviet occupation

THE FOURTH LARGEST ARMY IN THE WAR

Despite the relatively large size of its forces, Poland was unable to resist the German and Soviet armies.

MANPOWER	ARMY	CASUALTIES
100,000 soldiers	500 items	10,000 people

GERMANY

MANPOWER
1,500,000

GUNS 9,000	TANKS 2,750	AIRCRAFT 2,315

KILLED 16,400	WOUNDED 30,300	CAPTURED 0

POLAND

MANPOWER
1,000,000

GUNS 4,300	TANKS 880	AIRCRAFT 400

KILLED 66,000	WOUNDED 133,700	CAPTURED 680,000

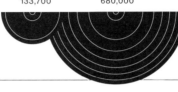

SOVIET UNION

MANPOWER
470,000*

GUNS 4,959	TANKS 4,736	AIRCRAFT 3,300

KILLED 1,500	WOUNDED 2,400	CAPTURED 0

* This figure refers only to the portion of the Red Army that was involved in the invasion of Poland.

INVASION AND OPPRESSION

Hundreds of thousands of Poles suffered under occupation.

● KALININ (now Tver)

WIELKA PIAŚNICA

● KATYN

STAROGRAD (aka Kocborowo, now Starograd-Gdański)

BYDOGOSZCZ
PALMIRY ●
✡ ✡ WARSAW
LODZ
RADOM ✡
✡ LUBLIN

● KATOWICE
✡ KRAKOW

● KIEV (now Kyiv)

● KHARKOV (now Kharkiv)

A German firing squad murders Polish civilians.

✡ Largest ghettos

● Mass execution sites

● Sites related to 'Katyn Massacre', April–May 1940

From the moment they marched into Poland, the Germans began to massacre thousands of Polish civilians. Hundreds of thousands of others were forced from their land and homes to make way for German settlers. Poland's large Jewish population was forced into overcrowded ghettos. The Soviet Union deported hundreds of thousands of Poles deep into the Soviet interior, and thousands more were shot.

🌐 A waiting game

The Allies, as Britain and France became known, gave little direct aid to Poland as it was destroyed. This was due not only to the speed with which Germany gained victory there, but also to the strategy that the Allies planned to follow in the event of war with Germany. Neither partner wished to repeat the terrible bloodletting of the Great War's Western Front. Rather, their aim was to stand firm and grip Germany in an economic blockade facilitated by the British Royal Navy's control of the sea. The expectation was either that Germany's economy would be unable to sustain its war effort for long, or that Hitler's grip on power would be too fragile to survive the strains of a war. Most in the Allied leadership thought that this process would take up to three years; others were more optimistic. The French commander-in-chief, Maurice Gamelin, expressed the view that 'Hitler will collapse the day war is declared on Germany ... the German Army will be forced to march on Berlin to suppress the trouble that will immediately break out.' On the new Western Front, the French Army made a token advance into German territory, while Britain's Bomber Command dropped propaganda leaflets on German cities instead of bombs. Following Poland's defeat, an uneasy quiet settled over the Franco-German border. French soldiers, now joined by a small British Expeditionary Force (BEF), found themselves locked in a state of dreary inactivity, as Europe endured one of its harshest winters for years. The world looked on in confusion at this strange phenomenon, dubbed the *Drôle de guerre* in France, the 'Bore War' in Britain and the 'Phoney War' by observing Americans. Even Chamberlain – who might have been expected to have an insight into Allied thinking – called it 'this strangest of wars'.

The Allies thought that Germany would collapse if starved of resources. Goods being shipped to Germany were declared 'contraband' and seized by the Royal Navy. These sample boxes were used to identify materials in ships examined by Contraband Control at Weymouth, Dorset. But Hitler's deal with Stalin gave Germany access to the supplies it needed, through the Soviet Union.

COBBER KAIN

The dreariness of the 'Bore War' was enlivened by twenty-one-year-old New Zealander Edgar 'Cobber' Kain. A pilot with the RAF contingent in France, Edgar became the British Empire's first 'air ace' – an airman credited with shooting down five or more enemy aircraft. He took this machine gun as a trophy of his first 'kill', a German Dornier 17 bomber that he shot down near Metz on 8 November 1939.

Edgar became a household name in Britain and New Zealand. By the time of the RAF's withdrawal from France in June 1940, Edgar had shot down sixteen German aircraft. Ordered to fly to England on 7 June, Edgar treated his comrades to a farewell display of low-level aerobatics, during which he accidentally hit the ground. He was thrown from his cockpit and killed.

War Comes to Scandinavia

The Allied strategists, however, had never considered the possibility of an agreement between the two political extremes represented by Hitler and Stalin. With Poland destroyed, these two tyrants now shared a land border, over which flowed all the goods and raw materials that the Allies had expected to be able to deny Germany. The Soviet Union supplied grain, oil and metals, and trans shipped other materials such as rubber, purchased with Japanese assistance in South East Asia. Stalin's motivation for helping Hitler was that he hoped to increase the security of the Soviet Union. It suited him to see the capitalist powers to his west embroiled in what he expected to be a lengthy and costly war. Given a free hand by the terms of

Winston Churchill poses on the steps of the Admiralty building in London. On becoming First Lord of the Admiralty at the outbreak of war, Churchill was returning to an office he had formerly held from 1911 to 1915. On arrival, he sent a signal to the entire Royal Navy: 'Winston is back.'

the pact with Germany, he forced the Baltic states – Estonia, Latvia and Lithuania – to accept Soviet military bases on their soil. A similar ultimatum, demanding territory from Finland, was rejected. In response, the Soviet Red Army invaded Finland on 30 November 1939. In what became known as the Winter War, the Finns held off massive but ill-coordinated Soviet attacks made in the extreme cold. The resolve of this small democracy to defend itself against overwhelming force earned admiration around the world. Britain and France even considered intervening in the region militarily. In this, however, they had an ulterior motive. The only way that they could send troops to Finland would be via northern Norway and Sweden. If the Allies could persuade these two neutral countries to accept such a plan, it might enable them to cut off crucial supplies of iron ore to Germany. This ore was mined in northern Sweden but, during the winter, could be shipped to Germany only via the ice-free harbour of Narvik in Norway.

Chief among the proponents of this idea was Britain's energetic navy minister, Winston Churchill. This political maverick had held high office in wartime and peacetime as a member of both the Liberal and the Conservative parties, having twice switched allegiance. By the 1930s, however, his political career was on the rocks. He was mistrusted by many, who regarded him as a 'genius without judgment'. He enraged his own party, the Conservatives, by setting himself up as the chief critic of the policy of appeasement. But when war came, his reputation for activity, as well as his credentials as a man who had demanded that Hitler be confronted, saw him return to the office that he had held between 1911 and 1915 – First Lord of

The bombardment of the Norwegian town of Bjerkvik by the Royal Navy typified the poorly organized Allied intervention in Norway. No Germans were present in the town and fourteen civilians were killed. To add insult to injury, Bjerkvik was then looted by a landing force composed of men from the French Foreign Legion.

the Admiralty. Churchill eventually persuaded the Cabinet that mines should be sewn in Norwegian waters to hamper German shipping. But events overtook this plan. In March 1940, following a renewed Soviet offensive, Finland was forced to sue for peace. Hitler too had been watching events in Scandinavia. He planned to take the initiative and not only secure his iron-ore supplies but also, by occupying the Norwegian coast, provide his navy with bases from which it could raid British shipping in the North Atlantic. On 9 April the German Army occupied Denmark, which, powerless to resist, became a German protectorate. Simultaneously, troops were landed by air and sea at various points in Norway.

The Allies hurried to respond to this unexpected development, with the Royal Navy tasked with escorting a joint Anglo-French force (including a contingent of exiled Poles) to assist the Norwegians. The operation soon descended into chaos, with poor coordination between the navy and the army and inefficient use of shipping. Men were landed in central Norway only to discover that their heavy equipment was absent or could not be got ashore. At the mercy of German air attacks, they soon had to be evacuated. The Allies had more success further north at Narvik. Here, the Royal Navy sunk ten German destroyers in the fjord, and British, French and Polish troops drove the German occupiers out of the town. But back in Britain, the impression that the Norwegian campaign had turned into a fiasco became widespread, as reflected in the words of the diarist Christopher Tomlin: 'The whole world is watching our battle in Norway. The whole business is a

nightmare ... Mother, Father and I feel it is murder: raw recruits sent there without artillery or supporting planes.' On 7 and 8 May 1940, Parliament debated the matter. Churchill's role in recent events largely escaped censure, but Chamberlain's war leadership came under heavy fire. He was forced to accept that he no longer had sufficient support to continue as prime minister. There was a strong feeling that Britain needed a government of all parties in this time of crisis. The Labour Party would not serve under Chamberlain, but would accept the leadership of either Churchill or the foreign minister, Lord Halifax. When the latter hesitated, Chamberlain advised the king, George VI, to appoint Churchill. On the evening of 10 May, sixty-five-year-old Winston Churchill became prime minister. He would form an administration from members of all three major parties. The inclusion of Labour politicians in senior posts was indeed essential to ensure that the trade unions – and therefore Britain's industrial workforce – stood solidly behind Churchill's direction of the war.

ABOVE The seizure of Norway opened up the North Atlantic to the German Navy. At the urging of Winston Churchill, neutral Iceland was invaded and occupied by British troops to prevent it from falling into German hands. This handkerchief was brought home as a souvenir by one of the British occupiers of this lonely outpost of the European war.

RIGHT Soldiers of the Norwegian Army. Mountainous terrain helped this tiny force to fight on for three months, meaning that Norway put up a longer resistance than any of the other countries invaded by Germany in 1939–40.

Germany Strikes in the West

The Germans advanced into Luxembourg, Belgium and the Netherlands using airborne troops to seize key locations. German aerial bombing terrorized soldiers and civilians alike. This beret was worn by the Chasseurs Ardennais, light infantrymen of the Belgian Army who defended the heavily wooded southern region of Belgium. In May 1940 they found themselves facing the bulk of Germany's tank forces, which were in the process of traversing the Ardennes in order to attack France.

On the day of Churchill's appointment, Germany launched its long-expected assault in the West, with the invasion of three neutral countries. Luxembourg was overrun, and airborne troops were landed in the Netherlands and Belgium, to pave the way for advancing land forces. Returning from his meeting with George VI, Churchill, with tears in his eyes (a not uncommon circumstance), confided to his police bodyguard, 'I hope it is not too late. I am very much afraid that it is. We can only do our best.' Thus, even as the new British prime minister was forming his war cabinet, German troops were pouring into the Low Countries. Within five days the Netherlands was forced to capitulate, with the final act of its defeat being the unnecessary flattening of the centre of Rotterdam by German bombers. News of this, accompanied by greatly inflated casualty figures, seemed to confirm pre-war fears about the horrors of aerial attack. But by this time, the attention of military leaders was focused elsewhere.

The Allies had had a long time to plan for the German attack. They aimed to meet the advancing German forces head-on in Belgium. The neutrality of the latter meant that they could not enter its territory until requested to do so, and could only move in once the German invasion was underway. As far as the Allies were concerned, there would be a showdown between the main German forces and their own best troops in central Belgium. This had also been the expectation of the German high command, but fears that the Allies had become aware of the plan, owing to a set of orders being lost in a plane crash, led it to change its mind. With Hitler's backing, an audacious scheme proposed by General Erich von Manstein was adopted. Now, the advance across the central Belgian plain would serve merely to draw the best Allied forces to the north-east. Meanwhile, most of Germany's tank forces – the panzer divisions – would advance through the wooded Ardennes region in the south of Belgium, aiming to strike at French defences along the River Meuse. If a breakthrough was achieved, the mobile German forces would thrust westwards towards the Channel coast, trapping the Allied forces that had advanced into Belgium. This strategy was extremely risky and did not have the wholehearted support of many German generals. Getting motorized forces through the narrow roads of the Ardennes would be a huge logistical challenge; and if the panzers broke through, they would be very vulnerable to French counter-attacks along their exposed southern flank.

Predictions about the difficulty of traversing the Ardennes proved correct; at one point, a 250-kilometre traffic jam stretched all the way from the Meuse back to the Rhine. But by 13 May 1940, the Germans were ready to strike. They were faced by low-category French units manned by reservists, many of whom had received their training two decades earlier. The French had plenty of artillery but were terrorized by German dive-bomber attacks. The Germans managed to establish three bridgeheads across the Meuse. By the time the French launched a counter-attack, German tanks had crossed the river at Sedan, precipitating a panic among the defenders. The Allied leaders could see the danger that the German breakthrough posed, but they struggled to move the armoured forces necessary to oppose it into position. The German tanks sped westward, leaving their supporting infantry to march along behind them as best they could. Senior German commanders

This watercolour was painted by the British war artist Edward Ardizzone. Ardizzone was one of the first artists to be commissioned when Britain, following a precedent from the Great War, set up the War Artists Advisory Committee. He was attached to the British Expeditionary Force in France. The painting shows British troops advancing into Belgium in May 1940, against a tide of exhausted refugees.

This is the uniform of an officer of the French general staff – the brains of an army. France's army was powerful and, in 1940, had more artillery and tanks than its German opponent. But its leadership expected to rely on tactics that had proved successful in the Great War and struggled to respond to the highly mobile warfare conducted by Germany's panzer divisions.

tried to check their momentum, in order to ensure that the flanks of the narrow wedge opened up by the panzers were secure from counter-attack. But the generals at the head of the advance refused to be stopped. On 20 May their leading units reached the Channel coast near Abbeville. They could not believe their luck in bringing such a high-risk strategy to completion.

At 7.30 am on 15 May, Churchill was awoken by a telephone call from the French prime minister, Paul Reynaud, who stated that 'we are beaten ... the battle is lost'. Hurrying to Paris the next day, Churchill asked the French commander-in-chief, Gamelin, to reveal the location of the French Army reserves, which Churchill believed could be used to cut off the German advance. 'There are none,' came the reply. The Allies' best troops, including most of the British Expeditionary Force, were now trapped in Belgium and the northernmost corner of France. Pressure from the Germans to their east and a chaotic transport situation, with the roads under air attack and clogged with terrified refugees, prevented them from fighting their way out towards the south-west. The chief of Britain's Imperial General Staff, Sir Edmund Ironside, wrote that 'right now it looks like the biggest military catastrophe in history'.

Perhaps predictably, the crisis prompted a breakdown in relations between France and Britain. The French, with their national existence at stake and feeling that the whole war could be won or lost at this point, demanded every possible assistance from Britain – particularly the full commitment of its air power. But Britain's leaders had one eye on what might happen if France were defeated, and wanted to keep enough men and machines in reserve in case the UK had to fight on alone. Generals of both armies blamed each other for failing to cooperate in the mounting of counter-attacks on the German panzers. On 26 May the British government authorized the commander of its Expeditionary Force, Lord Gort, to evacuate his men by sea. Gort himself had already been preparing for such an eventuality. The British decision infuriated the new French commander-in-chief, General Maxime Weygand, who commented sourly that 'every people has its virtues and defects. Apart from his distinguished qualities, the Englishman is motivated by almost instinctive selfishness.'

This photograph of tanks of the German 7th Panzer Division was taken by its commanding officer, Erwin Rommel. Rommel made his reputation as a general in the Battle of France. The tanks in the background are a Czech design, put into production for Germany following its 1939 occupation of Czechoslovakia.

Trapped at Dunkirk

Soldiers await evacuation on the beach to the east of Dunkirk. Owing to the difficulty of embarking men from the beach, most were evacuated from the port itself.

As they tightened their grip on the surrounded Allied forces, the Germans captured the ports of Boulogne and Calais. This left only Dunkirk as a point of embarkation for the trapped men. British and French troops managed to form a firm defensive perimeter around the town and the beaches to its east. They were able to do so because the German armoured forces had been obliged to halt for three days by an order from above. This order was issued because the German high command wanted to ensure that its tank units remained strong enough to complete the campaign against France. It is also likely that Hitler saw an opportunity to assert his complete control over military decision-making. He was persuaded that the Dunkirk bridgehead could be destroyed by his air force and fantasized about using anti-aircraft shells to slaughter the men exposed on the beaches. A second hindrance to the Germans was a large French force surrounded in the city of Lille, whose stout resistance required the attention of three panzer and four infantry divisions. But the Allies had to overcome another crisis on 28 May, when the Belgian Army surrendered to the Germans, temporarily exposing the eastern flank of the Dunkirk bridgehead.

In Britain, a National Day of Prayer had been held two days earlier, on Sunday, 26 May, with the Archbishop of Canterbury leading prayers for 'our soldiers in dire peril in France'. The evacuation from Dunkirk got fully underway the following day, but did not gather pace until a British naval officer discovered that it was possible to embark men from one of the breakwaters that protected the bomb-damaged harbour. More men were to escape this way than from the beaches. The evacuation, code-named Operation Dynamo, was commanded from Dover by Vice Admiral Sir Bertram Ramsey. He and his team worked around the clock to assemble and dispatch enough ships to save the trapped army. Civilian vessels proved invaluable. These included paddle steamers (some had already been taken

BILL OSBORNE

Bill, a Royal Engineer, was caught up in the retreat to Dunkirk. Amid the chaos, he tore this railway map from a café wall. If he became separated from his unit, the map would give him a chance to find his way to the coast.

Fearing that he would not survive, he wrote a hurried letter to his wife, telling her that 'if you ever fall in love with another man, may God bless you with happiness'. Despite his anxiety, Bill was rescued from Dunkirk and went on to serve in the army for the remainder of the war.

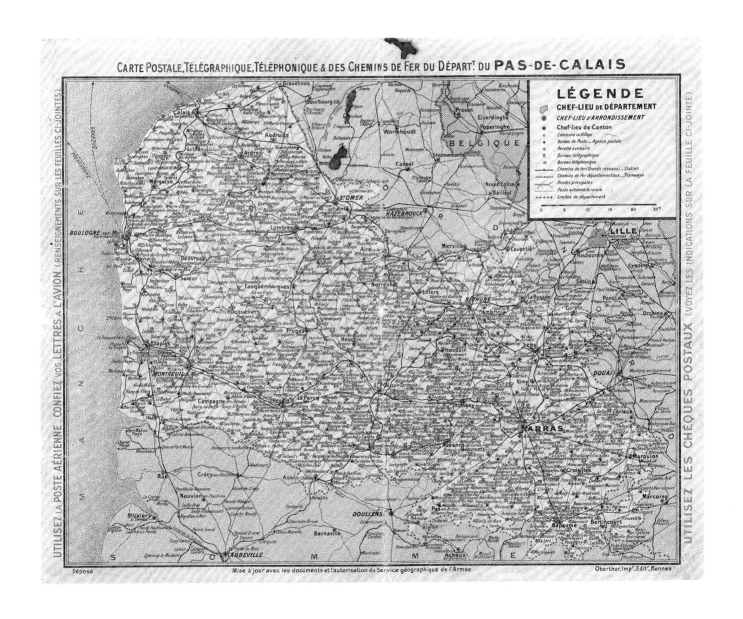

This fishing boat, *Tamzine*, is the smallest-known vessel of the more than 900 ships and boats used to evacuate British and French soldiers from Dunkirk. Towed across the Channel behind a larger vessel, *Tamzine* was used to ferry men from the shallow water just off the beaches to bigger ships further out. Most of the smaller boats were abandoned once their job was done, but *Tamzine* was towed home.

into naval service as minesweepers), trawlers and forty Dutch coasters known as schuyts (or 'scoots', to the sailors who manned them). Only very small boats could approach the sandy beaches, so civilian pleasure craft and small fishing boats were towed across to ferry men between the beach and larger boats. Most of these vessels were manned by the Royal Navy. Some civilians, including fishermen and lifeboatmen, volunteered to sail with their own boats, but many others were unwilling to go. Some made one or more trips but, understandably, refused to go again.

For the trapped soldiers, the main terror came from the air. Almost miraculously, however, low cloud and fog, in which the German planes could not operate, shrouded the area for six of the nine days of the evacuation. Even more fortunate was the absence of any strong winds, which kept the Channel unusually calm throughout the evacuation. Some of those evacuated cursed the Royal Air Force (RAF) for failing to protect them on the clear-weather days, but what they did not see was that the RAF lost ninety-nine of its precious fighters defending the airspace over Dunkirk. Fear of becoming a prisoner of the Germans drove some men to panic. While much of the embarkation was carried out in a remarkably orderly manner, at other times discipline broke down. The diary of one witness, Private Henry Linley, carries the following, hastily written entry for 30 May: 'Situation desperate. Every man for himself getting boarded.' French soldiers were evacuated too, on an equal footing with the British from 31 May, following a pledge made by Churchill to the French government. The last British troops were taken off French soil on the night of 2/3 June, and the operation ended on 4 June, when the 40,000-strong French rearguard laid down its arms. Over 338,000 men had been rescued, including 110,000 French personnel.

Most of the returning British troops expected to be shunned because, in their eyes, they represented such a humiliating defeat. They were amazed to be greeted as heroes. The press and the BBC celebrated their rescue as a miracle. The *Daily Telegraph* hailed a 'Defeat Turned to Victory' and, on the wireless, the English writer and broadcaster J. B. Priestley honoured the 'little holiday steamers' that 'made an excursion to Hell and came back glorious'. In the House of Commons, Churchill also called it a 'miracle' but cautioned against assigning 'this deliverance the attributes of a victory. Wars are not won by evacuations.' Hitler was not inclined to such equivocation, proclaiming, 'Soldiers of the West Front! Dunkirk has fallen ... with it has ended the greatest battle of world history.' At the same time, an almost forgotten battle ended far to the north, when Allied troops were evacuated from Narvik. After sixty-two days of resistance, the Norwegian Army was forced to lay down its arms.

MUHAMMED AKBAR KHAN

Muhammed was one of the first soldiers from the British Empire to reach the front line. He was in command of one of four Royal Indian Army Service Corps Animal Transport Companies sent to France in 1939. They and their mules were much sought-after during the winter of 1939/40 as providers of off-road transport.

In May 1940 Muhammed faced the challenge of leading his men – mainly Muslim Punjabis and Pashtuns – in the retreat to Dunkirk. He succeeded in evacuating all 300 of them, but they were heartbroken at having to leave their mules behind. The Indian muleteers, minus one company that had been captured in France, were reformed in Britain, where they took part in mountain-warfare exercises in Wales and Scotland. This portrait of Muhammed was painted in 1941 by the Australian-born British artist Henry Lamb.

The Fall
of France

The Germans now turned to completing their defeat of France. This proved more costly to them than had the initial invasion in May. Strong French resistance meant that the Germans now suffered 5,000 casualties a day – twice the number they had sustained daily up to 3 June. On 10 June, hoping to share in the spoils as one of the victors, Mussolini declared war on France and Britain. However, his soldiers made little headway against French defences on the mountainous border between the two countries. But the self-sacrifice of French soldiers proved to be in vain. The shock of the disaster in May had encouraged defeatism among some of France's leaders. In the course of the crisis, a hero of the Great War, Marshal Philippe Pétain, had been brought into the government as deputy prime minister. He and the commander-in-chief, Weygand, now agreed that the military situation was hopeless, and that France could be saved only if it sought an armistice while its forces were still in existence. Otherwise, they feared a breakdown of order. Reynaud, the prime minister, wanted France to keep fighting – from its colonies if necessary – but his cabinet voted to request an armistice. In a desperate attempt to avoid this outcome, Reynaud made an appeal to President Roosevelt to bring America into the war. Later the same day, German troops entered Paris. In a final effort to keep France fighting, Churchill offered an 'indissoluble union' between the two nations

Mussolini, although aligned with Hitler since May 1939 in the 'Pact of Steel', did not bring Italy into the war until 10 June 1940. Seeing France facing defeat, he hoped to share in the spoils. This magazine reports his declaration of war on France and Britain. However, Italian troops achieved little in the twelve days before France's surrender.

Luxuriating in his surprisingly swift victory over France, Adolf Hitler made an early morning tour of Paris – as much as a devotee of architecture as a conqueror.

of Britain and France. Pétain dismissed the concept as 'fusion with a corpse'. Reynaud resigned and was replaced by the elderly marshal.

On 22 June Hitler revelled in forcing French representatives to sign an armistice in his presence, in the very same railway carriage that had been used for the armistice of 1918. France was divided into occupied zones and an autonomous region that became known as Vichy France, after the spa town that was its seat of government. The Vichy regime, with Pétain as its figurehead, was a right-wing authoritarian state. It replaced the French republican motto of 'Liberty, Equality, Fraternity' with one of its own: 'Work, Family, Fatherland'. Hitler treated the new regime with respect, hoping that it could play a role in the new Europe he was creating.

The fall of France meant that British strategy lay in tatters. The UK had given no consideration before the war to the possibility of having to fight without a strong European ally. Many, chief among them the prime minister himself, turned their gaze towards the United States. But Roosevelt, although sympathetic to the Allied cause, was engaged in an election campaign that would see him become president for an unprecedented third term. Americans trusted him to steer their country through the crisis that was gripping the world, but he also promised to keep the US out of the war. The unexpectedly swift defeat of France undermined Stalin's strategy as well. The Soviet ruler moved swiftly to create further buffer zones on his country's western borders. The Baltic states were occupied and forced to become part of the Soviet Union, and Romania was bullied into ceding the border regions of Bessarabia and Northern Bukovina. Meanwhile, Stalin continued to give Germany the goods it demanded. He wanted to give Hitler no cause for reverting to enmity with the Soviet Union. The failure to crush Finland had made him aware that the Red Army was in no state to fight a major enemy until it had been reformed and modernized.

Others saw opportunities in the defeat of the Allies. Mussolini made plans for Italy to replace Britain as the leading colonial power in the Middle East. But the most powerful effects of these events were seen in Japanese policy. The weakening of the established colonial powers in South East Asia – Britain, France and the Netherlands – persuaded Japan's leaders that a great opportunity had arrived for Japan to create an empire in the region. Japan was infuriated by the economic sanctions that the United States had placed on it, in the hope of limiting its aggression in China. Seizing the resources of South East Asia would make these sanctions meaningless and might enable the war in China to be brought to a victorious conclusion. More immediately, Japan saw a chance to cut off most of the supplies being imported by the embattled Guomindang regime.

RACIAL VIOLENCE

Governments used racial prejudice to stir up hatred for their enemies. The Japanese treated the Chinese as a lesser race; in turn, Allied propaganda portrayed Japanese people as animals. Nazi Germany categorized the Slavs of Eastern Europe as less than human, and black Allied soldiers as monstrous. It also saw Jews both as a powerful threat and as racially inferior. Around the world, hatred of other people on the basis of their race led to extreme violence.

ABOVE More than 3,000 black African soldiers, recruited by France from its empire, were murdered after surrendering to the Germans in 1940. This album, with photographs of African prisoners of war, was kept by a member of the Waffen SS – the armed wing of the Nazi Party – which was heavily involved in the killings. When French-African prisoners appeared on newsreels in Germany, audience members shouted, 'Shoot these black beasts!'

These came either by rail from French Indochina (modern-day Vietnam, Laos and Cambodia), or by road from Burma (Myanmar). Japan bullied Vichy France into cutting the rail links and accepting a Japanese military presence in what is now northern Vietnam. It also demanded that Britain close the Burma Road. In its weakened position, the UK agreed to do so for a period of three months. It could ill afford to create a new enemy at this moment of crisis: the country faced more direct and imminent threats closer to home. (For a further discussion of these events, see Chapter 4.)

Control of the French and Norwegian coasts gave Germany the opportunity to challenge Britain's control of the seas. In particular, it now had bases that gave it direct access to the Atlantic Ocean, enabling it to unleash its warships, submarines and aircraft against British shipping. And in northern France, the German armed forces appeared to be making preparations to invade England. This outcome had been feared by the British government since late May. While the Dunkirk evacuation was underway, the Cabinet had discussed what should be done if France were defeated. Consideration was given to asking Hitler for peace terms – potentially using Mussolini as an intermediary. However, the Cabinet eventually agreed with the view championed by Churchill, that any deal acceptable to Hitler would so weaken Britain that it would be unable to resist further demands from him in the future. The UK would have to fight on. On 18 June Churchill made a radio broadcast, repeating a speech that he had made earlier in the day in Parliament. He told the nation that 'what General Weygand has called the battle of France is over ... the battle of Britain is about to begin'. Around the same time, an anonymous interviewee of the social-research organization Mass Observation gave the following grim assessment: 'I think we have reached what they call a crisis. Now they will have to prove that "Britons never shall be slaves". There is no doubt that we shall be exterminated.'

Following France's defeat, Britain had to decide whether or not to keep fighting. Winston Churchill thought that a peace agreement would make Britain a hostage to further Nazi demands. After tense discussions, his war cabinet agreed. This newspaper reported Churchill's stirring speech to the House of Commons, during which he proclaimed that Britain would fight on.

This anti-British propaganda poster, *N'oubliez pas Oran!* (Don't forget Oran!), was produced by the French Vichy regime. The British Royal Navy had attacked the French fleet at its base near Oran in Algeria, owing to fears that Germany would take control of it. This ruthless attack on a former ally showed the world – especially the US government – Britain's determination to keep fighting, but poisoned relations with the French. The Vichy government retaliated by ordering its air force to bomb Gibraltar.

N'oubliez pas Oran!

CHAPTER 3

BRITAIN'S WAR

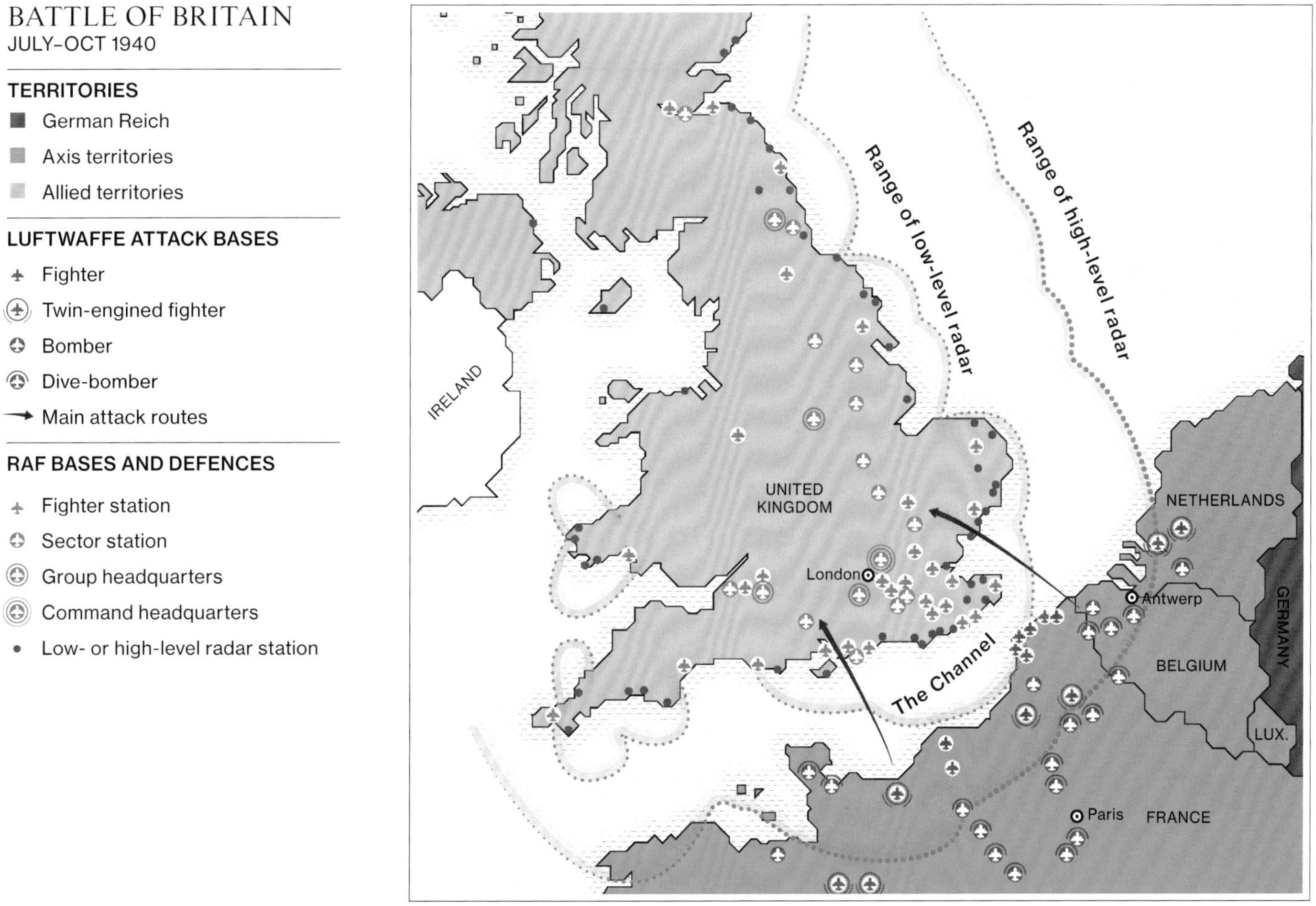

BATTLE OF BRITAIN
JULY–OCT 1940
TERRITORIES
German Reich
Axis territories
Allied territories
LUFTWAFFE ATTACK BASES
Fighter
Twin-engined fighter
Bomber
Dive-bomber
Main attack routes
RAF BASES AND DEFENCES
Fighter station
Sector station
Group headquarters
Command headquarters
Low- or high-level radar station
Range of low-level radar
Range of high-level radar
IRELAND
UNITED KINGDOM
London
The Channel
NETHERLANDS
Antwerp
BELGIUM
GERMANY
LUX.
Paris
FRANCE

Britain Alone?

Winston Churchill and
Franklin D. Roosevelt on board
HMS *Prince of Wales* during
the Atlantic Conference,
August 1941.

To a world stunned by the defeat of France, Britain offered the last resistance to Nazi Germany. But Britain was never truly alone. As countries in Europe fell under the domination of the Nazi regime, London became the centre of 'Free Europe', home to its fleeing citizens, exiled royal families and governments. By the summer of 1940, immigrants from Belgium, Czechoslovakia, Denmark, France, Luxembourg, the Netherlands, Norway and Poland had arrived in the UK. Many exiled troops and civilian refugees joined Britain's armed forces and civil-defence organizations.

JACQUES VOYER

In 1940 Jacques heard Charles de Gaulle, leader of Free France, on the radio. De Gaulle encouraged French people to resist German occupation and join his Free French Forces in Britain. Jacques was only sixteen years old, but ran away from school and lied about his age to join the Free French Forces as a wireless operator.

Jacques's role was to parachute into occupied France and send messages from the Resistance back to London. However, Jacques was caught while following a German troop convoy. Arrested and tortured, he refused to give up any information. Eight days later, on 27 June 1944, he was shot dead by a firing squad.

WILHELM MOHR

As German forces captured Norway in April 1940, Wilhelm escaped in a small fishing boat, making his way to Britain. As an experienced pilot, he was asked to set up a training base in Canada for escaped Norwegian pilots. The base became known as 'Little Norway'.

Wilhelm returned to Britain and took command of No. 332 Squadron. In an aerial battle over France in 1942, Wilhelm was wounded in the leg, but continued flying. This portrait of Wilhelm was sketched by Eric Kennington, an official war artist in both world wars.

⊕ Divided America

An America First Committee poster showing how political opinion in the United States was divided on the topic of entering the war.

Although the United States was neutral in 1940, its president, Franklin D. Roosevelt, gradually introduced measures that allowed the sale of arms to Britain. Initially, the UK bought large numbers of US weapons, but soon ran short of money. In March 1941 Roosevelt signed the Lend-Lease Act. The US would now lend countries weaponry and other goods, with payment to be negotiated after the war. By the end of 1942, the British depended on America for about a third of their steel, all their synthetic rubber and most of their oil. Other Lend-Lease supplies to Britain in 1942 included 170,000 tons of canned meat, 215,000 tons of lard and 224,000 tons of condensed and dried milk (for more on Lend-Lease, see Chapter 4).

Large numbers of American civilians tried to help as Britain felt the strain of war. They expressed their support through personal donations and fundraising. The New York socialite Natalie Latham started a knitting circle and sent bundles of children's clothes to Britain. Commemorative charms were sold to raise money. Samuel McVitty from Salem, Virginia, donated his Whitney rifle to the British Home Guard. In addition, just under 250 Americans volunteered for the RAF. In August 1941 Winston Churchill met President Roosevelt on board HMS *Prince of Wales* for the Atlantic Conference. There they agreed the Atlantic Charter, a set of principles 'for a better future of the world'. The Atlantic Charter made it clear that the US was supporting the UK in the war, and that it wanted to be part of developing a peaceful post-war world. One of the key principles was 'the right of all peoples to choose the form of government under which they will live'. This was encouraging news for independence groups across the British Empire, whose nations were still under the control of Britain.

Not everyone in the United States was so supportive of the war. Many Americans feared a repeat of the bloodshed of the First World War and campaigned vigorously to stay out. Anti-war groups feared that Roosevelt's support for Britain would lead them into another European conflict. In California, the Yanks Are Not Coming Committee issued pamphlets to labour-union members, calling on America's leaders to avoid the 'filthy mess' of war. The America First Committee was a national anti-war organization whose membership grew to around 800,000. A poster produced by the committee suggests that the liberty of US citizens would be 'war's first casualty'.

⊕ Alliance and Empire

ABOVE In this propaganda poster, a group of seven military personnel from different parts of the British Empire are shown marching together in uniform.

BELOW Indian women labourers, engaged in airfield-construction work at a base in Bengal, India, in 1944, pass mechanics working on an RAF Consolidated B-24 Liberator bomber.

At the onset of the Second World War, Britain was reliant on its empire for a variety of people, money and goods. This dependency only deepened with the outbreak of war. Pro-British propaganda stressed the commonality of the British Empire and the Commonwealth through such phrases as 'our destiny and yours are one'. Yet the relationship between Britain and its empire was marked by commodity scarcity, exploitation and continued inequality. Australia, Canada, New Zealand and South Africa were self-governing Dominions within the British Empire, and in September 1939 they agreed independently to fight alongside Britain. The British colonies in the West Indies, Africa and Asia were still largely governed from London and were forced to join the war. In India, the viceroy, Lord Linlithgow, proclaimed hostilities without consulting the Indian National Congress. Its leaders wanted a promise of independence before they would support the war and were angry at the way India had been sent into battle. Many began to oppose the war effort as a result. In the following years, Britain struggled to defend its empire, damaging its reputation as a protector of the people under British control, and strengthening their demands for independence.

The British Empire was a huge source of manpower. Recruitment posters and campaigns encouraged people to join the armed forces. Many travelled from across the empire to Britain to support the war effort. A Canadian division began to arrive in the UK from December 1939. In Africa, large numbers of men volunteered to fight. Among them was Isaac Fadeoyebo, who was sixteen years old when he enlisted in Nigeria: 'I simply saw military service as a good job. Without consulting my parents and caring less about the consequences I took a plunge into the unknown by getting myself enlisted in the army at Abeokuta.' Joe Culverwell from Zimbabwe claimed that 'the majority of my friends felt like me. They felt loyal to the crown, very British.' For many in the empire, war provided opportunities for travel, money and adventure. Samson Muliango from Zambia was thinking about the life he would lead when he returned from war: 'the government promised us all as a reward farms and lots of money if only we fought for the British Army.' However, as the war continued, pressure to find more troops resulted in conscription in many countries, and men were made to serve against their will. Batison Geresomo from Malawi remembers that 'when the conflict was about to come, the white man came in all the districts of Malawi to recruit soldiers. Some were taken by the chiefs' force and some went on their own wish.' A man from Swaziland described the way in which 'many men were grabbed along the roads to be drafted into the army. Government vehicles were speeding up and down the roads hunting for men.'

Few remaining original records document the plight of those forced to fight or provide manual labour. Many were illiterate or did not have the money to buy writing materials to keep a diary or send letters home. There were millions of South Asian people working behind the scenes to secure supply lines and support the Allies. These were non-combatants who worked as cooks, mechanics, road builders or miners. Their jobs were

ABOVE A group of women from Palapye, Bechuanaland (now Botswana), knit clothes for the Navy League, an organization established to raise the public's awareness of the importance of the British Navy.

BELOW, RIGHT This poster was created to thank the people of Jamaica, whose fundraising had enabled the country to present Britain with two squadrons of Blenheim bombers. The images on the poster show some of the bomber crews preparing for and conducting a raid on Germany.

BELOW This British wartime poster shows Mr K. Singh from Amritsar, India, being trained as a factory inspector in Britain. Many young Indian men trained as specialists in the UK before returning to India to apply their skills in their own country's factories. For many years, Mr Singh worked in a flour and cotton mill, and held the position of instructor fitter in the Lucknow Loco Works.

hard and dangerous. In many cases they were subjected to aerial bombing attacks, worked under poor conditions in climates where malaria and other tropical conditions were common, and had little medical support if they fell ill. For some people, earning enough money to eat was more important than writing an account of their wartime experience. As a consequence, the stories of these individual men, women and children, all of whom were essential to Britain's war effort, have often been forgotten or marginalized.

Manpower was not the only commodity that Britain was able to demand from its empire; it also put pressure on certain territories to increase their production of materiel, including aircraft, tanks and other weaponry. Over the course of the war, Canada produced 800,000 lorries, about a quarter more than were built in the UK. When Japan began attacking Britain's South East Asian interests in 1941, increased pressure was put on food and raw-material production in the African colonies, as a means to support the imperial war effort. After the Japanese captured Malaya (now part of Malaysia) in 1942, Britain lost control of that country's tin production and responded by establishing a forced-labour scheme in Nigeria. This led to the conscription of 118,000 Nigerian men to work in tin mines in poor conditions and with little pay. Britain would not have been able to continue fighting the war without the financial support of its empire. Millions of pounds were borrowed from governments, and even individuals donated to fundraising campaigns to supply Britain with mobile canteen vans, Spitfires and bomber aircraft.

The Empire

BRITAIN LOOKS TO ITS EMPIRE TO BOOST ITS WARTIME RESOURCES

With the outbreak of war, Britain's reliance on its empire for such resources as people, money, food and raw materials deepened significantly, extending to military equipment and supplies. Illustrated here are some of the main forms of assistance provided by the empire during the war, together with just a few examples of the many contributions made by individual nations.

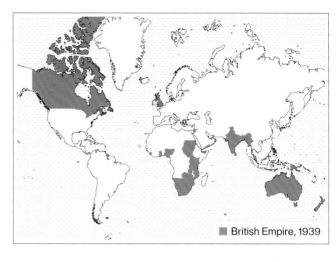

■ British Empire, 1939

MATERIEL

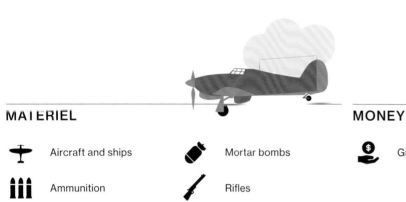

✈ Aircraft and ships ◗ Mortar bombs

ⅲ Ammunition ⚊ Rifles

Canada's war industry produced materiel worth $9 billion and, at its peak, employed 1.2 million people. By 1943 its rate of output of merchant vessels was second only to Britain's, and by the end of the conflict 116,000 Canadian workers had produced more than 16,000 aircraft for the Allied war effort. On the other side of the world, Australia sent Britain approximately 30,000 rifles, 200,000 mortar bombs and 100 million rounds of ammunition.

MONEY

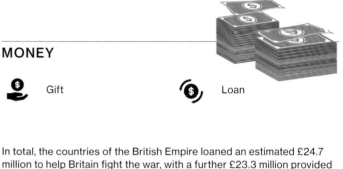

💲 Gift 💲 Loan

In total, the countries of the British Empire loaned an estimated £24.7 million to help Britain fight the war, with a further £23.3 million provided in the form of gifts. Individual contributions included a £50,000 gift from Bechuanaland (now Botswana) and £20,000 from Grenada towards the purchase of a fighter aircraft. Many nations also donated large sums of money to war charities; in Nigeria, for example, where local wages were only 2 shillings (10 pence) per day, the country's 25 million people donated £250,000.

FOOD

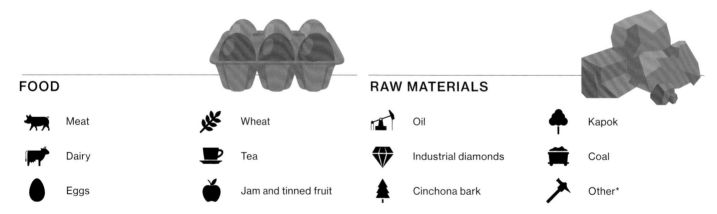

🐖 Meat 🌾 Wheat

🐄 Dairy ☕ Tea

🥚 Eggs 🍎 Jam and tinned fruit

Wartime Britain relied on its empire for a wide variety of foodstuffs. Canada, for example, provided 18–31% of its cheese (or 334,000 tons), 15% of its eggs, 39% of its bacon (1.3 million tons) and at least 57% of its wheat. Other major exporters included New Zealand (458,000 tons of meat in 1943; 30,000 tons of butter in June 1942) and South Africa (25,000 tons of jam; 28,000 tons of tinned fruit). Over the course of the war, 78% of the tea produced by Nyasaland (now Malawi) was sent to Britain.

RAW MATERIALS

🛢 Oil 🌳 Kapok

💎 Industrial diamonds 🗑 Coal

🌲 Cinchona bark 🔨 Other*

*Gold, silver, copper, iron, manganese, chromite, vanadium, cobalt, uranium, asbestos, graphite.

During the war, Ceylon (now Sri Lanka) was a major source of graphite, kapok (a cotton-like substance) and cinchona bark (the main ingredient of quinine). In the Caribbean, Trinidad and Tobago were the largest producers of Allied oil, supplying around half of the Royal Navy and RAF's wartime needs. In Africa, Southern Rhodesia (now Zimbabwe) was a major exporter of chromite, asbestos, coal, silver and iron, while the continent as a whole supplied large proportions of the world's key raw materials, including 98% of its industrial diamonds.

MILITARY PERSONNEL

Men and women from every corner of the empire were recruited to serve with the Allies. Examples included 50,000 women each from Canada and Australia, and 1,000 men from the Cayman Islands – equivalent to two-thirds of the adult population.

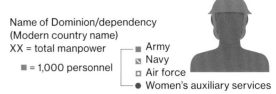

Name of Dominion/dependency
(Modern country name)
XX = total manpower

■ = 1,000 personnel

- ■ Army
- ◩ Navy
- ▫ Air force
- ● Women's auxiliary services

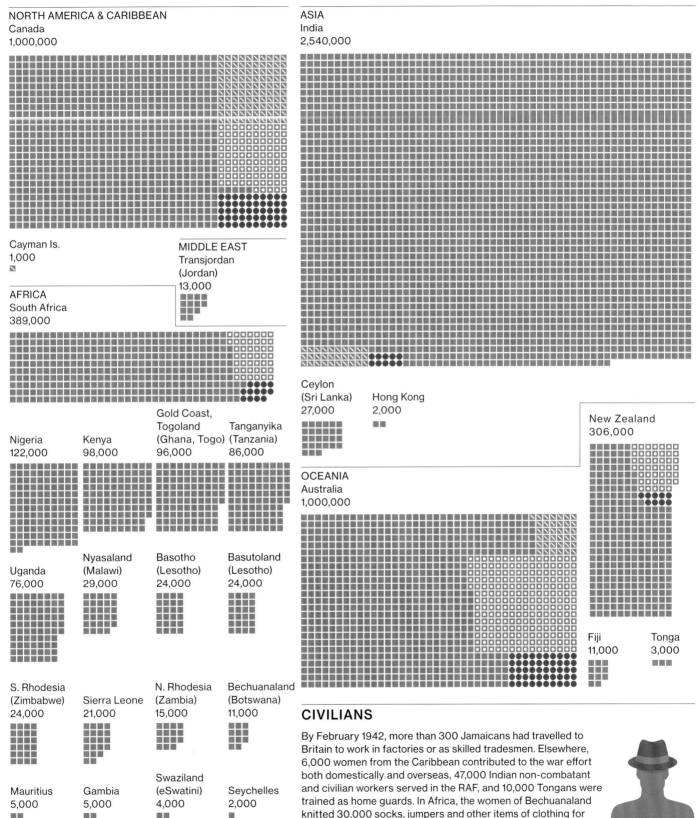

NORTH AMERICA & CARIBBEAN
Canada
1,000,000

Cayman Is.
1,000

AFRICA
South Africa
389,000

MIDDLE EAST
Transjordan
(Jordan)
13,000

Nigeria
122,000

Kenya
98,000

Gold Coast, Togoland
(Ghana, Togo)
96,000

Tanganyika
(Tanzania)
86,000

Uganda
76,000

Nyasaland
(Malawi)
29,000

Basotho
(Lesotho)
24,000

Basutoland
(Lesotho)
24,000

S. Rhodesia
(Zimbabwe)
24,000

Sierra Leone
21,000

N. Rhodesia
(Zambia)
15,000

Bechuanaland
(Botswana)
11,000

Mauritius
5,000

Gambia
5,000

Swaziland
(eSwatini)
4,000

Seychelles
2,000

ASIA
India
2,540,000

Ceylon
(Sri Lanka)
27,000

Hong Kong
2,000

OCEANIA
Australia
1,000,000

New Zealand
306,000

Fiji
11,000

Tonga
3,000

CIVILIANS

By February 1942, more than 300 Jamaicans had travelled to Britain to work in factories or as skilled tradesmen. Elsewhere, 6,000 women from the Caribbean contributed to the war effort both domestically and overseas, 47,000 Indian non-combatant and civilian workers served in the RAF, and 10,000 Tongans were trained as home guards. In Africa, the women of Bechuanaland knitted 30,000 socks, jumpers and other items of clothing for men serving overseas.

JO OAKMAN

During the Battle of Britain and the Blitz, Jo assisted people whose homes had been bombed. As an Air Raid Precautions (ARP) warden in Chelsea, west London, she brought people food and clothes and helped put out fires.

On one occasion, Jo's colleague Albert Thorpe sent her out on a routine patrol to check for fires. When Jo returned, she was shocked to discover that their wardens' post had been bombed and that Albert had been killed. She pasted his obituary in her diary to remember him by.

KILLED AT HIS POST

Chelsea Air Raid Warden's End

The Chelsea A.R.P. organisation has lost one of its earliest members by the death on Saturday week of Mr. Albert George Thorpe, 31 Smith-street, Chelsea. He was killed at his post. Born in London, and trained in the North of England as an engineer, Mr. Thorpe joined the Royal Army Medical Corps at St. Mark's Hospital early in the last war. He showed as keen an aptitude for nursing as he had for engineering.

Despite tempting offers to resume civil employment during the war, he preferred to remain in the Army, and he eventually saw service in France, Gallipoli, Egypt, India, Salonica, and various Red Sea and Aegean ports in H.M. hospital ship Egypt. He was nicknamed "The Admiral." After demobilisation in 1919, he took up nursing as a profession and attended many notable people. In the course of his duties he visited Australia and America, his travels in the latter country taking him from San Francisco and Hollywood to New York.

GEORGE ROBERTS

George was originally from Trinidad. After serving in the Middlesex Regiment during the First World War, George settled in London.

When the Second World War broke out, George was too old to join up again. Instead, he became an auxiliary firefighter on the home front, saving lives in Southwark, south London, during the Blitz. George also co-founded the fire service's education group.

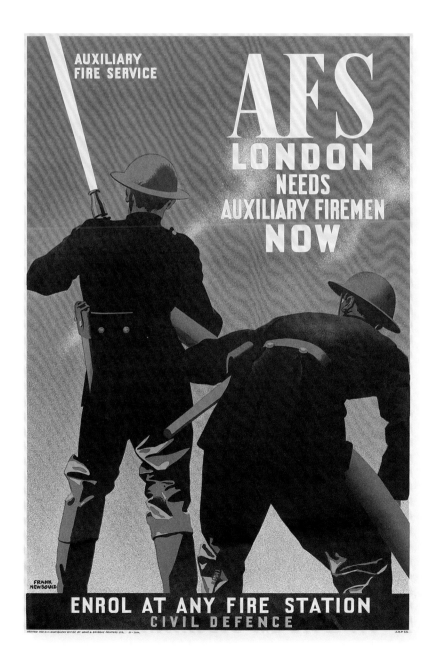

JAMES CRAWFORD

James was a veteran of the First World War, having served in the Cameron Highlanders and the Royal Tank Regiment from 1916. In 1940 he joined the Home Guard, volunteering for the 17th Battalion in Northfleet, Kent. While carrying out his duties as second-in-command, he continued to work as a GP in Gravesend Hospital.

The 17th Battalion's responsibilities included guarding the River Thames just west of the Thames Estuary, an area that would be of great strategic importance in the event of an invasion of Britain.

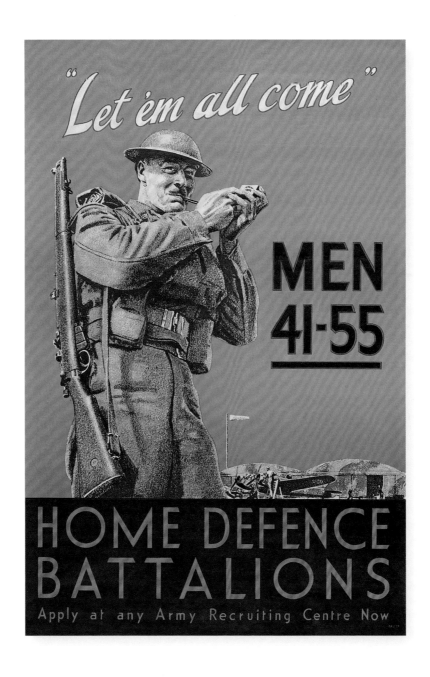

The British home front: volunteers wanted

Britain readied itself for the changes war would bring to life on the home front. In 1938 the government set up civil-defence organizations to deal with the impact of aerial bombing. Initially, the planning and provision of Air Raid Precautions (ARP) varied between cities and boroughs. Recruitment posters encouraged people to volunteer part-time as firemen or wardens, or to join the police force and ambulance service. These groups rapidly grew in size and importance. Many of these jobs involved being on the front line as bombs dropped on Britain. During the war, around 2,300 civil-defence workers were killed while on duty.

ARP wardens ensured that their neighbours and local areas abided by the black-out regulations, and distributed gas masks to the public. During a bombing raid, ARP wardens would deal with fires caused by incendiary bombs. These firebombs crashed through roofs and set buildings alight, so wardens would use a bomb scoop either to move a bomb to where it could do no harm, or to cover it with sand to put it out. As Elsie Warren, a civilian volunteering with the Women's Auxiliary Fire Service, recalled: 'When the incendiaries started to fall, scores of people rushed to tackle them. Everyone joined in, sharing stirrup pumps and sand, and bombs were soon extinguished.'

The Auxiliary Fire Service (AFS) was established to provide part-time support for local fire brigades. They set up stations in schools, garages and factories. To fight fires, the AFS at first used trailer pumps towed by taxis. In 1941 the AFS and local-authority fire brigades were combined into a National Fire Service (NFS). By 1943, more than 70,000 women had enrolled in the NFS. While they did not tackle major fires, they watched for fires on rooftops, drove fire trucks, managed the communications network, completed first-aid training and provided hot food in mobile canteen vans.

The Women's Voluntary Services (WVS) was formed in 1938 by Lady Reading to support communities affected by war. It played a pivotal role in evacuating and billeting children, organizing the young evacuees at railway stations and escorting them on their journeys. During the Blitz, the WVS ran rest centres that provided washing facilities, food and clothing to those whose homes had been destroyed in the bombing raids. By 1943 the WVS had more than a million volunteers, whose work ranged from helping with the collection of materials to be salvaged for the war effort, to the knitting of socks and gloves for merchant seamen.

Battle of Britain

⊕ Invasion threat

Many members of the Local Defence Volunteers (LDV) had to find their own weapons. At first, they were also without uniforms, so had to wear an armband like this over their clothing. In July 1940 Winston Churchill changed the name of the LDV to the Home Guard. Over time, it received better equipment and guidance.

An instructor explains how a rifle works to two members of the Local Defence Volunteers.

After Germany had defeated France in June 1940, Britain chose to fight on. While Germany put pressure on Britain to surrender, Hitler ordered an invasion plan – code-named Operation Sealion – to be drawn up. But invasion was intended as a last resort; Hitler would have rather agreed terms with the British without using military means. By holding out, the British knew that an attack from German forces could happen any day, and throughout the summer of 1940 people across the country anxiously watched for signs of the expected invasion. Hitler's army was only 35 kilometres from the coast of southern England, across the Channel in France. The British people frantically prepared to defend their country. They constructed anti-tank defences, built concrete pillboxes and stockpiled poison gas to use against German troops on the beaches of southern England. They removed signposts to confuse invading forces and went on the alert for German spies.

The British government also created a new, voluntary armed force, the Local Defence Volunteers (LDV), which would support the army if there was an invasion. Its name was later changed to the Home Guard. Soon, 1.5 million men who were too young or too old for military service had enrolled. The Home Guard patrolled factories and coastlines and checked identification cards at roadblocks. Its members were issued with khaki battledress, but shortages meant that they often found themselves without a steel helmet or overcoat. Small Home Guard units were trained in sabotage techniques to attack behind enemy lines in the event of invasion. But in quiet village streets, most noises in the night were false alarms.

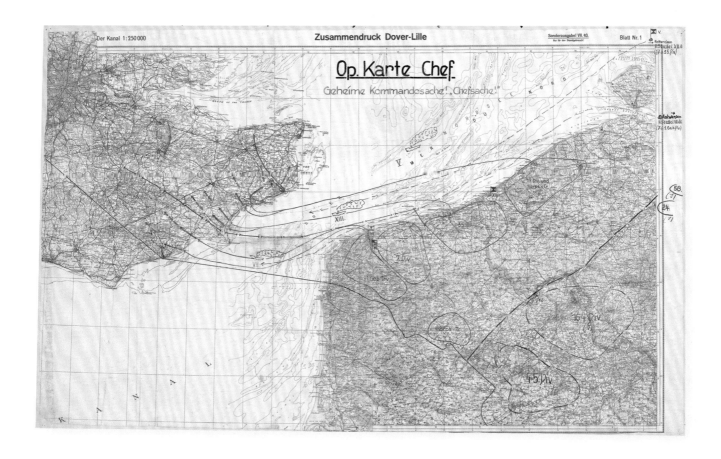

This map (above; detail right) was part of Operation Sealion, the Germans' planned invasion of Britain. It shows where German forces would land and advance. The Germans also compiled a book, *Die Sonderfahndungsliste G.B.* (Special Search List Great Britain), also known as the 'Black Book', which contained a list of people living in Britain whom they planned to arrest after the invasion. The list included prominent politicians, Jewish people and communists, as well as famous authors, actors and artists.

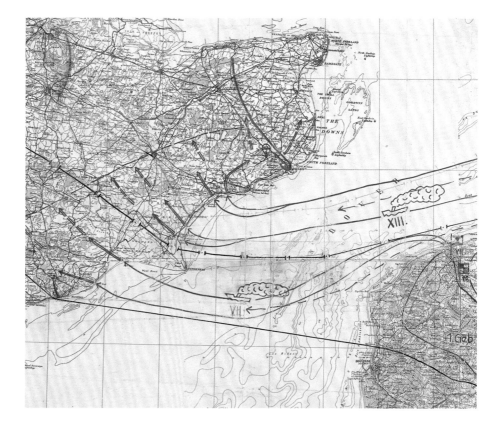

⊕ The battle

In the summer of 1940, Britain came under intense attack from the air as Germany's air force, the Luftwaffe, fought the RAF for control of Britain's skies. As part of Operation Sealion, the Germans knew that, before their invasion fleet could cross the Channel and land sufficient numbers of men along the south coast, they first needed to establish air superiority over southern England. Starting in July, German aircraft attacked British ports; then, in mid-August, they began bombing RAF bases. The aim was to seriously damage the RAF's ability to continue the fight by making it difficult for pilots not only to take off and land at their bases, but also to rest. In September, the Germans switched tactics and began bombing London by day. This gave RAF Fighter Command a much-needed chance to regroup. As a result, when the Luftwaffe launched a series of heavy raids on southern England on 15 September, it found the RAF was stronger than expected. The Germans suffered heavy losses and realized that a seaborne invasion of Britain would not be possible.

Throughout the Battle of Britain, the UK threw everything it had into defending itself. Among its arsenal was a well-organized air-defence network, the Dowding System, which gave the RAF a crucial advantage, ensuring that incoming raids were quickly detected, and that Britain's limited resources were deployed as effectively as possible. Radar (radio detection and ranging) was used to pick up and locate attacking enemy aircraft, while members of the Observer Corps scanned the skies and tracked the aircraft as they moved inland. The combined intelligence was sent to Bentley Priory – the hub of the Dowding System, located to the north of London – before being forwarded to the relevant RAF Group and passed on to a sector station, which would scramble fighter aircraft into action. Once these fighters had intercepted the German aircraft, fierce aerial battles known as 'dogfights' would break out. Pilots had to think quickly and work fast in these high-stakes encounters. Aircraft and pilots could be impaired in a range of ways, and if anything went seriously wrong

An Observer Corps post in action during the Battle of Britain. The corps consisted of around 30,000 members. Observers watched for incoming enemy aircraft and estimated what height they were flying at.

ABOVE The British war artist Paul Nash completed this oil painting, *Battle of Britain*, in 1941. He wanted to capture the overall impression of what he witnessed, not just a single event. As he explained, the intense clashes in summer skies above the English landscape and the 'smoke tracks of dead or damaged machines falling' were all intended to 'give a sense of an aerial battle'.

RIGHT A group of pilots from No. 303 (Polish) Fighter Squadron RAF, one of two Polish squadrons that fought in the Battle of Britain. A total of 145 Polish airmen took part in the battle, along with men from Australia, Belgium, Canada, Czechoslovakia, France, Ireland, New Zealand, Rhodesia (now Zimbabwe), South Africa and the United States. In total, the Battle of Britain involved almost 3,000 Allied airmen.

ABOVE This summer flying suit belonged to Ehrenfried Lagois, a Luftwaffe pilot who fought in the Battle of Britain. Ehrenfried, whose nickname was 'Fred', had been shot down during the Battle of France in May 1940 but had survived. Although he was well trained and experienced, he was under intense pressure – like other German airmen – to break Britain's RAF. Later in the war, Ehrenfried's aircraft was accidentally hit by German anti-aircraft fire. He crashed into the sea and died.

RIGHT This is a scale model of a British Hawker Hurricane. Between them, the British and German air forces had some of the best fighter aircraft in the world. The British also had the iconic Supermarine Spitfire, while German pilots flew the formidable Messerschmitt Bf 109E. Spitfires were faster, sleeker and could climb higher than Hurricanes, but the latter outnumbered the former and, although slower, were more robust. RAF pilots had to use all their skill and ingenuity to shoot down Messerschmitt fighter aircraft.

during a sortie, or mission, an emergency landing or bail out by parachute might be the only options left. But such escape routes were not always available, and large numbers of men were shot down and killed. Many pilots were seriously wounded – mainly from burns and bullets – and some faced the prospect of long-term disability.

In order to fight the Battle of Britain, the RAF needed pilots, ground crew and, above all, aircraft. Following appeals for help, men joined up as pilots and ground crew, while women volunteered for the Women's Auxiliary Air Force (WAAF). People gave millions of pounds to build new aircraft as part of a popular public campaign, the 'Spitfire Fund'. Crucially, Britain's aircraft production outpaced Germany's throughout the campaign. Airmen were at the heart of the battle. They needed skill, endurance and luck to survive. Pilots could be scrambled into action four or even five times a day, and were unable to get much rest. Many became mentally and physically exhausted.

Although known as the 'Battle of Britain', the campaign was in fact a truly multinational effort. In total, 574 men from outside the UK flew as RAF pilots during the battle. These included some of the top air 'aces' (pilots who had shot down at least five enemy aircraft) of the war, such as the Czech pilot Josef František, Witold Urbanowicz from Poland, and the New Zealander Brian Carbury. The average age of an RAF fighter pilot in 1940 was just twenty years old. Both air forces involved in the battle suffered heavy losses. Around 2,500 members of the Luftwaffe died and 544 RAF airmen – around one in six – were killed.

For German pilots, who had a tough job in trying to break the RAF, the battle was hard-fought and demoralizing. The Germans thought that the Luftwaffe was doing more damage than it actually was. This affected German airmen, who were being sent to fight a battle that, it seemed to them, they just could not win. Large numbers were shot down and taken prisoner, with the British noting the nervous exhaustion of German airmen captured at the height of the campaign. By October, it was clear that the Luftwaffe had failed to break through Britain's air defences. It had also lost too many aircraft. This meant that a seaborne invasion of the UK would not be possible before the winter set in. Britain had survived.

JOAN MORTIMER

On 31 August 1940, the RAF airfield at Biggin Hill in Kent was heavily attacked. Joan, a sergeant in the Women's Auxiliary Air Force, was in the armoury when the air raid started. Although surrounded by high explosives, she stayed at her telephone switchboard to send vital messages to the defence posts around the airfield.

Joan then picked up a bundle of red flags and hurried out to mark the unexploded bombs scattered around the airfield, continuing her work even when one went off close by. Joan was awarded a Military Medal (far left) for her bravery. Also pictured is her Defence Medal and War Medal.

FREDERICK HARROLD

Frederick was a British fighter pilot. On 28 September 1940 he set out in his Hawker Hurricane on his third operational flight, but German fighter aircraft shot him down. At first, he was believed missing, but his parents later received a telegram confirming that their only son had been killed.

Frederick was wearing this RAF jacket when he was shot down. Various other possessions – including religious medallions, a bent house key and a dented cigarette case – were found on his body. Frederick was just twenty-three years old when he was killed in action.

The Blitz

⊕ Britain under attack

Having abandoned their plans to invade the south of England, after failing to gain air superiority over the RAF, the Germans turned their attention to breaking Britain's will to stay in the war by attacking its war economy and the morale of its citizens. The Germans bombed the UK repeatedly from September 1940 until May 1941, targeting major cities, ports and armaments factories. British newspapers called the campaign the 'Blitz', taken from the German word *blitzkrieg*, meaning 'lightning war'.

Bombs struck night after night across the country, killing 42,000 people, shattering communities and damaging more than 2 million homes. London was the most-raided city, bombed for fifty-seven nights in a row. The densely populated, poorer areas of East London suffered particularly badly. But the Blitz was an attack on the whole country, and German bombers targeted other major British cities and industrial centres. Places repeatedly or severely hit included Belfast, Birmingham, Cardiff, Clydebank, Coventry, Hull, Liverpool, Manchester, Plymouth, Portsmouth, Sheffield and Southampton. In raids on Hull over two consecutive nights in May 1941, around 10 per cent of its population were made homeless. The Germans even coined a new word, *coventrieren*, following their destruction of the small city of Coventry during raids in November 1940. They then used the term to describe the razing of a city through bombing.

Never knowing where and when the raids would happen, the British people were put under intense strain. Often bombed at night after a full day's work, many became exhausted. It was difficult to find shelter in crowded cities and thousands of people took to sleeping in the surrounding countryside to escape the bombs, something that became known as 'trekking'. At one

ABOVE Ron Weir, aged six, wrote this letter to his grandmother from a communal air-raid shelter near Blackfriars in London. Packed with people, such shelters were often unpleasant and uncomfortable places to be. Air raids could last for hours, and spending time in a small shelter soon became boring. Ron records some of the things that he and the other people in his shelter had done to pass the time, including playing draughts and knitting. People would also play cards and other games, read, and listen to records or the wireless.

OPPOSITE, TOP The Morrison shelter became available in March 1941. It was a steel cage that doubled as a table and was designed for a family to sleep in. Although they took up space, they were more convenient than going to an outside shelter, and people kept blankets and clothes in them for quick use. In government tests, the Morrison proved to be effective. It was designed to withstand the upper floor of a house falling on top of it.

OPPOSITE, BOTTOM Alice Prendergast, of Balham, south London, waters vegetables on top of her Anderson shelter.

point in May 1941, it was estimated that around half of Liverpool's population were leaving the city each day for the relative safety of the surrounding countryside, so severe was the bombing. But many people chose to sleep in their own beds, only going to a shelter if the air-raid siren sounded. Some had shelters at home, either a Morrison shelter – a strong, metal construction that doubled as a table – or, for those with a garden, a corrugated-steel Anderson shelter. Both were free to low earners, and by September 1940, 2.3 million of the latter had been issued. Anderson shelters offered protection against anything other than a direct hit, but were cramped, cold, dark and often leaked. Increasingly, they were used less and less by families who, despite the risk, preferred the comfort of their house. Those without space for a shelter at home used shared public shelters, which could accommodate larger numbers of people. These could be in the basements of buildings; at places of work; large purpose-built shelters; or brick-built surface, or street, shelters. The last of these were often flimsily constructed and gave little protection from the bombs. Moreover, when these larger, group shelters received a direct hit, it resulted in mass loss of life.

With lots of people – often strangers – crowded together in communal shelters for hours at a time, tempers would sometimes fray and fights could break out. In the capital, people used ready-made subterranean spaces to shelter from the air raids: the London Underground. The British government initially banned use of Underground stations as places of refuge but were forced to relent once it became clear that Londoners were ignoring the ban on a nightly basis. In September 1940, an estimated 177,000 people were taking cover in the Underground each night. Long queues formed outside Tube-station entrances during the evening as people sought room on the crowded platforms; at some stations, a permit was needed to guarantee a place.

ABOVE A British family shelters in an alcove of Christ Church in Spitalfields, London, 6 November 1940. This is one of a series of photographs taken by the British photographer Bill Brandt, who was commissioned by the Ministry of Information to capture life in air-raid shelters.

At first, those people whose homes had been destroyed by the bombing struggled to find help. The raids made huge numbers homeless, and it was difficult for them to know where and how they should get the help they needed in order to put their lives back together. Changes were introduced and, in time, agencies providing emergency assistance with housing, food and clothing became better organized. Much of the help for air-raid victims was provided by volunteers, such as those who worked for the Citizens Advice Bureau, which offered information and practical assistance.

But not everyone possessed this community spirit, and crime levels actually rose during the Blitz. The bombing heightened divisions between the wealthy and those living in densely populated, poorer neighbourhoods, who tended to suffer more. Some people took advantage of the disorder, committing such crimes as looting, profiteering and fraud. Newspapers of the time frequently recorded the various instances of Blitz-related crime. Looting of property from bomb-hit houses and work premises was a fairly common offence, adding insult to injury for those whose homes or livelihoods had been damaged. 'Hang a Looter' cried the front page of the *Daily Mirror* on 26 November 1940, with the lead article going on to state that fines and imprisonment were doing nothing to deter people from committing this 'filthy crime'. Although many offences were carried out by known criminals and opportunists, there were also instances of people in positions of authority taking advantage of the trust placed in them. Members of the armed services, war reserve policemen, auxiliary firemen and ARP rescue workers were among those convicted of stealing possessions or materials from damaged premises or victims of bombing. And looters were not always adults: children, too, were found guilty of this crime. Wartime profiteering – charging inflated amounts of money for in-demand items – and the illegal trading of food and goods (the black market) were other crimes that tested Britain's over-stretched police force and criminal justice system during the Blitz.

Before the war, the British government had been worried about how mass bombing might affect the population. It kept a close eye on public morale through Home Intelligence – a department of the Ministry of Information that reported on people's attitudes during the war. Further, unofficial records of the British public's opinion of the Blitz were kept by Mass Observation, which used volunteers to observe and report on how people were coping. There is no single consensus that can be drawn from these assessments, and people responded to and experienced the Blitz in a variety of ways. The so-called Blitz spirit was not a complete myth and did exist to some degree. However, in places that suffered significant damage or were reduced to rubble, morale did at times deteriorate, even coming close to breaking. In some of the hardest-hit places, where large loss of life occurred, resources were too stretched to provide for individual burials. Instead, mass funerals took place, at which the whole commu-

ABOVE An injured woman is helped to a reception centre from a first-aid post, following the bombing of her home during an air raid on Liverpool in May 1941.

RIGHT During the nine months of the Blitz, more than 45,000 tons of explosives were dropped on Britain. The bombs varied in size and impact. Large parachute mines and high-explosive bombs caused huge devastation, while strangely shaped butterfly bombs, such as this one, were smaller but deadly. Incendiary bombs were dropped in vast quantities in order to start fires that not only destroyed buildings but also guided German bombers at night.

OPPOSITE, BOTTOM At around 1 am on 17 April 1941, a German landmine struck buildings in Brixton Road, south London. It caused thirteen casualties and totally destroyed the offices of the solicitors' firm where John Turner worked. An official report recorded that, several hours later, fires were still burning. These scissors were all that John could salvage from the wreckage. He used them for years, regarding them as lucky to have survived such devastation. Thousands of homes, offices and factories were destroyed through bombing and it often took months to repair them.

nity could pay their respects to those killed in the bombing. A mass funeral was held in Coventry to bury the dead from the raid on 14 November 1940, and after the devastating attack on Clydebank in March 1941, twenty-two unclaimed bodies were buried in a mass grave at Dalnottar Cemetery.

Amid the destruction, many worked to rebuild, rehouse and rescue the victims of bombing. When explosive devices failed to detonate, the bomb-disposal teams that went to make them safe did so knowing that they could be killed at any moment – indeed, a number of them were. People who were trapped under the rubble of bomb-hit homes were saved by men who knew that the remains of the buildings could collapse on them as they tunnelled through the debris. Many who carried out rescue work and bomb disposal displayed great bravery. A new award – the George Cross – was created by George VI during the Blitz to reward the most notable acts of heroism.

🌐 Evacuation

A group of evacuees from Bristol arrive at their destination. About 175 children were evacuated from Bristol to the Kingsbridge area of Devon, south-west England.

The biggest ever mass movement of people in Britain took place in the summer of 1939. More than 3 million people – mainly children – were moved from cities at risk of bombing. They were evacuated to the safety of small towns and the countryside. When there were no major air raids for a year, many evacuees returned home. Later, however, in 1940, heavy bombing and the threat of invasion drove them out of the cities again. Evacuation brought together people from very different backgrounds. Their experience was not always a happy one.

The government had been researching the idea of evacuation since the 1930s, but it was in the summer of 1938 that the Anderson Committee developed the scheme, dividing the country into evacuation, neutral and reception areas. Parents in the evacuation areas, usually larger urban areas like London, were encouraged to evacuate their children to the reception areas, which tended to be more rural. Priority was given to school children, mothers with children under five, pregnant women, teachers and some disabled people. The government needed the help of railway officials, teachers and the police, as well as the Women's Voluntary Services (WVS) and billeting officers, to support such a massive movement of people.

Evacuation was announced over the radio on 31 August 1940. Parents were sent letters by schools or local authorities encouraging them to register for the voluntary scheme. A document was issued that listed the items children should take with them; these included a gas mask, a change of underwear, pyjamas, a toothbrush, a comb, a towel, soap, a face cloth, handkerchiefs and a warm coat. But many families struggled to provide their children with all of the items on the list. Some middle-class hosts were appalled at the condition the children arrived in, and the Mass Observation archive contains accounts of evacuees who were infested with lice or had never eaten at a table with a knife and fork. In addition, some of the more homesick children tended to wet their beds, with host families assuming it was a sign of bad character or neglectful parents. The WVS produced leaflets giving advice on how to help children settle in and prevent bed-wetting. There is evidence, however, to suggest that some reports were exaggerated in an effort to claim an additional laundry allowance from the government. Criticism was also directed towards evacuated mothers, who were often accused of being lazy and negligent. Devon's education inspector noted evacuee children being 'seen outside the local public houses in the evenings' while their mothers were inside. *Spectator* magazine reported that many evacuated mothers were the 'lowest grade of slum woman'.

Starting in June 1940, the government's Children's Overseas Reception Board (CORB) evacuated more than 2,600 children to Australia, Canada, New Zealand, South Africa and the United States. But in September that year, a German submarine sank the SS *City of Benares*, a passenger ship, as it sailed to Canada. Of the ninety evacuees on board, seventy-seven died. The CORB scheme was stopped. Some families, however, continued to make private arrangements to relocate children overseas. Removal vans in city streets became a common sight as wealthier people organized accommodation in country hotels or with family and friends.

This Ministry of Health poster was designed to discourage families from bringing their children back to the cities from which they had been evacuated. A large number of evacuees were brought home during the early stages of the war, but were re-evacuated when heavy bombing began in 1940.

DOROTHY DAVIES

Dorothy Davies was thirteen years old when she was evacuated from London to the village of Fittleworth in Sussex. The woman who owned the house where Dorothy stayed was seventy years old and had just had a stroke. Dorothy was billeted with her friend, and together they had to cook, clean and look after the woman.

Despite the hard work, Dorothy enjoyed the fresh air and freedom of the countryside. She embroidered this tea cosy with an image of two girls happily picking flowers.

JOHN SADLER

One evening in August 1940, thirteen-year-old John was going to bed when his father came in to tell him that he would be evacuated the following day. Shocked, John soon found himself aboard the SS *Llanstephan Castle* on the way to South Africa.

John used the materials from his model aircraft kit to build a model of the ship. He showed it to the captain, who encouraged John to visit the ship's carpenter. Together they used paint from the actual ship to finish the model and mount it.

⊕ A nation at war

RIGHT The government used posters such as this one to urge civilians to produce their own food.

BELOW A woman pins a luminous flower on to her jacket at a London department store. Blackout restrictions led to the creation of innovative new accessories to help people be seen in the dark.

OPPOSITE, BOTTOM The Women's Voluntary Services played a leading role in the National Salvage Scheme, organizing household collections and introducing rewards to encourage children to take part. This silk scarf, designed by Jacqmar of London, was intended to increase awareness of the scheme, and bears the slogan 'Salvage your Rubber'. Rubber could be recycled into aircraft tyres or wellington boots.

·· every available piece of land must be cultivated

GROW YOUR OWN FOOD
supply your own cookhouse

With Britain at war, life changed dramatically. Men, women and children had to carry identity cards and gas masks at all times. A nationwide 'blackout' made it harder for German bombers to spot cities at night. Street lights were turned off and car headlights masked. Light from windows was blocked out with thick curtains, cardboard or paint. Faced with having to fumble their way home in the dark, people wore luminous armbands, buttons or flowers to prevent accidents.

As an island nation, Britain imported vast amounts of food and supplies from overseas. With German U-boats stalking British merchant ships in the Atlantic, delivering these resources was dangerous. The government looked at ways of producing more food on the home front. The 'Dig for Victory' campaign, for example, used posters to encourage people to grow their own food. Vegetable plots sprung up in gardens across the country. Food rationing began on 8 January 1940, when bacon, butter and sugar were limited. By 1943, the list of rationed foods had expanded to include milk, eggs, cheese and cooking fat. People were issued with ration

ABOVE The British National Savings Committee created the Squander Bug, a character intended to discourage wasteful spending. Poster and newspaper campaigns encouraged people to 'squash the bug' and buy war savings certificates to help finance the war instead. The Squander Bug seen here, complete with a Hitler moustache and swastika tattoos, was used as an air-rifle target.

books and were required to register with local shops. The shopkeeper would then remove the relevant coupons from the ration book when items were purchased. The rationing of food and other goods affected everyone. It was a popular policy that was supposed to mean 'fair shares for all', but shortages, long queues and the black market caused much grumbling.

With fabric in short supply, clothes were also strictly rationed. The government introduced a utility clothing range, based on cheap, simple designs that used less material. Pockets and lapels were made smaller and trouser turn-ups banned. While it was in operation, the utility scheme saved about 5 million square metres of cotton per year. A 'make do and mend' campaign encouraged people to patch-up old clothes. During the war the demand for ordinary materials used in manufacturing increased significantly. The National Salvage Scheme encouraged people to recycle rags and metal so they could be made into clothes, weapons and machine parts; the scheme also urged them to save their kitchen waste to help feed animals.

Fighting Back
🌐 Bombing Germany

The British public was encouraged to back the bombing campaign against Germany. The 1941 film *Target for Tonight* was made in the style of a documentary and featured real servicemen. Although it inspired public support, it was misleadingly positive. The film followed a Wellington bomber crew on a successful – but fictional – raid against a German oil plant. It was so popular that this souvenir pamphlet containing stills from the film was published.

In the summer of 1940, with much of Europe under German control, Britain's chances of victory seemed bleak. Undaunted, the British looked to ways in which they could take the fight back to the Germans. Some military and political leaders thought that Germany could be bombed into surrender, with Churchill stating that the way to defeat Germany was 'an absolutely devastating, exterminating attack by very heavy bombers upon the Nazi homeland'. RAF Bomber Command was tasked with destroying German industrial targets – including factories and synthetic oil production plants – in order to weaken Germany's capacity to fight.

Britain's bombing force, however, was not strong enough to inflict significant harm. It did not have enough men or aircraft and lacked the technology to find and hit targets, so the early air raids caused only minor damage overall. Moreover, British RAF bomber aircrews incurred heavy casualties, which weakened morale. As German defences grew ever stronger, Bomber Command suffered an unsustainable rate of loss. British crews had outdated bomb-aiming technology, making precision bombing almost impossible. A 1941 government study, the Butt Report, found that only one in three aircraft dropped its bombs within five miles of the target. Although the raids had little real impact, there was moral outrage in Germany at the civilian deaths caused by British bombs. On 25–26 August 1940, RAF bombers raided Berlin for the first time. Although the attack caused very little damage, it was met with shock by Berliners, who had been assured by Hermann Goering, a senior Nazi leader and commander-in-chief of the Luftwaffe, that enemy bombers would never reach the German capital. William Shirer, a US journalist who was in Berlin at the time, wrote in his diary on 28 August: 'The Berliners are stunned. They did not think it could happen.'

British government propaganda built up the bombing campaign as a positive, proactive means of hitting back against a seemingly all-conquering enemy. The true results of the bombing campaign – the RAF's high rate of loss and an underwhelming impact on Germany's war machine – were hidden

JOHNNY SMYTHE

Johnny grew up in Freetown, the capital of Sierra Leone. Sponsored by the Sierra Leone government, he volunteered for the RAF in 1940 and travelled to Britain to train as a pilot. He later became a navigator.

Johnny's twenty-seventh mission, in November 1943, was an attack on the German city of Mannheim. During the raid, his aircraft was badly damaged by German anti-aircraft defences. He was wounded and forced to bail out. Johnny and his crew were captured and spent the rest of the war in a prisoner of war camp. He was released in 1945.

from the British public. Many people supported it, in reprisal for the impact German bombing was having on British towns and cities during the Blitz. But the campaign also had its detractors, including religious leaders, and a sizeable proportion of the British population was opposed to enemy civilians being bombed.

⊕ Spies, raids and codebreaking

In July 1940 the British established a secret organization to work against the Germans in occupied Europe. The Special Operations Executive (SOE) was led by Hugh Dalton, the minister for economic warfare, who was told by Winston Churchill to 'set Europe ablaze'. SOE recruited, trained and armed special agents and sent them to work with resistance groups, carry out sabotage and conduct espionage. Agents, all of whom served voluntarily, were drawn from both the armed services and civilian life. After intense training, including weapons handling, unarmed combat and the use of explosives, an agent would be given a mission and parachuted into enemy territory, armed with false identity papers. They were provided with specialist equipment and weapons – many of which were invented by SOE during the war, including plastic explosive, radio transmitters concealed in suitcases, and 'time pencils' (small, timed detonators) – in order to work against and spy on German occupying forces.

Operating behind the lines in German-occupied Europe was extremely dangerous. Many captured agents were tortured and executed. Of the 470 SOE agents sent to France, 118 did not return. Unusually for wartime Britain, women were allowed to serve in an equal capacity to men. Female agents underwent the same training as their male counterparts. In total, thirty-nine women were sent by SOE to operate in France, thirteen of whom did not survive. As a new and somewhat unorthodox organization,

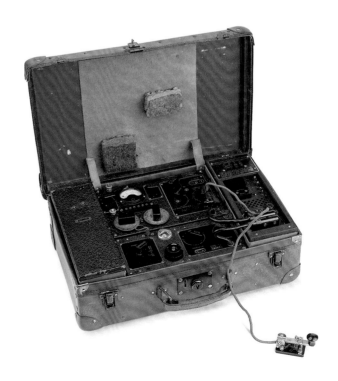

This suitcase radio was used by Special Operations Executive (SOE) wireless operators to send vital messages back to Britain. They used Morse code to transmit encoded communications about supply drops, operational updates and personnel. The wireless operator's role was important but extremely risky, as their transmissions could be picked up and their location exposed. As a result, the survival time of wireless operators in the field could be measured in terms of weeks.

BEN COWBURN

Ben was a British agent for the Special Operations Executive (SOE), recruited in 1940 and sent to France because he spoke fluent French. If caught, he would have faced almost certain death: SOE agents wore civilian clothes during their missions and could therefore be shot as spies. Like all agents in German-occupied territories, Ben had a fake identity so he could blend in. He used this forged ID card to pass as 'Jean Villeneuve'. He travelled to France four times. During these missions, he sabotaged a German submarine and six railway engines. On one occasion he caused chaos by putting itching powder in some German troops' laundry.

TO THE ATTACK!

This poster depicts one of the British Commando raids in Norway in 1941. Norway was targeted because it produced huge quantities of fish oil, used in German war production. The Commandos destroyed vast amounts of this oil in attacks on the Lofoten Islands in March and on Vågsøy in December. The raids forced the Germans to send more troops to guard the Norwegian coast, instead of deploying them against the Soviet Union.

SOE came under attack from competing entities. The Secret Intelligence Service (SIS, now MI6) viewed it with suspicion as a rival to its already-established underground intelligence work. Bomber Command saw use of its precious aircraft for SOE missions as a nuisance. It was only with tenacity – and the continued backing of Churchill – that SOE survived these threats. By the end of the war, it was a significant and sizeable operation that had boosted morale in occupied countries and successfully waged a secret war against the Germans.

In May 1940 Dudley Clark, who worked for the professional head of the British Army, General Sir John Dill, wrote a secret memorandum that set out his idea for a new force that could fight against the Germans in occupied Europe. As the British Army was being evacuated from Dunkirk, he wrote: 'There seem enormous possibilities of creating untold havoc among enemy air bases and communications if we resort to guerrilla warfare on a big scale.' The force he was proposing would carry out reconnaissance and small-scale raids against the Germans, as well as targeted attacks behind enemy lines. Churchill quickly agreed to the idea, and the force, known as the Commandos, was formed. At first it was relatively small and could operate only in a limited capacity, but in time it grew in size and capability. Early Commando members were army volunteers and were typically very active and physically fit. They received intensive training in Scotland, in weapons handling, survival and close combat. Commando raids in Norway in 1941 kept the Germans on the alert and raised morale in Britain and German-occupied Europe. As the Commandos grew in strength and experience, they achieved greater successes, including, in March 1942,

FRED HAM

Fred joined the Commandos from the Gloucestershire Regiment. He was an expert climber and later became a Commando climbing instructor.

Fred carried this knife with him when he took part in a raid on Norway's Lofoten Islands in March 1941. Fred and his comrades destroyed 800,000 gallons of valuable fish oil, took more than 200 German prisoners, and captured important information. They also returned to Britain with 300 Norwegians who had volunteered to fight against the Germans.

the destruction of the dry dock at Saint-Nazaire on the west coast of France to prevent the Germans from using it. But these activities also served to enrage Hitler, who, in October 1942, issued a directive stating that, 'From now on, all men operating against German troops in so-called Commando raids in Europe or in Africa are to be annihilated to the last man.' Later in the war, Commandos were used as assault troops to spearhead large-scale attacks and were deployed in locations across the world.

While undercover agents and commandos took the fight to the enemy, an army of codebreakers was at work to find out its intentions. At Bletchley Park, a country house and estate in Buckinghamshire, Britain's brightest minds found ways to read encoded German messages, in one of the best-kept secrets of the war. Bletchley Park housed the British government's Code and Cypher School, in which top-secret work was carried out to decipher the military codes used by Germany and its allies. Women as well as men worked at Bletchley Park – the hub of Britain's codebreaking activity – and all had to keep their wartime work completely secret. Enemy messages were first intercepted by members of the Y Service, a chain of wireless intercept stations around Britain and across the world. Once an encrypted message had been transcribed, it was sent to Bletchley to be decrypted and analysed.

Perhaps the most famous of Bletchley's achievements was the breaking of the 'Enigma' code. The Enigma (of which there were several models) was a type of enciphering machine used by members of the German armed forces to send messages securely. From early in the war, a team at Bletchley worked on cracking the codes the Germans used for Enigma messages, to discover their plans. Two leading mathematicians, Alan Turing and Gordon Welchman, designed a machine known as the 'Bombe', which helped to significantly reduce the work of the codebreakers. From mid-1940, German Luftwaffe signals were being read, and the intelligence gained from them was helping Britain to fight the war. Turing also worked to decrypt the more complex German naval communications that had defeated many others. Although breaking the Enigma code is the most well-known of Bletchley Park's accomplishments, cracking the 'Lorenz' cypher was arguably more important to the outcome of the war. Lorenz machines were used to encipher German strategic messages of high importance. Although the cypher was highly complex, it was possible to break. But working through the messages by hand proved too time-consuming. An engineer, Tommy Flowers, invented 'Colossus', a very early type of electronic computer, which sped up the process and allowed these valuable Lorenz communiques to be understood.

Members of the German armed forces used Enigma machines to encrypt messages in secret codes they believed were unbreakable. Although Polish mathematicians had worked out how to read Enigma messages and had shared this information with the British, the Germans increased the machine's security at the outbreak of the war by changing the cipher system daily, making the task of British codebreakers more difficult.

⊕ War-weary Britain

People in Britain became increasingly tired of war and austerity. By 1942 they were no longer under threat of invasion or constant air attack. Yet the government continued to make more demands on people's lives. Wartime restrictions and shortages of food continued.

The thoughts and opinions of the British public were captured through an independent social-research project run by Mass Observation. People were encouraged to keep diaries or answer questions about rationing, bombing, doubts over victory, crime and even sexual behaviour. The government monitored these insights to gauge public attitudes towards the war, propaganda campaigns, and the restrictions it was imposing.

⊕ The mobilization of women

Another significant change to lives on the home front was the mobilization of women for the war effort. In many countries their labour kept factories, farms and transport running. Women also served in the armed forces, mainly in support roles, although in the Soviet Union women fought on the front line. In some countries war work for women became compulsory. The wages they earned gave many women newly found independence. But their jobs could be dangerous, dreary and exhausting, and many were expected to look after families as well.

From December 1941, Britain conscripted women into the war effort. Unmarried women under thirty had to join the armed forces or work on the land or in industry. By 1943, women up to the age of fifty could be mobilized. Many women gained new skills and higher incomes, but gender inequality continued. Marion Mills, a member of the Auxiliary Territorial Service (see below), was proud to say that 'women found that they could master a variety of hitherto unknown tasks, not just adequately, but with skill and dedication.'

Women's Land Army recruits at the Northampton Institute of Agriculture learn how to milk a cow, 1942.

ROSEMARY THOMPSON

'Have you any rats you want catching?' Rosemary would ask, as she travelled through the countryside with the Women's Land Army (WLA). Rosemary's job was to pump gas or poison into the hedgerows of farms around Devon in order to kill the rats that were eating the crops. She would then return the next day to collect the dead animals.

In a letter to her parents, Rosemary commented that, having spent so much time in orchards, she had eaten enough apples to turn her 'insides into a barrel-full of cider'. The job did not always go according to plan: on one occasion, Rosemary's friend accidently gassed five chickens instead of rats.

MARIAN MILLS

After joining the Auxiliary Territorial Service, Marian became a radar operator with an anti-aircraft unit stationed at Dartford in Kent. At night, when the 'action stations' alarm was sounded, Marian's job was to dash to the power unit and turn it on with a heavy cranking handle. Once they had power, a radar transmitter and receiver searched for the target. As a woman, Marian was not allowed to shoot the anti-aircraft guns, despite being on the front line as shells and debris fell around her.

Mrs Cheatle from Sheffield operates a lathe at a munitions factory in Yorkshire, 1942.

Recruitment posters for the Women's Land Army (WLA) offered prospective members a healthy outdoors lifestyle, something that would have appealed to the many women who had been living in towns or cities. The reality, however, was hours of hard manual work, with long days and minimal holiday. Basic accommodation was often provided on farms, but, owing to the high recruitment rate, by 1944 there were 22,000 women living in 700 hostels. At its peak in 1944, approximately one-quarter of the 80,000 members of the WLA were employed in some type of dairy work. Other roles included pest control, especially the containment of rats, which posed a serious threat to supplies of food and animal fodder on farms. In order to increase food production, areas of land that had previously been considered unsuitable for growing crops were drained and transformed with heavy machinery. Land girls, as WLA recruits were often called, were taught to operate excavators and tractors for this purpose. Around 6,000 women were employed in the Timber Corps, sourcing and cutting the wood that was urgently needed for telegraph poles and rebuilding projects.

The Auxiliary Territorial Service (ATS) was a branch of the British Army for women. Just like their male counterparts, ATS recruits completed four weeks of basic training. Although they were not allowed to fight, a wide range of jobs was available to them, including cook, telephonist, driver, postal worker and ammunition inspector. Owing to the shortage of men of fighting age, ATS members took over support jobs as radar operators, military police or on anti-aircraft gun crews. This put women on the 'front lines' of the British home front, and hundreds of ATS recruits were killed on duty. Famous members of the ATS included Mary Churchill, Winston's youngest daughter, and Princess (later Queen) Elizabeth, who trained as a lorry driver and mechanic.

Janet Holland and Eileen Eteson, officers with the Auxiliary Territorial Service, operate a searchlight, 1944.

The Mobilization of Women

Unmarried women under 30 had to join the armed forces or work on the land or in industry. By 1943, women up to the age of 50 could be called on to serve. In addition, hundreds of thousands of women volunteered in almost every aspect of wartime life.

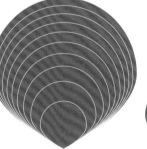

100,000

1,000,000	200,000	182,000	80,000	74,000	168*
WVS	**ATS**	**WAAF**	**WLA**	**WRNS**	**ATA**
Women's Voluntary Services	Auxiliary Territorial Service	Women's Auxiliary Air Force	Women's Land Army	Women's Royal Naval Service	Air Transport Auxiliary
Women who joined the WVS often had family responsibilities that prevented them from joining the armed services. Members volunteered for such tasks as escorting evacuee children.	ATS personnel worked as radar operators and military police, crewed anti-aircraft command posts, and fulfilled a wide range of essential operational duties.	WAAFs undertook a variety of roles, including compiling weather reports, maintaining aircraft, serving on airfields and working in intelligence.	The land girls did a wide range of jobs, including milking cows, lambing, ploughing, gathering crops, digging ditches, catching rats and carrying out farm maintenance work.	Wrens played a major part in the planning and organization of naval operations. From 1941, they also served at Bletchley Park, operating machines used in codebreaking.	Female members of the ATA served as pilots or flight engineers. Pilots' responsibilities included flying military aircraft from factories to front-line bases.

* Number of women involved in each service by 1943, except ATA: the figure of 168 is for the whole of the war.

WOMEN IN EMPLOYMENT
BRITAIN, 1939–1943

Most women in the labour force took over factory jobs that had been held by men.

Government figures show that women's employment in the UK increased during the Second World War from about 5.1 million in 1939 (26% of all women of working age) to just over 7.25 million in 1943 (36%). By September that year, 46% of all women aged between 14 and 59, and 90% of all able-bodied single women between the ages of 18 and 40, were engaged in some form of work or National Service.

1939
5.1 million

1943
7.25 million

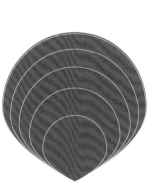
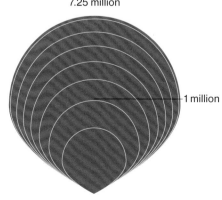

1 million

Approximately 950,000 British women worked in munitions factories during the Second World War, in roles that encompassed engineering, explosives, chemicals and shipbuilding. Factory work was often well paid, but women endured long shifts, sometimes up to seven days a week. Workers were also at serious risk from accidents involving dangerous machinery or highly explosive materials; indeed, accidents caused by the latter were common. Handling such chemicals as sulphur turned the women's skin and hair yellow, earning them the nickname 'canary girls'.

The Women's Royal Naval Service (WRNS), whose members were known as Wrens, initially recruited women in order to allow men to serve at sea. This was reflected in its recruitment posters, which featured such slogans as 'Join the Wrens today and free a man to join the Fleet'. Although few served at sea, Wrens did operate small ships close to shore. Their responsibilities included driving, cooking, clerical work, and operating radar and communications equipment. Many Wrens were also involved in planning naval operations, including the D-Day landings in June 1944. Some were drafted into signals intelligence and called on to operate machines used in codebreaking at Bletchley Park.

Women who joined the Women's Auxiliary Air Force (WAAF) worked closely with RAF pilots and aircrew, interpreting photographs of enemy targets, plotting aircraft movements, forecasting the weather for air operations and debriefing returning aircrew. A large number of them were trained in highly skilled roles as mechanics, electricians or engineers. Unlike many of the other services, the RAF and WAAF did not have a colour bar to prevent people of different ethnic backgrounds from enlisting. Although WAAFs did not serve as aircrew, women were allowed to fly as pilots in the Air Transport Auxiliary (ATA). ATA pilots were responsible for flying military aircraft from factories to front-line bases or damaged aircraft to repair yards. They flew anything from temperamental fighters to four-engine heavy bombers. Pilots in the ATA were nicknamed 'Ancient and Tattered Airmen': as well as women, they included men who had been rejected by the RAF for being too old or having a disability.

LOUIE WHITE

Louie trained at the Leeds Mechanical Institute as a milling-machine operator, and in 1942 went to work at the Blackburn Aircraft factory at Roundhay Road, Leeds. Her boss, George, was impressed with her ability to check the dimensions of aircraft parts using a micrometer. When Louie was promoted to inspector, she bought her own micrometer and George engraved her name on it.

Louie often worked the night shift, starting at 7 pm and finishing at 7.30 am. After only a few hours' sleep, she would do the shopping or housework; she even found time to join the local section of the Women's Home Guard. In June 1943 Louie heard that her husband, Jack, an air-gunner with the RAF, had been killed. Louie was a widow at just twenty-five years old.

EVE ALBU

Eve served in the Women's Royal Naval Service (WRNS), travelling the country and giving eye tests to pilots in naval air stations. While cycling towards Lee-on-Solent, Hampshire, Eve heard the hum of a German fighter aircraft overhead. A hail of bullets splattered across the road in front of her. Eve threw herself over a wall, rigid with fear until the aircraft had gone.

Eve loved her job in the WRNS but was forced to leave when she married her husband, Ian Robertson. Women were expected to leave paid employment when they married or had their first child.

LILIAN BADER

Lilian, who was born in Liverpool, applied to join the Navy, Army and Air Force Institute (NAAFI) and worked briefly in the canteen at Catterick Camp, Yorkshire. However, she was dismissed because of her Jamaican heritage.

Lilian gave up hope of 'doing her bit' until she heard on the radio that the RAF was accepting West Indian recruits. Lilian became one of the first women to qualify as an RAF instrument repairer in the Women's Auxiliary Air Force (WAAF). During her training, she received the news that her brother Jim, who was serving in the Merchant Navy, had been killed at sea.

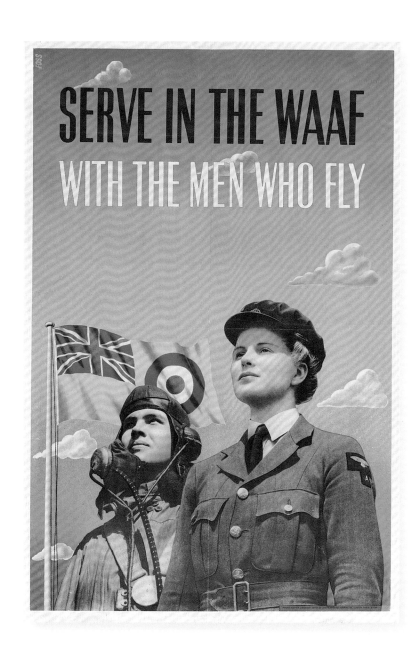

JOAN HUGHES

Joan celebrated her seventeenth birthday by becoming the youngest licensed female pilot in Britain. In 1940, at the age of twenty-one, she became one of the first eight women to be accepted into the Air Transport Auxiliary.

Joan worked as an instructor at the Advanced Flying Training School in White Waltham near Maidenhead, Berkshire. While taking off in a Stirling four-engine bomber, one of the tyres punctured on the runway. Onlookers feared for her life, but were impressed by Joan's ability to keep such a large aircraft under control.

⊕ Later raids on Britain

The Luftwaffe continued to bomb Britain after the Blitz. Between April and June 1942, the Luftwaffe targeted areas of cultural or historical significance, including the cities of Exeter, Bath, Norwich, York and Canterbury. These attacks were known as the 'Baedeker Raids', after the famous German travel guides. Some well-known historic buildings were destroyed, such as the Guildhall in York, but many were not; as a result, the Luftwaffe's attempt to break British morale failed. In 1944 Hitler ordered a concentrated attack on the Greater London area, known as the 'Baby Blitz'. However, most bombs failed to reach their target, and British air and ground defences ensured that relatively little damage was done. It was clear that Germany could not match the scale of the Allied air forces, which were conducting a strategic bombing campaign day and night against German cities.

Rescue teams listen for survivors among the ruins of a house in Upper Norwood, south-east London. The house had been destroyed by a V-1 flying bomb.

The first German V-1 flying bomb landed in London on 13 June 1944. Over the following seven months, V-1s landed mainly in London but also in the Belgian city of Antwerp. These *Vergeltungswaffen* (revenge, or retribution, weapons) were the first missiles of their kind. They killed more than 5,000 people and seriously injured some 16,000. The V-1 flying bomb was nicknamed the 'doodlebug' or 'buzzbomb', after the distinctive, motorbike-like sound of its engine. When the V-1 reached its target, its engine shut off – an unexpected consequence of the missile entering its final dive – leaving people below to guess where it might fall. British defences against the V-1 included anti-aircraft guns and more than 2,000 barrage balloons, which were intended to catch the missiles in the cables tethering them to the ground. Fighter pilots even dared to tip the wings of the V-1s with those of their own aircraft, knocking them off course and reducing the number of casualties. To calm Londoners' nerves, districts under V-1 attack received extra supplies of beer. The V-1s, and the even more destructive V-2 rockets, were made by forced labourers in underground factories, where as many as 20,000 of these labourers died.

THIS PAGE This harness and lead (above) belonged to Rex (shown on the left in the photograph below), a German shepherd search and rescue dog. Rex searched the spaces in London's bombed-out houses that humans could not reach. When he found someone, Rex would alert the Air Raid Precautions wardens by barking or digging with his paws. In April 1945 Rex received the Dickin Medal (below) – a gallantry award given to animals – for saving sixty-five lives.

FRANK HANNAN

Frank joined the Royal Canadian Air Force at the age of twenty-two, and was posted to Yorkshire in England as a bomb-aimer. From March to May 1944, Frank flew operations in support of the preparations for D-Day, which included mine-laying and bombing railways.

On 26 June 1944 Frank scored a direct hit on a V-1 launch site in Ardouval, north-west France, which he recorded with excitement in his logbook. Frank wrote his name across the front of his flying helmet.

CHAPTER 4

GLOBAL WAR

WESTERN THEATRE
1941–1942

■ Axis powers and their allies
▨ Held by Axis powers, Dec 1941
▧ Allied powers and their allies
□ Neutral countries

AXIS ADVANCES
→ 1941
┈▸ 1942
╌▸ Nov 1942

ALLIED ADVANCES
→ 1941
┈▸ Nov–Dec 1942

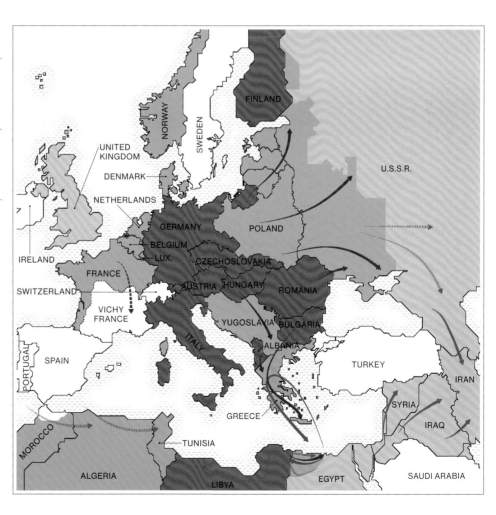

War in Africa, the Middle East and the Mediterranean

🌐 Clash of empires

With Britain besieged in 1940, Benito Mussolini saw an opportunity for Italy to supplant it as the leading power in the Middle East. A huge Italian force of 250,000 men was assembled in Libya, with the object of invading Egypt. The latter country was officially independent, but significant British military forces were stationed there. They protected the Suez Canal and shielded oil reserves and refineries in Iraq and Iran. Egypt also provided an important harbour, at Alexandria. From there, Britain's Mediterranean Fleet contested control of the eastern Mediterranean with the Italian Navy. The UK would not give up Egypt without a fight. The British land commander in the region, General Sir Archibald Wavell, was forced to defend Egypt with just 36,000 men. In mid-August, however, as the Battle of Britain reached its climax, Britain's leaders took the risky decision to send to Egypt almost half of the tanks currently available to defend Britain against German invasion. On 13 September, while these tanks were still at sea, the Italians marched. Untroubled by British opposition, they advanced more than 90 kilometres into Egypt. But there, at the coastal town of Sidi Barrani, they stopped, settling down to build a base from which they could renew their advance.

This Italian minefield marker was recovered from Sidi Barrani in Egypt. There, on 10 December 1941, the Western Desert Force, composed of Indian and British soldiers, attacked an Italian army five times its size. It captured 38,000 Italian soldiers at a cost of only 624 casualties.

Wavell had no intention of allowing the Italians to dictate the course of the campaign. He planned to attack them once the new tanks had arrived. On 9 December, the British 7th Armoured Division and the 4th Indian Division broke through the Italian positions south of Sidi Barrani and advanced towards the coast. Italian troops began to surrender in large numbers. The British followed up their victory by crossing into Libya and driving the Italians back along the coast. In late January 1941 the 7th Armoured Division crossed the desert to the south to cut off the Italian retreat. This trapped the Italian 10th Army, which was forced to surrender. Wavell's small force had beaten an Italian army of 300,000 men, capturing 133,000 of them.

This was not the only Italian threat to Britain in Africa. An equally large Italian army was based in Italian East Africa, from where it could threaten British control of Kenya and Sudan. In August 1940 the Italian East African Army invaded British Somaliland, forcing its evacuation. But for Wavell, this threat was a secondary one. Unlike the Italian forces in Libya, the East African Army could not be reinforced from Italy. Only in early 1941, once the limited local forces had been strengthened by arrivals from Egypt (notably the experienced 4th Indian Division) and elsewhere in the British Empire, did Wavell make his move. Italian East Africa was

These are the badges of soldiers brought from across the British Empire to invade Italian East Africa. They attacked in late 1940 from Kenya and Sudan. The experienced 4th Indian Division came fresh from victory in Egypt. Further troops came direct from India, Britain's African colonies and South Africa. By November 1941, the Italian Empire in East Africa ceased to exist. From top, left to right: 4th Indian Division cloth badge; 5th Indian Division cloth badge; 1st South African Division cloth badge; Sudan Defence Force cap badge; 7th King's African Rifles cap badge; Royal West African Frontier Force cap badge.

invaded from three directions – from Sudan in the north and west, and from Kenya in the south. Both combatants made heavy use of troops raised in their empires. Britain shipped in soldiers from India and other parts of Africa, while colonial troops made up two thirds of Italy's forces. Italian resistance was poorly coordinated, although resilient in the chief battle of the campaign, at Keren in Eritrea. Italian leaders feared Ethiopian reprisals against their settlers and colonial officials, so frequently proved eager to arrange the surrender of towns to British forces. By November 1941 Italian power in the region had been destroyed, and the exiled emperor, Haile Selassie, was restored to his throne. Most significantly for Britain, ending an Italian presence in the Red Sea enabled President Roosevelt to declare that it was no longer a 'combat zone'. Ships from the neutral United States could now deliver war material direct to the British in Egypt.

ABOVE Ethiopian *Arbegnoch* (Patriot) soldiers gather to witness the return of their emperor, Haile Selassie, from exile.

RIGHT Soldiers of the 4th Indian Division in action in Eritrea.

⊕ Britain overstretched

These Polish, British, Indian, Australian and Czech soldiers were among those who fought in the siege of Tobruk.

In the spring of 1941 Britain's victories against Italy were overshadowed by a series of crises and disasters. In October 1940 Italy had mounted an invasion of Greece from Albania, over which it had established control in 1939. The Greek Army not only managed to defend its mountainous border but also, in terrible winter conditions, drove the invaders back into Albania. Hitler, fearing a collapse of Axis power in this theatre of war, came to Mussolini's rescue. He persuaded Bulgaria to act as the base for a German invasion of Greece and sent a small but well-equipped force to North Africa under his favourite general, Erwin Rommel. Britain had already sent aircraft to aid Greece; it now planned to send a land force there. At worst, it was thought that this decision would show the UK in a good light to the watching United States; at best, it might encourage neutral Yugoslavia and Turkey to turn against Germany. On 27 March 1941 the Yugoslav government, which had just agreed to become an ally of Germany, was overthrown in a coup. An enraged Hitler now decided to crush Yugoslavia 'with pitiless harshness', as well as Greece. The German invasion of both countries commenced on 6 April. Both were overwhelmed in little more than three weeks. Most of the British, Australian and New Zealand expeditionary force in Greece managed to escape by sea to the island of Crete. As in Norway and France, a British campaign had once again culminated in a desperate evacuation.

Even as the Greek disaster was unfolding, Britain suffered a defeat in Libya. Showing the sort of initiative that was lacking in the Italian generals to whom he was supposedly subordinate, Rommel attacked and drove the British all the way back to the borders of Egypt. The British had been weakened by the need to send troops and aircraft to Greece. Rommel benefited from the arrival of strong Italian reinforcements in Libya, although his own *Afrika Korps* were at the heart of his highly mobile campaign. Britain was saved from a worse defeat only by the fact that the 9th Australian Division held on to the vital port of Tobruk. Their presence there meant that Rommel could not risk a further advance into Egypt. As if Wavell did not have enough

Two British soldiers made this banjo for their makeshift band. They were helping to defend the crucial port of Tobruk in Libya during a seven-month siege by Axis forces in 1941. For most of this time, the principal element of the Tobruk garrison was the 9th Australian Division. Their successful defence of the port prevented an Axis advance into Egypt.

A Maori soldier of the New Zealand Division is helped ashore after being evacuated from Crete. The Royal Navy lost nine ships during the battle for the island.

problems, a nationalist takeover in Iraq now threatened to take that country over to the Axis side. Troops had to be sent to oust the new government. With the Germans attempting to channel aid to Iraq through Vichy-France-controlled Syria, Wavell was also forced to mount an invasion of the French colony. At the same time, pressure from Churchill impelled him to make two abortive attempts to drive back the Italian–German army and relieve Tobruk.

The most startling event of this taxing period for Britain was the daring German capture of the island of Crete, garrisoned by many of the troops evacuated from mainland Greece. The defenders failed to cope with an assault led by airborne troops, beginning on 20 May 1941. Yet again an evacuation had to be mounted. This time, however, 18,000 men had to be abandoned, and the Royal Navy paid a heavy price in lost ships. In 1940 Britain's Mediterranean Fleet had seized the initiative against the Italians, despite the latter having more modern warships. But now, air and submarine attacks began to wear it down, ship by ship. Its base at Malta became untenable owing to heavy bombing attacks. More ships were lost in the western Mediterranean when convoys were sent from Gibraltar to keep Malta supplied. Finally, as 1941 drew to a close, Italian divers entered Alexandria harbour on manned torpedoes and put two British battleships out of action. The land campaign in North Africa now acquired even more significance.

TOTAL WAR

DESTRUCTION

The war saw devastation on an unprecedented scale. Whole cities and towns were ruined by aerial bombing or shellfire. Countless villages were deliberately burned to the ground. People's homes, workplaces and schools were destroyed, as were such essential services as transport, water and drainage. Those living in areas shattered by war faced years of struggle to restore their homes and lives.

RIGHT This drawing by the British war artist Leslie Cole shows the aftermath of an attack on the city of Senglea, on Malta's Grand Harbour. The island of Malta was the most bombed place on Earth during 1942, which marked the climax of an Italian and German bombing campaign that the Maltese people had endured since June 1940. More than 30,000 buildings were destroyed or damaged.

JOHN CLOUDSLEY-THOMPSON

Not long after celebrating his twenty-first birthday in May 1942, John was in command of a tank of the 4th County of London Yeomanry. At the Battle of Gazala in Libya, his tank was one of almost 400 destroyed in a terrible British defeat. Severely injured, he managed to scramble clear of the tank. Three of his crew, however, had been killed.

John narrowly avoided having his leg amputated. While recovering, he made this model of the Crusader tank in which he so nearly died.

⊕ The desert war

The war in North Africa was confined largely to the coastal fringe of the region. In the open terrain, infantry units unsupported by tanks or anti-tank guns were almost helpless against motorized or armoured forces. Consequently, the war there became a war of movement. The fighting see-sawed backwards and forwards between eastern Libya and western Egypt. Control of the small ports along the Libyan coast was crucial for bringing in supplies of fuel. Nearby airfields were key to establishing air superiority over the battlefield and interdicting seaborne supply lines. An army that suffered defeat in battle usually needed to withdraw for hundreds of miles to re-establish a firm basis of supply.

Britain had poured ever increasing resources into the region. Churchill hoped to open up the Mediterranean by driving the Axis powers out of North Africa. It was also an area to which Britain could ship troops from its empire with relative ease, and a place where it could be seen to be prosecuting the war with vigour. As one British general put it: 'we can't beat Germany in the Middle East ... but we can fight Germans there.' Wavell's failure to defeat Rommel saw an impatient Churchill replace him with General Sir Claude Auchinleck in July 1941. Auchinleck succeeded in relieving Tobruk, but soon he too found himself out-manoeuvred by Rommel. In June 1942 the Axis forces broke through the British Empire positions around Gazala in Libya and threw Auchinleck's Eighth Army into a panicky retreat into Egypt. At the time Churchill was visiting the United States – an ally since its entry into the war at the end of 1941 – and was actually in the White House when the terrible news arrived that Tobruk had fallen, with 35,000 men entering Axis captivity. A sympathetic Roosevelt immediately ordered the dispatch of 300 of the latest American tanks to Egypt. This was all the more generous given the scathing reports that the US military attaché in Egypt was filing regarding the poor performance of the British and Empire forces. The situation was not helped by the fact that the Italians were decoding the attaché's messages and passing detailed information about British dispositions to Rommel. Such useful intelligence only served to enhance Rommel's reputation as a military genius, a celebrity status that was as readily accepted in Britain's desert army as it was in Germany.

This 25-pounder gun saw action at a pivotal moment in the war in North Africa. In the summer of 1942, Germany won a major victory in Libya, driving the British back into Egypt. But the German and Italian advance was stopped by British Empire troops at the First Battle of El Alamein in Egypt. During the battle, the 11th Field Regiment, Royal Artillery, used this gun as an emergency anti-tank weapon.

The Eighth Army's respect for Rommel was not matched by a similar admiration for its own officers. Repeated defeats and retreats had demoralized many of its men, who were fighting a long way from home in physically challenging conditions. There were scenes of confusion and disorder during the retreat into Egypt in June 1942. Some men began to desert their units to lurk in the comparative safety of Cairo or Alexandria. The situation became so serious that Auchinleck and other senior commanders began to argue for the return of the death sentence for desertion or cowardice. However, enough of the army's fighting spirit remained for Auchinleck to stabilize the situation by defeating a renewed Axis attack at the First Battle of El Alamein.

This did not save him from an increasingly exasperated Churchill. Ordering another change of leadership, Churchill appointed General Sir Harold Alexander commander-in-chief in the region. To lead the Eighth Army, Churchill was persuaded to choose a relatively unknown figure, with no experience of the fighting in North Africa: Lieutenant General Bernard Montgomery. 'Monty', as he was known, could hardly have differed more from the reserved and reticent figures cut by Wavell and Auchinleck. He deliberately set himself up as a 'personality' to whom soldiers could relate – assisted by lavish handouts of cigarettes. Taking the tactics and organization of his army back to basics, he insisted that he would undertake operations only 'within the capabilities of the troops'. He also refused to be chivvied by Churchill into attacking before he was fully prepared.

The Axis forces in Egypt were in a dangerous position at the end of a long and vulnerable supply line. Having failed to break through the El Alamein position, Rommel could not go forward and, for political reasons,

ABOVE Winston Churchill with generals Sir Harold Alexander (left) and Bernard Montgomery (right).

RIGHT A group of South African airmen return from a mission in their American-supplied Douglas Boston bomber. Close cooperation between Britain's Desert Air Force and its army was key to the outcome of the war in North Africa.

This watercolour, by the British soldier Jack Chaddock, shows troops advancing at El Alamein. The Second Battle of El Alamein lasted for two weeks, during which British Empire troops gradually wore down the Italian and German defenders and forced them into retreat.

could not order a retreat. His men were increasingly afflicted by illness. Fly-borne sickness affected both sides, but the British took greater care to stop its spread by digging effective latrines. At El Alamein, fighting was concentrated in a 32-kilometre gap between the sea and the Qattara Depression – impassable to vehicles – to the south. In front of their positions on this narrow front the Germans and Italians sewed 300,000 land mines. On 23 October 1942 Montgomery launched his long-planned attack against this heavily fortified line. In a gruelling set-piece battle, the Axis forces were ground down to a point where they could no longer hold their position. On 4 November Rommel ordered a retreat that proved to be irreversible. Churchill had at last got the desert victory he so desired. And it had come in the nick of time. Just four days later, British and American forces landed in French North Africa and began advancing on the Axis forces from the west. The time for winning purely British victories was over.

Germany Invades the Soviet Union

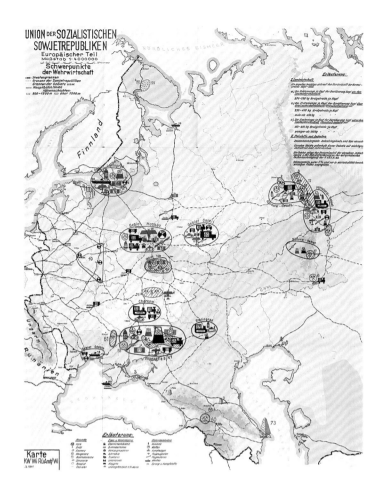

The Germans planned to exploit conquered territory in the Soviet Union ruthlessly. This high-command planning map shows the location of war-related resources and industries in the western Soviet Union. But it also hides a darker purpose. The regions tinted yellow are those producing a surplus of food; this would be taken for Germany. The brown-tinted regions normally imported food; people here would be allowed to starve. One Nazi minister wrote: 'the Russian has stood poverty, hunger and austerity for centuries. His stomach is flexible; hence no false pity!'

Scarcely had Hitler enjoyed his supreme moment of triumph over France when his mind turned to another potential conquest. This was not Britain, whose sea and air defences made invasion an unappealing prospect to the German Army, but Germany's partner, the Soviet Union. In late July 1940 Hitler informed his generals of his intention to 'smash' the Soviet state. He justified this proposal by pointing to the raw materials and other resources that Germany would gain. He further suggested that a Soviet defeat would remove Britain's last hope and force it to make peace. In reality, Hitler was inspired by long-held ideological and racist convictions. He wanted to destroy the 'asocial criminal system' of communism and build a Germanic empire in the East. It would be peopled by German settlers, who would act as the overlords of any of the indigenous population who were not killed or driven away. In less than a year, as preparations for the attack were being brought to completion, this conception had become central to Nazi thinking. Heinrich Himmler, the head of Germany's security and police services, told his subordinates that the coming war against the Soviet Union would be 'a racial struggle of pitiless severity, in the course of which 20 to 30 million Slavs and Jews will perish through military actions and crisis of food supply'.

🌐 Operation Barbarossa

Code-named Barbarossa (after the twelfth-century Holy Roman Emperor), the invasion of the Soviet Union was the largest military operation in history. The build-up could hardly have been concealed from Soviet observation, and Stalin received multiple warnings of the impending attack from spies, foreign powers and even deserters from the German Army. While he did not dismiss the likelihood of war, he clung to the idea that Hitler would not risk it as long as Germany was benefiting from its trade deals with the Soviet Union, and as long as Britain stood undefeated to the west. He was sustained in this state of denial by his political cronies. On 21 June 1941 Lavrentiy Beria, head of the NKVD, wrote to Stalin, saying: 'my people and I, Josef Vissarionovich Stalin, firmly remember your wise prediction: Hitler will not attack in 1941!' Within hours, a massive German air attack had destroyed most of the front-line planes of the Soviet air force before they could even get airborne. Three million Germans began to cross the recently established western borders of the Soviet Union. They were joined by allies: in the south, 300,000 Romanians; in the far

A photograph taken during the German advance into the Soviet Union, showing a smashed Soviet motorized unit. On the left, a dazed man is taken prisoner.

These German photographs, being in colour, offer a rare opportunity to view the 1941 invasion of the Soviet Union as the invaders themselves would have seen it.

ABOVE German troops pass through a village. The vast majority of German soldiers invading the Soviet Union were forced to march huge distances on foot. These bicycle-equipped men are part of an infantry reconnaissance unit.

RIGHT A roadside ditch contains the bodies of dead Soviet soldiers.

BELOW A German anti-tank gun in action. The standard German 37-millimetre anti-tank gun proved useless against the most modern Soviet tanks. Its crews called it the 'doorknocker'.

BELOW The Germans issued their soldiers with straw overboots to protect them from frostbite in the bitter Russian winter. Such efforts were insufficient to save 250,000 German soldiers from frostbite in the winter of 1941/42.

BOTTOM Soviet troops drive the Germans back from Moscow. These men are lucky enough to be supported by the latest model of Soviet tank – the powerful T34.

north, 500,000 Finns seeking revenge for their defeat in 1940. Smaller contingents were contributed by Italy, Hungary and Slovakia.

In Germany, both in the army and among the Nazi leadership, there was confidence that victory would be swift and that the whole Soviet system would collapse, 'like a house of cards'. Extraordinary initial successes supported this optimism. The Soviet Red Army was ill-prepared and proved unable to respond effectively when its battlefield communications were disrupted. As in the Battle of France, fast-moving German tank and motorized formations created havoc, surrounding huge numbers of confused and poorly led Soviet soldiers. By 1 September, nearly a quarter of a million Red Army soldiers had been killed and, strikingly, more than 2 million captured. Nevertheless, things were not going as smoothly for the invaders as they had hoped. They had underestimated the number of troops at Stalin's disposal, the fighting spirit of the Red Army and the resilience of the Soviet system. Germany's own losses were significant, and the vast size and poor transport infrastructure of the Soviet Union began to overstrain the German Army's resources. It was able to beat off repeated Soviet counter-attacks and continue its advance, but its leaders now belatedly began to understand the nature of the war they had initiated.

RIGHT This shirt was worn by a Soviet prisoner held in Majdanek concentration camp in Nazi-occupied Poland. During its invasion of the Soviet Union in 1941, the German Army made little effort to feed or house captured soldiers. Some – communist officials and Jews – were shot. Most simply starved, or died of disease or exposure. Later in the war, Soviet prisoners were kept alive but only to be exploited as a source of labour.

TOTAL WAR

CRIMES AGAINST PRISONERS OF WAR

International rules enshrined in the Third Geneva Convention governed the treatment of prisoners of war (POWs). In many cases, those regulations were respected. The Soviet Union and Japan, however, were not signatories to the convention, and prisoners held by these countries endured hard labour, hunger and disease. Many thousands lost their lives. Other combatants also failed to apply the rules. At the end of the war, thousands of German prisoners held by British, US and French forces in makeshift camps died of neglect.

But the worst atrocity against POWs was committed by the German Army. During 1941 it captured 3 million Soviet soldiers. Two-thirds of them were dead within six months – murdered, or the victims of criminal neglect.

ABOVE Soviet prisoners bury the emaciated corpses of their comrades at Stalag 319. At this camp alone, at Chelm in occupied Poland, 60,000 prisoners died.

In September, the Germans were encouraged when they captured Kiev and took another huge haul of prisoners. By the end of the month they were ready to mount a final drive to take Moscow. Their attack was initially successful, encircling yet more of the Red Army; but rain and snow – or, more specifically, the terrible mud it created – slowed them down. When the ground froze hard, they advanced once more. One unit penetrated as far as Khimki, less than 30 kilometres from the Kremlin. In Moscow there had been panic and looting, but Stalin made it clear that he was staying put. His decision to stand firm was encouraged by reports from his spies that Japan had no plans to invade Siberia. This allowed him to move his final reserves of men from the Far East to his western front. On 5 December these troops counter-attacked. Overstretched, taken by surprise and ill-equipped for the freezing conditions, the Germans were driven back. Only the determination of some units to fight on while surrounded, and Hitler's demands that there should be no retreat, prevented a rout. Nevertheless, after more than two years of war, the Red Army had inflicted the first major land defeat on Germany.

⊕ A million murdered

From the outset, Hitler's war in the East had a brutal impact on the civilian population there. While many people, especially in the Baltic states and Ukraine, hated Stalin's regime, they soon found that Germany and its allies were anything but 'liberators'. Hitler himself expressed the opinion that 'the vast area must be pacified as quickly as possible; this will happen best by shooting anyone who even looks sideways at us.' His generals subscribed to this view as well, fearing the possibility of 'partisans' operating at their rear as they advanced. Anyone suspected of such resistance faced summary execution; villages accused of harbouring partisans were burned down. Special units, *Einsatzgruppen*, consisting of men from the Nazi security organizations – the SS, the SD and the Order Police – were tasked with shooting anyone thought likely to cause trouble. They had already honed their murderous skills during the occupation of Poland. The campaign of terror they unleashed in the Soviet Union soon began to focus on the local Jewish population. Their leaders assured themselves that 'where the partisan is, there the Jew is too, and where the Jew is, there is the partisan also'. They began by shooting Jewish men, but within a few weeks the murders were extended to women and children too. People from some Roma communities were subjected to the same treatment.

The *Einsatzgruppen* swiftly realized that they could recruit help from local people. The latter were motivated by antisemitism, a desire for Jewish property, or the fact that they associated Jews with the hated Soviet regime. In western Ukraine the Romanian occupiers mounted their own campaign of terror against Jews. The killers could also count on the support of the German Army. Field Marshal Walther von Reichenau told the soldiers of his Sixth Army that they were the carriers of 'an inexorable racial idea' and urged them to 'have full understanding of the necessity for harsh but just punishment of the Jewish sub-humans'. In the *Einsatzgruppe* shootings, people were generally murdered at short distances from their homes, having been marched to the killing site on foot. The size of the massacres varied according to the size of the local Jewish population. The *Einsatzgruppen* leaders exchanged tips with one another regarding the most efficient means of killing large numbers of people. At the biggest single massacre, at the Babi Yar ravine outside Kiev, almost 34,000 people were shot over the course of two days. In total, it is believed that more than 1.5 million people were murdered in this way during 1941 and 1942. The war in the Soviet Union had transformed the Nazi policy towards Europe's Jews from one of persecution to one of outright annihilation.

An *Einsatzgruppe* in action, 14 September 1941. These men are shooting Jewish women in a pit near Dubăsari in Transnistria.

🌐 The road to Stalingrad

During the early part of 1942, Stalin pushed his generals to keep attacking the Germans all along the vast front, which stretched from the besieged city of Leningrad in the north to the Crimea in the south. His insistence on multiple attacks diluted their effect, although they continued until May, when an attempt to liberate Kharkov met with disaster. Hitler too was devoting an increasing amount of his energies to the war in the East. In the wake of the Soviet counter-attack at Moscow, he had dismissed the commander-in-chief of the German Army and taken the role himself. Realizing that the Soviet Union could no longer be smashed in a single campaign, he approved plans for an attack in the south. Its chief goal was to seize the principal Soviet oilfields, located in the Caucasus region. If successful, it would also cut off supplies being sent from the United States and Britain to the Soviet Union via Iran, which had been occupied by an Anglo-Soviet invasion.

Commencing on 28 June 1942, the German attack showed every sign of achieving complete success. The Red Army was forced into a retreat that appeared unstoppable. The Western Allies – America and Britain – feared that the Soviet Union would be knocked out of the war. Stalin announced savage punishments for soldiers of all ranks who retreated without orders. One phrase from his order, 'not one step back', was seized on as a slogan to help galvanize Soviet resistance. Crucially, although the Red Army retreated, it was now agile enough to avoid large-scale encirclements and surrenders. By the early autumn, the Germans were pushing towards the oilfields to the south and the River Volga to the east. But their advance had once again outpaced their resources, and they fell just short of seizing the oil. Meanwhile, they were becoming increasingly fixated on the city of Stalingrad – named for the Soviet dictator in

Red Army soldiers move through shattered Stalingrad. The streets, houses and factories of the city were bitterly contested for five months.

Starting on 19 November 1942, the Red Army attacked to the north and south of Stalingrad, surrounding 265,000 German soldiers. Hitler sent this signal ordering them to hold on. In February 1943, 91,000 starving and sick survivors surrendered. The Germans were driven back to where they had stood a year previously.

commemoration of his defence of the city during the Russian Civil War. Although it had scarcely featured in the original German plan, Stalingrad was an important industrial centre and, because it ranged along the western bank of the Volga, it offered a useful anchor for the flank of the southward German advance. The Germans succeeded in conquering most of the city but, by feeding in reinforcements across the Volga, the Red Army held on, drawing more and more German resources into the battle. Bitter fighting raged in the streets and wrecked factories. Even individual buildings became the scene of long struggles, with men of either side frequently occupying different floors of the same structure. The defenders were eventually reduced to holding strips of riverbank no more than 800 metres deep. But still they fought on.

Elsewhere, the Soviet high command was planning a counter-attack. For the first time in the war, they were able to make careful and relatively unhurried preparations for a major operation. On 19 November they struck. With their enemy hugely overstretched, they were able to concentrate overwhelming quantities of tanks and guns on either side of Stalingrad. Significantly, the initial attacks fell on Romanian formations, which lacked modern tanks and were short of anti-tank guns. Bursting through these weak defences, the two Red Army pincers met on 23 November. The Germans in and around Stalingrad were trapped. This operation was one of an ambitious series of attacks planned by the Soviet leadership.

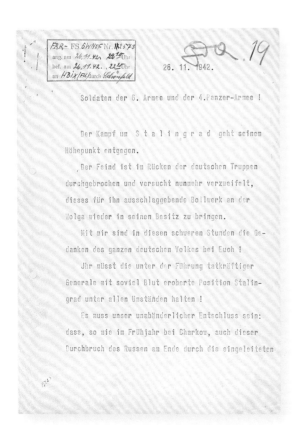

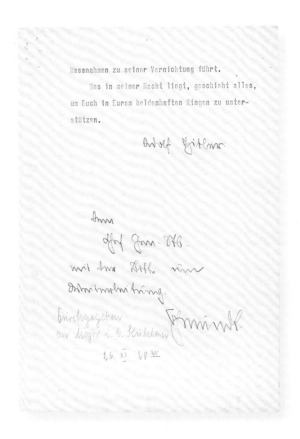

A second major offensive – against the centre of the front to the west of Moscow – turned out to be a dismal failure. But there was still a chance of exploiting the victory at Stalingrad. Plans to smash the entire southern wing of the German armies had to be scaled down because of the resources needed to maintain the encirclement of Stalingrad, where the Red Army had surrounded far more men than it had expected. But a powerful attack to the north-west of the city – this time crushing another German-allied formation, the Italian Army in Russia – compelled the Axis forces to withdraw hurriedly from all the territory they had gained during the previous summer. The men trapped in Stalingrad were doomed. Starving, sick and without medical supplies, they surrendered on

VITTORIO CARESSA

As an officer in the *Armata Italiana in Russia* – an Italian force sent to fight the Soviet Union – Vittorio found himself hundreds of miles from home. His letters to his family reveal the disturbing realities of life at the front. In one letter to his sister Marcella, Vittorio describes Russian children reduced to starvation: 'Three or four lost boys and girls who follow me ... I feel so sorry for them, you should see what they eat, if we drop a piece of macaroni on the ground, even if it's covered with piss they eat it greedily, I saw them eating grass like goats ... If you only knew and could see what war is!'

Vittorio was killed on 19 January 1943, when the *Armata Italiana* was virtually destroyed in the battles that followed the encirclement of Stalingrad.

German soldiers about to enter Soviet captivity after the surrender of the Stalingrad 'pocket'. The poor health of those surrendering and the harsh conditions faced by prisoners in the wartime Soviet Union meant that few of them would survive the war.

2 February 1943. Of the 265,000 men who had been surrounded, just 91,000 survived to enter Soviet captivity.

In a series of mobile operations, the Germans were able to re-establish a firm front in eastern Ukraine by the end of March 1943. But they had suffered a terrible defeat that had left the outcome of the war against the Soviet Union hanging in the balance. Hitler faced an agonizing decision about what to do next. Meanwhile, the Red Army had learned valuable lessons about conducting large-scale mobile operations. During 1941 and 1942, the Soviet Union had survived two German onslaughts that had looked potentially fatal. It now began to make plans to drive the invaders from its soil.

FRITZ LÜDERITZ

German Army sergeant Fritz faced an uncertain fate when his unit was surrounded at Stalingrad. In a Christmas letter to his fiancée, Wilma – his 'dear Bunny' – Fritz wrote: 'one day a Christmas must come that we can both spend together. This year Santa Claus has completely failed us. But I knew it could not be otherwise, he cannot come to Stalingrad.'

Fritz and Wilma took advantage of a law that allowed soldiers to wed their fiancées by proxy when far from home. But Fritz was destined never to return home to take up his married life.

Rapid Japanese Conquests in Asia and the Pacific

⊕ The war in China

RIGHT Residents of Chongqing after a Japanese air attack.

BELOW After the fall of Hong Kong, Lung Kai Ming – shown here with his wife and child – escaped to Guilin in China and became a pilot in the Flying Tigers.

As we saw in Chapter 1, when Japan invaded China in 1937, it successfully captured the major Chinese cities of Shanghai and Nanjing, forcing the Chinese nationalist leader, Chiang Kai-shek, to retreat with his government further inland. Thousands of refugees fled to the mountain city of Chongqing, where the Guomindang had set up a temporary wartime capital. However, Japanese aircraft targeted the city, and in May 1939 more than 4,000 people were killed in the resulting air raids. The Chinese forces managed to halt the advancing Japanese with a series of desperate counter-attacks. In 1938 Chiang's troops destroyed dykes on the Yellow River, flooding the area and killing Japanese soldiers. But the floodwater also destroyed farmland and crops, driving people from their homes. Approximately 4 million Chinese people became refugees and victims of famine during the war.

Japan was surprised by the Chinese resistance, and the costs of the war were already higher than it had

SOONG MEI-LING

Soong Mei-ling was one of the world's most powerful women. As the wife of China's nationalist leader, Chiang Kai-shek, she travelled to the United States to win support for her husband and the plight of China. Having lived in America, she spoke excellent English.

Soong became the first Chinese national and only the second woman to address both houses of the US Congress. She established schools for the orphans of Chinese soldiers and encouraged the formation of the Flying Tigers (see below and opposite, bottom).

In 1941 Clair Chennault, a retired US Army Air Force general, recruited around a hundred volunteer pilots in America to fight in China. These pilots, nicknamed the 'Flying Tigers', became the First American Volunteer Group (AVG) of the Chinese Air Force. Flying Tigers pilot Robert Smith took this photograph while flying his aircraft with his knees.

expected. It predicted that in order to avoid several more years of fighting in the vast interior of China, it would have to isolate the country from outside support, primarily from the United States. By the end of 1939, the Japanese had succeeded in cutting off the seaports in China, leaving only two supply routes: a rail line from Haiphong harbour in French Indochina, and a road from British-controlled Burma. Then, in 1940, events in Europe presented new opportunities for Japan. Nearly all of South East Asia was under the control of three colonial powers – the British, the French and the Dutch. But when France fell to Germany in June 1940, and Britain appeared weakened, Japan took advantage of the situation. It expanded into South East Asia, occupying airbases in French Indochina with the agreement of the French Vichy government. Japan cut China's access to supplies from Haiphong. It then turned its attention to the Burma Road, threatening Britain with war unless its leaders closed it. Churchill did not want to fight the Japanese as well as Germany at this moment of crisis, and agreed to close the road. China was now alone.

⊕ Political alliances

Japan's ambitions to control China were opposed by the United States, so it conducted a series of diplomatic moves in an attempt to neutralize US interference. On 13 April 1941 Japan signed a five-year non-aggression pact with the Soviet Union. By eliminating the Soviets as a threat in Asia, Japan was indicating that the only opposition to its plans came from the United States. The Japanese also aligned themselves with Germany and Italy. They signed a pact that obligated Japan to enter the war on the side of the Axis powers if America joined Britain in the conflict. Japan's attempt to intimidate the United States by signing these pacts backfired, however. President Roosevelt reacted by freezing all Japanese assets in America. Japan therefore lost the money it needed to buy war supplies. The US then banned all trade with Japan, preventing the Japanese from buying American oil or steel – materials that the country depended on for its military operations. Japan's oil reserves would not last long, so General Hideki Tojo, Japan's new prime minister, was faced with a choice: either give in to US demands and withdraw from China, or prepare for war with America.

The Japanese chose the latter option and began to plan simultaneous attacks against key locations in Asia. They endeavoured to cripple the US Pacific Fleet at Pearl Harbor, preventing it from responding to attacks on the British naval base at Singapore, as well as on American air and naval bases in the Philippines, Wake Island and Guam. The Japanese believed that by the time the British and Americans had recovered enough to launch a counter-attack, the costs of recovering their lost territory would be too great. Japan would be in control of the raw materials it needed, would have built up strong defences, and would be in a greater position to negotiate with the Western powers, forcing them to accept Japanese control of Asia.

A surrendering British soldier is searched by Japanese troops in Malaya, January 1942.

Japanese Conquests in Asia

ESTABLISHING A SPHERE OF INFLUENCE

By 1941, Japan had been locked in a bitter war with China for four years.
Seeking a quick victory in South East Asia, it launched a series of attacks
on key outposts, starting with a surprise attack on the US Pacific Fleet
at Pearl Harbor. Just a few months later, Japan had seized the natural
resources it needed to continue fighting in China.

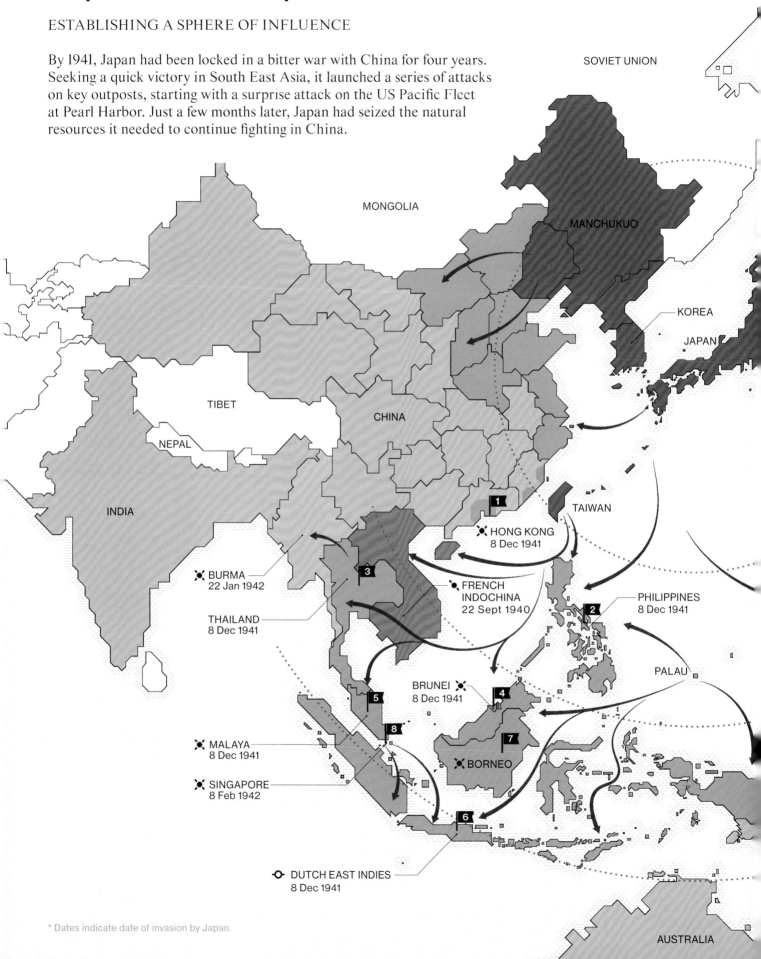

SOVIET UNION

MONGOLIA

MANCHUKUO

KOREA

JAPAN

TIBET

CHINA

NEPAL

INDIA

TAIWAN

HONG KONG
8 Dec 1941

BURMA
22 Jan 1942

FRENCH
INDOCHINA
22 Sept 1940

PHILIPPINES
8 Dec 1941

THAILAND
8 Dec 1941

PALAU

BRUNEI
8 Dec 1941

MALAYA
8 Dec 1941

BORNEO

SINGAPORE
8 Feb 1942

DUTCH EAST INDIES
8 Dec 1941

AUSTRALIA

* Dates indicate date of invasion by Japan.

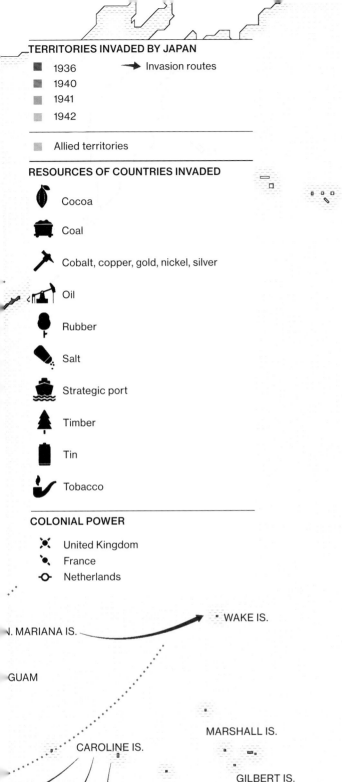

N. MARIANA IS. — WAKE IS.

GUAM

MARSHALL IS.

CAROLINE IS.

GILBERT IS.

NEW GUINEA

SOLOMON IS.

PAPUA

VANUATU

FIJI

1. HONG KONG ✕

The loss of the strategic port of Hong Kong to the Japanese represented the first time a British colony had surrendered to an invading force.

2. PHILIPPINES

In 1941 the Philippines was the world's second-largest producer of nickel. Its other exports included copper, petroleum, silver, gold, salt, cobalt and timber.

3. THAILAND

Thailand's pre-war exports included tin and rubber. However, Japanese occupation brought substantial economic loss and widespread social disruption. Between 1942 and 1945, 6% of Thailand's GDP came from forced labour, the printing of money and seized capital.

4. BRUNEI ✕

By 1935, Brunei was the third-largest oil producer in the Commonwealth. Its abundance of oil, as well as rubber, therefore made it a prime target for the Japanese during their invasion of South East Asia. Over the course of the war, Japan succeeded in extracting more than 1.5 million tons of oil from the country.

5. MALAYA ✕

In 1941 Malaya produced 38–40% of the world's rubber, and 58% of its tin, with a total export business worth £131 million. Losing this territory to Japan caused great damage to British prestige and business around the globe.

6. DUTCH EAST INDIES ⦵

At the outbreak of war, the Dutch East Indies accounted for 3% of the world's oil, producing 60 million barrels in 1940. It also exported such non-ferrous materials as bauxite, the chief commercial ore of aluminium.

7. BORNEO ✕

At the start of the war, Borneo's exports included oil, tobacco, cocoa, rubber, coal, timber, gold, Manila hemp, copra (coconut) and processed sago. In 1940 the country's oil fields, combined with those of the Dutch East Indies, produced 65 million barrels of oil. The loss of Borneo, together with Indonesia, Java and the Philippines, meant that Britain was removed from 90% of the world's rubber production, as well as 60% of global tin production.

8. SINGAPORE ✕

At the outbreak of war, Singapore was an important source of tin, petroleum and rubber. Following the Japanese occupation of Singapore in 1942, however, exports of these essential war materials came to a halt.

⊕ A surprise attack on Pearl Harbor

On 7 December 1941 Japan's ambassadors in Washington DC received a diplomatic note from Tokyo breaking relations with America. They were ordered to destroy the code machines in the Japanese embassy and deliver the note to the US secretary of state, Cordell Hull, at 1 pm local time. The US intelligence services also received the note, and knew it meant one thing – war would be declared imminently. Warnings were sent to American commanders in both the US Army and the US Navy. No one knew where an attack might be launched. But the Japanese ambassadors did not deliver their note until 2.20 pm. By this time, it was 8.30 am in Hawaii, and an attack on the US Pacific Fleet at Pearl Harbor had been underway for nearly half an hour. According to the accepted rules of warfare, Japan had attacked the United States illegally, striking at America before declaring that a state of war existed.

Located in the Pacific Ocean, Hawaii is roughly 3,200 kilometres from the US mainland, and 6,400 kilometres from Japan. No one believed that Japan would start a war with an attack so far away. For this reason, the naval facilities at Pearl Harbor were relatively undefended. Almost the entire fleet was moored in the harbour, and hundreds of aircraft were parked wingtip to wingtip on the surrounding airfields. The attack began at 7.55 am, on a quiet Sunday morning. A fleet of six Japanese aircraft carriers launched a first wave of 183 fighters, bombers and torpedo aircraft.

The USS *Arizona* following the Japanese attack at Pearl Harbor.

When Japanese bombs penetrated the armoured deck of the USS *Arizona*, its ammunition stores exploded, ripping the battleship apart. Fierce fires burned for days. Of the 1,512 crewmen on board, 1,117 were killed. This piece of the *Arizona* was salvaged from the wreckage. The majority of the ship remained submerged.

They intended to inflict heavy damage on the eight US battleships and three US aircraft carriers believed to be moored in the harbour. In less than two hours, more than 2,400 Americans had been killed and 1,100 wounded. Every battleship had sustained significant damage, airfields had been put beyond use, and the Japanese had achieved their objective and won a significant victory. However, the US Pacific Fleet had not been entirely destroyed. Crucially, none of its aircraft carriers were at the base, and a number of maintenance and repair yards, fuel-storage facilities and the dry dock were not attacked, allowing work to begin on salvaging the battleships straight away.

The American public was outraged by news of the Japanese attack. Although divided over neutrality before Pearl Harbor, the US Congress was now united in declaring war on Japan. President Roosevelt addressed a joint session of the US Congress on 8 December, announcing that 'yesterday, December 7, 1941 – a date which will live in infamy – the United States of America was suddenly and deliberately attacked by naval and air forces of the Empire of Japan ... No matter how long it may take us to overcome this premeditated invasion, the American people in their righteous might will win through to absolute victory.' Three days later, on 11 December, Germany declared war on the United States; in response, the United States declared war against Germany.

Following the attack on Pearl Harbor, pre-existing racial tensions against Japanese people in the US magnified. Anti-Japanese propaganda fuelled suspicions that Japanese Americans were not loyal to the United States or were acting as spies. An editorial in the *Los Angeles Times* warned that Japanese Americans will aid Japan 'by espionage, sabotage and other activity ... they need to be restrained'. On 9 February 1942, Roosevelt issued Executive Order 9066, which forced people with Japanese ancestry to leave their homes and report to assembly centres. They were then moved to internment camps, or War Relocation Centres, located in California, Arizona, Colorado, Wyoming, Idaho, Utah and Arkansas. Approximately 117,000 Japanese Americans were forced into these internment camps. Many were compelled to sell their homes and businesses for a fraction of their worth, not knowing whether they would be allowed to return.

JACK FELDMAN

Jack was stationed at Hickam airfield in Pearl Harbor. He wrote home to his parents in Philadelphia two days before the attack, saying: 'As company I have a .45 automatic, and I've been instructed to use it in the event of sabotage.'

The Japanese bombed and machine-gunned Hickam airfield to destroy US aircraft. *Life* magazine recorded Jack as one of the first Americans to be killed during the assault. Jack's family received this memorial certificate.

IN GRATEFUL MEMORY OF

Private Jack L. Feldman, A.S.No. 13027061,

WHO DIED IN THE SERVICE OF HIS COUNTRY AT

Hickam Field, Territory of Hawaii, December 7, 1941,

HE STANDS IN THE UNBROKEN LINE OF PATRIOTS WHO HAVE DARED TO DIE

THAT FREEDOM MIGHT LIVE, AND GROW, AND INCREASE ITS BLESSINGS.

FREEDOM LIVES, AND THROUGH IT, HE LIVES—

IN A WAY THAT HUMBLES THE UNDERTAKINGS OF MOST MEN

Franklin D Roosevelt
PRESIDENT OF THE UNITED STATES OF AMERICA

🌐 Rapid Japanese conquests in Asia

ABOVE This flag was carried at the surrender of Singapore in February 1942 (see below); it was then kept secretly in Changi prison. On 12 September 1945, the same flag was hoisted over the surrender of Japanese forces at Singapore Town Hall.

BELOW Lieutenant General Arthur Percival and his party carry the Union Jack on their way to surrender Singapore to the Japanese, 15 February 1942.

In the Pacific, the Japanese were executing their plan to control Asia by striking key Western outposts simultaneously. Many Asian people in these countries were discriminated against under European or US rule. To justify their invasion and occupation strategy, Japan promised these countries and their populations independence from the control of Western powers. Japan declared that it would create a self-sufficient bloc of Asian nations that would be culturally and economically united under the 'Greater East Asia Co-Prosperity Sphere'. Ultimately, however, real power would remain with the Japanese, who would impose a harsh regime throughout the countries they invaded. Large numbers of people would eventually suffer, as food and raw materials were diverted to the Japanese war effort.

Within hours of the attack on Pearl Harbor, Japanese forces had launched aerial attacks on the Philippines and begun landing troops on its islands. The Filipino and American forces under General Douglas MacArthur abandoned the capital city of Manila and retreated to the Bataan peninsula. Three months of fighting followed as the Japanese tried to defeat the US stronghold. The Americans were running out of food and ammunition, but with the destruction of the fleet at Pearl Harbor, reinforcements would not come. Recognizing the desperate situation, Roosevelt

Civilians in Singapore
take refuge in an air-raid
shelter during a Japanese
bombing raid.

ordered MacArthur to evacuate the Philippines and head to Australia. Approximately 60,000 to 80,000 American and Filipino troops were left behind and captured as prisoners of war. They were marched more than 90 kilometres to camps and loaded on to trains. During what became known as the 'Bataan Death March', prisoners received little to no food or water. They were brutally beaten, and many died.

Meanwhile, on the same morning that Pearl Harbor was attacked, the British colony of Hong Kong was targeted by the Japanese. The Hong Kong garrison was defended by British, Indian, Canadian and Chinese troops. They were outnumbered by the Japanese, who engaged them in bitter fighting, yet the garrison held out for seventeen days before surrendering on Christmas Day 1941. This was the first time a British colony had surrendered to an invading force. In Malaya, another British colony, Japanese troops began a series of amphibious landings on the Malay Peninsula. Malaya was a vital provider of the world's rubber and tin – materials essential to Japan's control of Asia. Nimbly navigating the tough jungle terrain on bicycles, the Japanese quickly broke the British defences. HMS *Prince of Wales* and HMS *Repulse* were stationed at Britain's naval base in Singapore, east of the Malaya coast. They sailed out to confront the Japanese amphibious support ships but were attacked by Japanese aircraft from their bases in French Indochina. This was the first time in history that warships had fought alone against an aerial attack, and it was generally believed that they could not be sufficiently damaged in such a skirmish. However, in just two hours, both the *Prince of Wales* and the *Repulse* had been sunk. This was a devastating turn of events for Britain. The Singapore naval base was now vulnerable. By February 1942, 130,000 British troops had surrendered at Singapore, an outcome that Winston Churchill described as the 'worst disaster and largest capitulation in British history'.

On 8 December 1941 Japanese paratroopers started landing on Borneo in the Dutch East Indies (now Indonesia) in order to seize key airfields. Dutch, American, British and Australian forces attempted to defend the island, but the Japanese overran them, taking thousands of Allied soldiers prisoner. In February 1942 the Japanese identified the small town of Darwin in Australia as a base from which the Allies could try to defend the Dutch East Indies. Japanese aircraft launched an attack on Darwin, killing around 250 people. Fears of an imminent invasion of Australia spread as the town's inhabitants fled inland. Cargo ships that had been moored in Darwin harbour were damaged and could not support defensive measures in Java or the Philippines. Free to occupy the Dutch East Indies, Japan now had control of the oil it needed to continue fighting.

Next, it turned its attention to the British colony of Burma. As well as being a rich source of oil, Burma possessed minerals such as cobalt and a surplus of rice. Control of the country would allow the Japanese to protect the flank of their main attack in Malaya and Singapore and give Japan control of the Burma Road, which, as we saw earlier, was being used to provide supplies to Chiang Kai-shek and his nationalist forces in China. By March 1942, the Japanese had captured Burma's capital and the strategic port of Rangoon. British troops were reinforced by Chinese soldiers under the command of Lieutenant General Joseph Stilwell of the US Army, but they were soon forced to retreat over the border into India, suffering heavy losses. Thousands of Burmese civilians lost their homes and livelihoods during the Japanese attacks. Refugees escaped to India, bringing with them tales of the British defeat. Japan had transformed the map of Asia and seemed unstoppable.

American prisoners are escorted by Japanese soldiers on the Bataan Death March, 1942.

⊕ The Allies take the offensive

This sketch shows Sergeant Sanopa of the Papuan Constabulary, who rescued a group of Australians stranded in the mountains. Papuan and New Guinean men engaged in reconnaissance patrols against the Japanese. Papuans were also praised for their dedication to the sick, acting as stretcher-bearers and carrying wounded men through the jungles to safety.

By 1942, the Japanese had succeeded in gaining control of the natural resources they needed to continue fighting in China. They had achieved their objective of striking hard and fast at Allied bases, and assumed it would take the Allies months or even years to respond to the multiple defeats. A total Japanese victory seemed assured. However, the Americans planned a counter-attack that would strike at the very heart of the Japanese mainland. Although the US had suffered greatly at Pearl Harbor, the three aircraft carriers of its Pacific Fleet (the USS *Lexington*, USS *Saratoga* and USS *Enterprise*) had escaped the attack. In addition, the USS *Yorktown* was made available from the Atlantic Fleet, giving the US significant naval and air power. Its leaders decided to use an aircraft carrier to launch an attack on the Japanese mainland.

The mission was planned by Lieutenant Colonel James Doolittle. Doolittle's bombers took off from the carrier on a one-way trip, because they were too big and heavy to land back on the carrier; moreover, the carrier itself had to retreat as soon as the aircraft had taken off, otherwise it would be an easy target for the Japanese. This meant that the pilots had to drop their bombs on Japan and then fly to China to land. Although the raid caused minimal damage to Tokyo, it sent a clear message that Japan was vulnerable to air attack, and greatly boosted American morale. However, the attack also had devastating repercussions for the people of China. Japanese troops attacked the coastal areas of China where many of the US bomber crews had landed. Chinese civilians who were discovered to have helped the Americans were tortured and killed.

US aircraft carriers and their support ships scoured the vast Pacific for signs of where the Japanese would attack next. Intercepted Japanese naval codes indicated that they intended to capture Port Moresby, an Australian possession in New Guinea. Control of Port Moresby's naval and air bases would give the Japanese a stronghold in the Coral Sea and access to Australia's north coast. With Japan already in control of bases in Java and Borneo, Australia would be neutralized. The United States sent a carrier force to oppose the offensive. Although the Japanese sunk more Allied ships in the resulting battle, they suffered heavy losses and were prevented from invading Port Moresby by sea.

KELVIN KOOREY

Kelvin – an Australian soldier known as 'Kel' to his friends – was fighting on the Kokoda Track in New Guinea with the 2nd/3rd Pioneer Battalion when a sniper's bullet hit him in the head, piercing his helmet and lodging in his jaw. Kel staggered to an airfield that was evacuating troops to the Australian base at Port Moresby. When an uninjured officer pushed past him to take the last place on the aircraft, Kel cried, 'No you're not, mate! I'm going.' Kel was sent home to Australia for surgery and made a full recovery.

An Australian 25-pounder gun gets stuck in the mud as it is hauled through the jungle on the Kokoda Track, September 1942.

More significantly, two Japanese aircraft carriers, *Shōkaku* and *Zuikaku*, were too damaged to take part in the Battle of Midway the following month, on 4–7 June 1942. Midway was the last American base in the Pacific other than Hawaii. A Japanese victory would eliminate the United States as a strategic power in the Pacific, and allow Japan to establish its Greater East Asia Co-Prosperity Sphere. Once again, intercepted Japanese coded messages gave the Allies detailed intelligence on the Japanese plan, which was to assemble a huge battle fleet to lure the American carriers into a trap and occupy Midway. The plan relied on ships engaging one another in the traditional style of naval warfare; however, the US counter-offensive was fought with aircraft, launched from its ships, so that the fleets did not fight within sight of each other. This new concept of naval warfare proved successful, and the American victory at the Battle of Midway was a turning point in the war in the Pacific.

Dominance of the sea allowed the Allies to begin their first major land offensive against Japan, at Guadalcanal in August 1942. Meanwhile, the Japanese tried once more to capture Port Moresby, this time with an overland advance. They landed troops at Buna in July 1942, intending to cross the Kokoda Track, a 96-kilometre mountain path through dense jungle, to reach Port Moresby and isolate Australia from the United States. The track was a dangerous and exhausting battlefield. Food and weapons had to be

Victorious troops of the US Marine Corps make their way out of the jungles of Guadalcanal in the South Pacific following their conquest of the Solomon Islands in February 1943.

brought up the steep mountain with mules, but the mud and torrential rain made the advance slow. Eventually, the Japanese retreated to Buna and established defensive positions. Buna finally fell in January 1943.

The US marines who landed on the island of Guadalcanal on 7 August 1942 found a large airfield, which they renamed Henderson Field, in honour of a marine who had died at Midway. Japanese reinforcements flooded the island, forcing the Americans to create defensive positions on a ridge about 1.5 kilometres from the airfield. Bloody battles for control of the ridge ensued, while naval forces struggled for control of the sea around the island. Eventually, by December 1942, the Americans gained control of Guadalcanal, with Japan evacuating its remaining forces by February the following year. The Allies were now on the offensive. They had changed the direction of the war and stopped the rapid Japanese advance in the Pacific.

SHELAGH BROWN

Shelagh, a British national, was interned for three and a half years in Japanese camps on Sumatra and Bangka in the Dutch East Indies (now Indonesia). She suffered bouts of malaria and struggled to survive starvation. To boost morale, two women in the Sumatra camp, Nora Chambers and Margaret Dryburgh, started writing out classical music from memory. They and other women in the camp used their voices to imitate orchestral instruments, creating a vocal orchestra of which Shelagh was a member. They performed three concerts before too many members had died for the orchestra to continue.

⊕ Prisoners of war held by the Japanese

As the Japanese triumphed across Asia, they interned more than 130,000 European and US civilians. Government officials, employees of international companies, teachers, missionaries and the families of servicemen were rounded up and sent to internment camps. More than 14,000 civilians died, mainly from disease and malnutrition.

Military servicemen who were taken as prisoners of war (POWs) by the Japanese were forced to undertake hard labour. During the construction of the Thailand–Burma 'Death Railway' in 1943, inadequate rations led to starvation. About 90,000 South East Asian civilian labourers and 12,000 Allied prisoners died during its construction. POWs were expected to work for long hours. They were subjected to random beatings and torture by their guards. 'It became common for our men to be literally driven with wire whips,' wrote British POWs in a report. Disease – including dysentery, malaria, beri-iberi and cholera – was rife and often proved fatal. A minor scratch could lead to tropical ulcers. Prosthetic limbs were made from scrap materials for patients

Police Sergeant Robert Bulpin secretly covered this jersey with the signatures of the 382 British, US, Belgian, Dutch and Greek nationals who were imprisoned in a Japanese camp in Shanghai. Internees faced harsh punishments if they were caught recording their experiences. For many, however, the act of signing their name was proof that they had lived; it also offered hope that they would not be forgotten if they died within the camps.

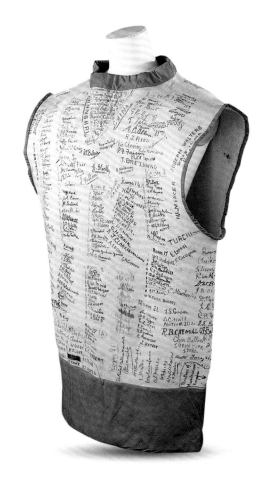

whose diseased limbs had to be amputated. Malnutrition caused diseased gums and tooth loss, and prisoners made dental plates from melted-down water bottles. Doctor Stanley Pavillard, a medical officer in the British Army, was taken prisoner after the fall of Singapore. He was sent to work on the Death Railway and treated sick prisoners with the meagre drugs and equipment he had in his medical case. He distilled water to stop the spread of cholera and performed blood transfusions. In one risky operation, he removed an appendix with a razor blade by torchlight. When Pavillard became sick himself, he continued to visit his patients while being carried on a stretcher.

THIS PAGE Prisoners held by the Japanese tried to make the best of their situation by staging concerts and plays. Great effort went into designing the theatre programmes and costumes. British POW Charles Woodhams, a former dancer, produced shows in Changi camp, Singapore, and in the Wampo and Kinsaiyok camps on the Thailand–Burma 'Death Railway'. Charles wore a dress made from a mosquito net while dancing with an officer onstage.

ABOVE Emaciated British
prisoners of war in a Japanese
hospital for POWs at Nakom
Paton, Thailand, 1945.

RIGHT In Japanese prisoner-of-
war camps, a minor scratch could
lead to tropical ulcers. Prosthetic
limbs such as this one were made
from scrap materials for patients
whose diseased limbs had to be
amputated.

The Battle of the Atlantic

🌐 Lifeline

Britain's war strategy was based on control of the sea. Initially, it had looked to starve Germany of resources by enforcing a naval blockade, but the German conquest of Norway and France had turned the situation on its head. With bases from which it could strike at British shipping under its control, Germany began to impose a blockade of its own. This threatened Britain's ability to keep fighting. Even after making huge efforts to increase its agricultural output, the UK still needed to import over half of what its people ate – largely from the Americas. Raw materials for industry needed to be shipped from across the British Empire and beyond. The oil used in Britain came from the United States, the world's biggest producer. Germany attempted to cut this seaborne lifeline by attacking ships bound for the British Isles with aircraft, surface vessels and submarines. The UK was able to counter the first two of these threats, improving the anti-aircraft defences of merchant ships and, after sinking the battleship *Bismarck* in May 1941, driving the surface raiders from the Atlantic. But the submarine threat remained.

At the outbreak of war, the German Navy possessed just eighteen operational submarines, or U-boats (*Unterseeboote*). During 1940, their limited numbers and use of faulty torpedoes restricted their impact. Early in the following year, however, they began to sink alarming numbers of merchant ships heading for Britain. In March 1941 Winston Churchill told Admiral of the Fleet Sir Dudley Pound, 'we have to lift this business to the highest plane over everything else. I am going to proclaim the Battle of the Atlantic.'

It was across the north of that ocean that Britain's most vital supply route lay. Here, shipping heading to and from the UK was formed into convoys, a system employed with success in the Great War. In the vastness of the ocean, a convoy was effectively as difficult for U-boats to locate as a lone ship. And merchant ships grouped together in a convoy could be protected by a naval escort. In 1940–41, however, Britain was desperately short of the small naval vessels most suitable for such escort duties. One of the first major contributions of the neutral United States to the British war effort was the supply of fifty elderly destroyers. In return for these badly needed ships, Britain gave America leases on sites in its New World colonies for military and naval bases. The Royal Navy also commissioned a new small warship, the Flower-class corvette. This very basic and rather slow vessel's chief virtue was that it was quick to build. It soon provided the backbone of Britain's convoy protection, with 294 being built in the UK and Canada. Aircraft were a proven deterrent to U-boat attack, but Coastal Command, whose task it was to patrol the seas, was the 'Cinderella branch' of the Royal Air Force. It had few modern aeroplanes and even fewer with the range required to escort convoys beyond coastal waters.

The construction of escort vessels and acquisition of new aeroplanes would take time. In 1941, therefore, the

Feeding 45 Millions–
FOOD CONVOY

danger posed by U-boats was acute. But Britain was saved by the fact that Hitler diverted his submarine fleet to other areas during the summer – first to the Baltic and northern Norway, in support of the invasion of the Soviet Union, then to the Mediterranean to buttress operations there. President Roosevelt pushed US neutrality to the limit in his efforts to help Britain. He established a 'security zone' on the eastern seaboard of America, where the US Coast Guard assumed responsibility for protecting shipping. In the summer of 1941, he took the extraordinary step of extending this zone two-thirds of the way across the Atlantic. Hitler, reluctant to provoke the United States, stopped his U-boats from attacking anything in this zone.

The commander of the German U-boat fleet, Admiral Karl Dönitz, understood that the only way to beat Britain at sea was to sink merchant ships faster than they could be built. It was in this context that the United States once again stepped in to provide vital help to Britain, by building ships for it. In 1940 Britain had placed an order in America for sixty freighters of a simple design, which its own shipyards did not have the capacity to build. American modifications resulted in a vessel that could be built extremely quickly, even by those with no experience of shipbuilding. President Roosevelt described the result as a 'dreadful looking object' but, branded as the 'Liberty Ship', it remained in production throughout the war, with an astonishing 2,710 being built.

Britain relied heavily on signals intelligence to protect its shipping. The codebreakers at Bletchley Park were able to decipher German naval communications during 1941, but lost this ability for most of 1942, when a more sophisticated enciphering machine was introduced. However, even if their messages could not be understood, radio transmissions made by U-boats allowed their locations to be pinpointed by radio direction-finding. Britain's 'Y Service' used land-based receivers for this purpose, while, from late 1941 onwards, some ships were equipped with 'Huff-Duff' – a high-frequency direction-finder that allowed them to locate nearby U-boats. Signals intelligence was passed to the Submarine Tracking Room at the Admiralty in London. There, the raw information was blended with inspired guesswork

This painting, *A Rescue-ship in the Atlantic, March 1943*, shows a scene witnessed by the British war artist George Plante at the climax of the Battle of the Atlantic. Plante served as a Merchant Navy radio operator and twice survived a torpedo attack. The painting shows the aftermath of a night attack by U-boats. From the deck of a rescue ship, a blazing tanker can be seen on the horizon. Survivors of another sinking can be seen at bottom right, cleaning themselves up after being rescued from oil-covered water.

to reroute convoys away from lurking U-boat 'wolf packs'. This was the most effective means of protecting shipping during 1941 and 1942.

When Hitler declared war on the United States on 11 December 1941, the U-boats were unleashed against American shipping. They enjoyed a hugely successful period, sinking thousands of tons of vessels off the eastern seaboard of America, before a convoy system was belatedly put in place. The focus then returned to the North Atlantic. Dönitz now had 300 operational U-boats, meaning that he could have eighty or more on patrol at any one time. His recent successes had earned him the enthusiastic backing of Hitler, who went so far as to claim that 'the submarine in the end will decide the outcome of the war'. It was no longer just a case of starving Britain out, but of preventing America from using it as a base for the liberation of Europe. U-boat sinkings in the North Atlantic rose to unprecedented levels. In October 1942, in a despairing letter to Roosevelt, Churchill wrote: 'the spectacle of all these splendid ships being built, sent to sea crammed with priceless food and munitions, and being sunk – three or four a day – torments me day and night.' By the year's end, British imports stood at just one-third of pre-war levels, with the UK possessing only two months' worth of oil. Terrible Atlantic storms at the turn of the year provided respite, but the threat had not disappeared. In January 1943 Hitler confirmed his backing for the U-boat campaign by making Dönitz chief of the whole German Navy. In the coming year, 400 U-boats would be available.

⊕ Winning the Battle of the Atlantic

By March 1943, shipping losses to U-boats in the North Atlantic had once again risen to a level that the Allies could not long sustain. But this masked the fact that Germany was in the process of losing the tactical and technological battle.

One reason that Britain had begun the war with inadequate escort vessels and maritime aircraft was its reliance on ASDIC, an echo-sounding system subsequently better known as sonar. But the U-boats circumvented it by attacking at night, on the surface. Creeping noiselessly among the ships of a convoy, they caused chaos when they struck. They could not be detected by ASDIC, and the darkness and confusion made them difficult targets for escort vessels.

But ASDIC was not Britain's only technological asset. An airborne radar, ASV II, was capable of detecting surfaced U-boats (a shipborne version, Type 271, became available in late 1941). Because U-boats tended to travel on the surface only at night, ASV II did not become fully effective until 1942, when an airborne searchlight – the Leigh Light – was introduced. It was used to illuminate U-boats detected by ASV II, so that they could be attacked. The Germans responded by introducing Metox – a device that detected ASV II transmissions. However, March 1943 saw the arrival of ASV III, invisible to Metox and capable of detecting even a periscope protruding from the waves.

Urgently needed improvements were also made to anti-submarine weaponry. The dropping of depth charges in the vicinity of an ASDIC 'contact' remained a standard method of attack, but relied on guesswork and luck because the U-boat below would be in an ASDIC blind spot. From 1942, 'Hedgehog' – a device that threw anti-submarine bombs ahead of the ship that carried it – enabled ASDIC contact to be maintained with the target. Aerial munitions were in even greater need of improvement, as the original British anti-submarine bomb was hopelessly ineffective. From mid-1942, new aerial depth charges became available, filled with a powerful new explosive, Torpex.

When Admiral Sir Max Horton, a former submariner, was put in command of the Western Approaches (the area of sea to the west of the British Isles), he instituted a vigorous programme of training to get the best out of these new weapons systems. With growing numbers of new and faster anti-submarine vessels available to him, he formed 'Escort Groups'. These independent formations of anti-submarine ships could respond to U-boat activity and hunt down their opponents without worrying about convoy protection. Some were based around newly available small aircraft carriers – Escort Carriers – built in American shipyards. Horton was confident that these new resources would bring results. Even as sinkings reached terrifying heights in March 1943, he wrote: 'although the last week has been one of the darkest on the sea ... I am really hopeful.'

The final and most decisive piece in the jigsaw was the availability of long-range aircraft. By 1943, the U-boats were concentrating their efforts on the part of the North Atlantic that lay beyond the range of most Allied aircraft – known to the Allies as the 'Air Gap' or, more sinisterly, the 'Black Pit'. It was well known that

From early 1942, some anti-submarine vessels were equipped with a 'Hedgehog', a multiple anti-submarine bomb launcher. This is a Hedgehog bomb. The bombs were fired forward, so that the ship could chase a U-boat while maintaining sonar contact with it.

aircraft were key to beating the U-boats, but Coastal Command had been able to deploy only a handful of planes capable of patrolling this gap. This was because Bomber Command demanded, and largely got, the use of all four-engine bombers. However, in the spring of 1943, the dire situation in the Atlantic saw Coastal Command being given forty new very long-range (VLR) aircraft in the form of modified US Liberator bombers. Their ability to stay airborne for up to eighteen hours enabled them to 'loiter' over the Air Gap, either attacking U-boats themselves or helping Escort Groups to find them. Their effect was immediate. In fact, their very presence forced U-boats to spend more of their time submerged – greatly reducing their endurance and effectiveness.

In May 1943 all these efforts and technological achievements bore fruit, with forty-one U-boats being sunk that month. A sudden transformation had taken place. The German Navy could formerly count on sinking many thousands of tons of shipping for each U-boat lost. Now, more U-boats were being sunk than Allied merchant ships. Instead of being a defensive measure, the convoy had become the means of forcing the U-boats to expose themselves to destruction. Dönitz, who lost his own son in a U-boat sunk by a Liberator on 19 May, was forced to withdraw his boats from the Atlantic. Never again would Germany's submarine fleet offer a critical threat to Allied shipping.

These photographs, taken from an RAF Liberator bomber of No. 224 Squadron, show the sinking of U-boat U-628 on 3 July 1943. This attack took place off the coast of Spain. U-boats wishing to get out into the Atlantic from their French bases began to hug the Spanish coast when they discovered that it made them harder to pick up on the radar carried by Allied anti-submarine aircraft.

FREDERIC WALKER

Frederic Walker, nicknamed 'Johnnie' after the popular brand of whisky, was Britain's leading 'U-boat killer'. By the climax of the Battle of the Atlantic in the spring of 1943, Johnnie was in command of 2nd Escort Group. This submarine-hunting formation comprised six sloops of the Black Swan class – part of a new generation of anti-submarine vessels that combined heavy armament and a long range with the ability to out-pace U-boats. Johnnie was driven by a relentless determination to defeat the U-boats, and ships under his command sunk twenty of them. He was promoted to captain and was awarded the Distinguished Service Order four times. He died in July 1944 of a stroke brought on by overwork.

🌐 Surviving the Battle of the Atlantic

The Battle of the Atlantic was a test of endurance for all who fought in it. Even without the life-threatening presence of the enemy, the sea and the weather presented a challenge. Indeed, boredom and physical discomfort were endemic, in a way that actual combat was not. For example, between May 1942 and May 1943, 105 out of 174 Atlantic convoys did not sight a single U-boat.

Experiences varied. In larger or more modern vessels, conditions could be reasonable. Veteran merchant seamen knew to avoid undertaking voyages in older ships if possible. For naval personnel, manning small escort vessels, such as Flower-class corvettes, in a heavy North Atlantic swell was a miserable experience, as it was seldom possible to get dry. Overhead, only a minority of aircrew enjoyed the reassurance of having four engines. The head of Coastal Command, Sir Frederick Bowhill, noted that 'we are asking a tremendous lot of the pilots to fly continually long distances over the sea, hour after hour, in aircraft that they know will not fly on one engine.'

For the Allies, the Battle of the Atlantic was a multinational one. Britain's merchant service had always recruited seamen from across the world. Consequently, many of its personnel were Lascars, Chinese or Arabs, or hailed from Britain's Caribbean or African colonies. Merchant seamen were civilians but, from 1941, were compelled to stay in the merchant service for the duration of the war. The diversity of the combatants was further increased by the contribution of sailors from countries lying under German occupation. Even neutral Sweden leased merchant ships to the Allies. In December 1941 the US Navy and Coast Guard entered the fray, although American merchant seamen had already been facing U-boat attacks as they sailed in

ABOVE This winter cap was issued to Canadian sailors. The Royal Canadian Navy was rapidly expanded to help protect convoys in the North Atlantic. Canadian sailors patrolled waters that were among the U-boats' most favoured hunting grounds.

BELOW This practical denim jacket was worn by a German U-boat petty officer. Its design was based on the British Army Battledress 'blouse', examples of which – from captured military stores – had proved popular after being issued to U-boat crews. In the cramped and dangerous conditions of a U-boat, relationships between officers and men were informal, and each wore whatever he found most comfortable.

convoys bound for Britain. An extraordinary contribution was made by the Royal Canadian Navy (RCN), which, starting almost from scratch, grew rapidly until it was providing almost half of the anti-submarine vessels in the North Atlantic in mid-1942. Unfortunately for the RCN, this rapid expansion meant that its men were perennially short of training, and that its ships often lacked the technology that the battle increasingly required. At the end of 1942, with Britain and the United States better placed to take up the strain, the Canadians were withdrawn from the battle so that they could re-equip and retrain.

Although most convoys avoided contact with the enemy, those that became the target of a U-boat wolf pack could expect to be attacked again and again, night after night. Terror and confusion would reign as ships exploded and burning oil covered the sea. Frequently, ships would fire off 'snowflake' flares, intending to illuminate the attackers, but often making themselves a clearer target. Even less enviable was the fate of 'stragglers' – ships that could not keep pace with their convoy. They made easy, unescorted targets and there was little chance that anyone who survived an attack would be picked up. Early in the war, some U-boat captains had taken lifeboats in tow, or otherwise assisted shipwrecked men. Dönitz put a stop to this, asserting that 'rescue contradicts the most fundamental demands of the war for the annihilation of enemy ships and crews ... Be hard. Think of the fact that the enemy in his bombing attacks on German towns has no regard for women and children.'

Unsurprisingly, the morale of Allied seamen began to suffer under the relentless pressure of crossing the North Atlantic with the threat of injury or death never far away. Sometimes, in the chaos of U-boat attack, panicking men abandoned undamaged ships in the belief that they had been torpedoed. On at least one occasion, a crew refused to re-board, meaning that their seaworthy vessel and its cargo had to be abandoned. Steps were therefore taken to make better provision for those who were shipwrecked. Lifeboats were fitted out with improved supplies of food, medical equipment and even waterproof radios. Rescue ships were introduced. These were freighters that had been converted to accommodate and feed up to 150 men, and equipped with large sick bays and sometimes small operating theatres. Sailing at the rear of convoys, rescue ships picked up survivors from damaged or sinking vessels. However, they could also become the target of attack themselves.

On the other side of the struggle the German submariners faced even greater discomfort and a much higher possibility of violent death. Conditions inside a U-boat were cramped in the extreme, fostering an informal camaraderie between the fifty or so officers and men of the crew. Once located by enemy ships or aircraft,

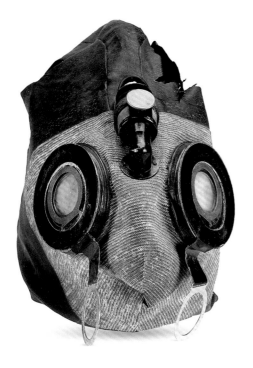

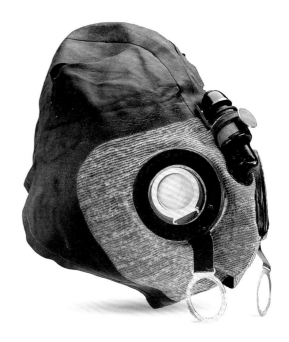

One of the threats faced by men forced to abandon ship was the oil from sinking tankers, which formed a slick on the surface of the sea. Sometimes the oil would be burning. Britain's Eagle Oil Company devised this mask to protect the mouth, nose, eyes and ears of anyone forced to jump into oil-covered water.

U-boats could quickly become deathtraps. The crew knew that if the hull was breached by a bomb or depth charge, they were likely to die. Only if their vessel was caught on or near the surface might they have a chance to abandon it. Little wonder, then, that the morale of these men declined as it became ever more difficult to evade detection and attack. Desperate demands by Dönitz for more aggression from his captains had little effect.

Of the 830 U-boats that saw wartime action, 696 were destroyed; and of their 40,900 crewmen, 25,870 were killed – a 63 per cent loss rate. In return, U-boat attacks claimed the lives of 30,248 merchant seamen and a similar number of naval personnel and airmen. But, in this longest-running battle of the war, the Allies had triumphed by mid-1943. The threat posed by the U-boats to Britain's ability to keep fighting had been overcome. Furthermore, now that the Allies controlled the Atlantic, American troops and supplies could be shipped across it with relative impunity. This ensured that the Allies could carry the war back to mainland Europe.

A U-boat crew is eager to know what their captain is seeing through the periscope.

POON LIM

Lim, from the Chinese island of Hainan, was one of many foreign seamen to work in the British Merchant Navy. A German submarine sunk his ship, the SS *Benlomond*, on 23 November 1942. Grabbing a life jacket, Lim leapt from the ship just before it exploded and clambered on to an empty life raft. When the raft's supplies ran out, Lim was forced to survive by catching seabirds, fish and even a shark. He was finally rescued by fishermen off the coast of Brazil after surviving for more than four months alone on the raft. He is pictured here after his return to Britain to receive the British Empire Medal.

Life under Axis Occupation

The Axis powers were united by a common goal: to conquer new territory. By rapid, violent expansion, they captured vast parts of Europe and East Asia, subjugating the millions of people who lived there. By mid-1942, Nazi Germany occupied an area stretching from France to Russia, and from Greece to Norway. Imperial Japan controlled even more territory. Life under Axis occupation varied according to where someone lived and how they were viewed by their occupiers. At the very least, people had restrictions imposed on their daily lives. But those the Germans or Japanese considered racially inferior endured slave labour, forced military service, sexual violence, deliberate starvation and deportation. Millions were murdered, and Europe's Jews were targeted for annihilation. Some people collaborated with their occupiers, while others risked their lives by resisting.

⊕ Europe

In Europe, people's experience of German occupation depended largely on where they lived. Nazi ideology informed the policy and practice of German occupation, as nations were viewed in terms of a racial hierarchy. The differing approaches can be broadly split into those of Eastern and Western Europe, although there were further variations within these areas. Across the continent, many suffered from shortages of food and other goods, as Germany prioritized the feeding of its own people over those it controlled.

German rule was the most moderate in the west, having either a hands-off or a supervisory nature. People were subject to limits on their civil freedoms, and existing state apparatus was generally left in place to continue administering each country, albeit with German supervision. Partly because Hitler viewed the western nations more favourably than the peoples of Eastern Europe, and partly due to strategic military and political concerns, countries such as France, the Netherlands and Belgium escaped the more extreme types of occupation that Germany practised elsewhere. Denmark had the least oppressive experience of all and was largely allowed to continue to rule itself unhindered. In France, German forces initially occupied only the north of the country, with most of the south ruled by the collaborationist government at Vichy.

In Eastern Europe, German rule was much harsher and all-encompassing. Huge numbers of people were executed, imprisoned or deported, and it was here that the Nazis murdered the majority of Europe's Jews. Hitler's disdain for 'Slavic' and Polish people ensured that they were dealt with ruthlessly. The Nazis viewed the Poles as inferior to Germans and sought to eradicate Poland's culture and subjugate its people, who experienced oppression, food shortages, deportation and widespread cruelty. Perhaps the most vehement treatment was reserved for the people of the Soviet Union, where Hitler's deep-seated hatred of Russians was mirrored in the conduct of the Wehrmacht, Germany's armed forces, and the SS, the Nazi paramilitary organization, during the German invasion and occupation.

An executed Polish man is left hanging in the doorway of a house in German-occupied Poland. German troops stand and look at his corpse.

This was waged as a war of annihilation, in which civilians, partisans and Jews were all killed in vast numbers.

Belorussia and Ukraine also suffered particularly harsh periods of occupation. Massacres and destruction of settlements contributed to Belorussia's high death toll; it is estimated that as much as a quarter of the population were killed. Ukraine was depopulated through deliberate starvation and murder, under both a brutal localized Nazi regime and a Romanian occupation that terrorized the Transnistria region. In contrast, the Baltic states – Latvia, Lithuania and Estonia – seen as places that could potentially become 'German', were treated better. Elsewhere, such as in parts of the Balkans, Germany occupied lands and then divided them up with its allies, which included Romania, Italy and Bulgaria.

People in Eastern Europe were subject to forced deportations, as part of Germany's plans to 'Germanize' its newly conquered territories by evicting local inhabitants and moving German people on to the land. Western Poland was cleared of large numbers of its existing population for incoming German settlers, while elsewhere ethnic Germans were brought 'back' into

NEDERLANDERS

VOOR UW EER EN GEWETEN OP !- TEGEN HET BOLSJEWISME DE WAFFEN SS ROEPT U !

The Netherlands was invaded and occupied by the Germans in May 1940. As in other German-occupied countries, thousands of men volunteered to serve in the German Army and the Waffen SS, encouraged by posters such as this one. The text at the bottom of the poster translates as 'For your honour and conscience! Against Bolshevism the Waffen SS is calling!'.

the German Reich. As part of 'Germanization', people were categorized into various grades of 'German-ness' and, in some areas, the local language was banned in favour of German.

At the heart of German policy across the continent was the Nazi obsession with ridding Europe of its Jewish 'problem'. This even took precedence over military concerns, sometimes to the detriment of Germany's overall war effort: Jews were killed even when it would have made more sense to use them as labour. As vast areas of Eastern Europe were conquered, their large populations of Jews came under German control. What started as a process of 'death by bullet' turned into systematic mass murder in a series of death camps. Jews were often rounded up and killed by local auxiliaries and police, as well as by German troops. Jews were also deported from Western European countries to be murdered in the east. Some countries, such as Hungary and Italy, resisted pressure to deport their Jewish populations. As well as Jews, large numbers of Roma in the east were also rounded up, imprisoned and killed.

Across occupied Europe, it is estimated that as many as 20 million people worked for the German war machine as a result of the Reich's forced- and slave-labour programmes. People in Eastern Europe were rounded up and sent to Germany, where they worked in poor conditions. Western European countries also contributed workers, such as the thousands of French people drafted in under a compulsory labour scheme. As Germany began to lose the war against the Soviet Union, greater numbers of people were forced to work for the Reich under ever worsening conditions. Many slave labourers were literally worked to death.

All over Europe, resistance movements worked to defy German rule. Resistance was often highly risky, especially armed attacks on German officials. Such attacks were counter-productive, as the Germans' retaliation was far worse and often involved the killing of civilians. Resistance in Western Europe included such actions as strikes, food riots and the writing of anti-German graffiti, as well as underground armies. In the eastern territories, however, people fought back against German aggression from the start by forming partisan movements. Partisan activity unnerved the Germans so was brutally quashed, particularly in the Soviet Union. Civilians were often killed in reprisal for armed resistance. Huge numbers of people lost their lives for this reason across Poland, Ukraine and Belorussia.

Conversely, there were those who collaborated with their German occupiers, helping them to impose Nazi ideology. People informed on others and assisted in the identification of Jews, even participating in the latter's murder. Owing to the vastness of the region they were ruling, the Germans relied on existing civilian and police administrations to help them. They could also count on the support of politicians and governments sympathetic to Nazism. People from occupied nations also fought for Germany. Men from countries including Belgium, the Netherlands, France, Hungary, Yugoslavia, Poland and Ukraine served in the Waffen SS, the military branch of the SS. Large numbers of Soviet citizens also fought on the German side.

LUCILLE HOLLINGDALE

Lucille risked her life on a daily basis. Each day, she cycled 120 kilo-metres with a basket full of food and clothing, searching for Allied airmen shot down over German-occupied France. As members of the French Resistance, Lucille and her British husband, Henry, helped more than 200 airmen escape the country.

In 1943 the couple were betrayed to members of the Gestapo, who arrested Lucille and beat Henry so badly he later died. Lucille was held in various concentration camps; she was also tortured by the Gestapo for information about the Resistance but told them nothing. Although she was eventually released and survived the war, her maltreatment meant that her health suffered for years afterwards.

 **Asia**

Burmese civilians evacuate Rangoon following the invasion of their country by the Japanese Army in January 1942. Thousands of civilian refugees fled northwards to India to escape the threat of Japanese brutality.

By the 1930s, Japan was in critical need of more resources than it could produce by itself. Its leaders decided to take them by force. Following the example of those European powers that had exploited overseas territories for centuries, Japan invaded and seized control of a large number of countries across East Asia and the Pacific in order to gain access to raw materials such as oil and rubber. The Japanese promised liberation from European rule to the places they occupied. But they themselves then exploited these areas, seizing resources for Japan to such an extent that local populations had inadequate rations and even starved. Many civilians were imprisoned in internment camps with high death rates. Huge numbers were made to fight or work for the Japanese, and hundreds of thousands of women and girls were forced into sexual slavery. The Japanese committed various atrocities, including summary executions, torture, rape and mutilation. Unknown millions died under Japanese rule, the largest proportion in China.

As a whole, the countries occupied by Japan suffered more under the Japanese than they had under the colonial powers. The Japanese forced local populations to supply them with the bulk of what they produced – particularly rice – at fixed low prices. They also commandeered vital supplies and equipment and forced large numbers of labourers to work for them instead, which led to an agricultural and economic downturn. The result was widespread shortages, inflation, the rise of black markets, malnutrition, disease and unemployment. Meanwhile, attempts by the Japanese to force their own language and religion on local populations backfired, instead often sending people towards their own nationalist movements. The Japanese ruthlessly purged occupied countries of those who were, or were deemed to be, anti-Japanese and anyone who resisted occupation.

The nature of the occupation imposed by the Japanese varied across the region. The reasons for this included Japanese racial views, political expediency and military priorities. However, the impact of occupation on civilians at a local level was extensive and depended on how the Japanese decided to rule each country.

MILOVAN ĐILAS

Milovan was a commander in one of Yugoslavia's resistance groups, the communist-led Yugoslav Partisans. The Partisans fought the Axis occupation forces that invaded Yugoslavia in April 1941, as well as other nationalist groups in a vicious civil war.

Milovan was respected within the Partisans and was trusted by their leader, Tito. Milovan was chosen to lead the Partisans' anti-Axis uprising in Montenegro. But the rebellion failed, and Milovan fell out of favour and was dismissed. He later regained his place in the Partisan leadership and once again took up the fight to liberate Yugoslavia. Milovan was part of the country's communist regime after the war, but was ostracized again and imprisoned. He later became a successful writer.

Chinese people suffered the most at the hands of the Japanese. From the first military actions in the 1930s up until the defeat of Japanese forces, Chinese civilians were subject to oppression and wide-ranging atrocities. Japanese troops were trained to despise the Chinese and view them as racially inferior 'sub-humans' deserving of high levels of brutality and dehumanization. During their invasion of China, they were responsible for widespread massacre, rape and looting. Japan's long-running war against China created millions of refugees, perhaps as many as 80 million; devastated the landscape; and destroyed infrastructure and industry on a vast scale. The exact number of Chinese people who lost their lives is not known. Most estimates range from 8 to 14 million, and China's own official figures suggest as many as 20 million.

The Philippines had been under US influence up until the Japanese conquered it in May 1942. The occupation was a catalyst for political unrest in the country and resulted in a number of different factions coming to the fore, including communists and pro-US elements. The Filipino people fought a highly effective guerrilla campaign that prevented the Japanese from ever being fully in control. In 1945 the Philippines was the scene of the worst urban battle in the eastern Asia-Pacific theatre. The capital, Manila, was all but destroyed, while hundreds of thousands of civilians died in the fighting.

Vietnam, part of French Indochina, was partially invaded by Japanese troops in 1940; Japan then expanded the reach of its control there the following year. The region had been part of the French colonial empire since the nineteenth century, and the Japanese allowed French sovereignty to continue in what was an uneasy shared occupation until 1945. The local population was exploited by both the Japanese occupiers and the French colonial government – for example, in food-buying policies that favoured the Japanese and French and left locals in poverty. One impact of this confused shared rulership was a famine that raged in northern Vietnam in 1945, in which an estimated 2 million people died.

The British colony of Singapore fell to Japanese forces in February 1942. The occupation affected Singapore's citizens in a number of ways, but its most severe impact was on their food supplies. The Japanese seized food for themselves, so only a small amount was left for the local population. Although there was never a famine, food availability was inadequate and

RIGHT American soldiers dash for cover during street fighting in Manila in February 1945. The Philippines capital was all but destroyed, and huge numbers of civilians were killed.

OPPOSITE, TOP A civilian lies dead after being hit by shrapnel during a Japanese air attack on Singapore, December 1941.

OPPOSITE, BOTTOM This painting, *British Women and Children Interned in a Japanese Prison Camp, Syme Road, Singapore* (1945), is another work by the British war artist Leslie Cole. Allied civilians were held in Japanese-run camps throughout the areas occupied by Japan, usually in terrible conditions.

there were frequent shortages. As a result, many suffered from malnutrition and disease and the death rate soared. People became desperate and resorted to buying and selling on the black market, while the Japanese punished looting with beheadings.

The Dutch East Indies fell to Japanese forces in March 1942. At first, the Japanese were welcomed as liberators who would bring the harsh Dutch colonial rule to an end. But the Indonesian people suffered under what turned into a period of Japanese oppression and exploitation of the country. Huge numbers were forcibly conscripted as labourers, known in Japanese as *rōmusha*, or as auxiliary soldiers, known as *heiho*. This practice also occurred in other areas under Japanese occupation. The exact number of Indonesians who were made to become *rōmusha* is unknown, but it was most likely in the millions. It is estimated that more than 4 million Indonesians died under Japanese occupation.

There were several aspects of Japanese occupation that constituted war crimes, and which were common to most, if not all, of the countries they ruled. One was the execution of civilians by Japanese troops, including the massacre of Australian military nurses and Allied prisoners of war that occurred at Banka Island in February 1942. Another was sexual violence, perpetrated by the Japanese against girls and women of the countries they occupied. It is estimated that between 100,000 and 200,000 women and girls were victims of an official, military-organized system that forced or tricked them into becoming sex slaves for the Imperial Japanese Army. Their nationalities included Korean, Chinese, Taiwanese, Filipino, Indonesian, East Timorese, Dutch and Melanesian.

The Japanese relied on forced labour drawn from their occupied territories to undertake the construction of railways (including the infamous Death Railway, discussed earlier), airfields and other projects important to their war effort. Unknown numbers of people were made to live and work in terrible conditions, which cost many their lives. They toiled long hours

under the watchful gaze of Japanese guards, who meted out harsh punishments to anyone they thought was working too slowly.

Around 130,000 Allied civilians were interned by the Japanese, and it is estimated that as many as 15,000 of them died as a result of this captivity. They were held in hundreds of camps across the region occupied by Japan. Conditions were usually appalling, and internees suffered from disease, starvation, malnutrition, overcrowding and poor sanitation, all of which contributed to the high mortality rates.

Further atrocities committed by the Japanese across East Asia included the torture and killing of prisoners of war, as well as biological and chemical warfare, experiments on human subjects, and even cannibalism. Evidence has been uncovered of Japanese soldiers resorting to the last of these in New Guinea as their military situation became increasingly desperate. The Japanese also used outlawed chemical and biological weapons in their war in China, including poison and tear gas.

Millions of civilians suffered under Japanese occupation. Indeed, so harsh was Japan's rule that various types of resistance rose up against it.

One such was Force 136, part of the Special Operations Executive. Run by the British in cooperation with the Chinese government, Force 136 operated in several countries, including Malaya, Borneo and Thailand. In addition, there was a successful guerrilla movement in the Philippines, as well as the Malayan People's Anti-Japanese Army, the Viet Minh and the underground Free Thai Movement. Conversely, some people worked with the Japanese, either fighting for them voluntarily or serving them in administrative roles.

COLLABORATION AND RESISTANCE

After a country had fallen to invading forces, its citizens had to decide how to react to living under occupation. Most people tried to carry on as normal. Some, however, chose to collaborate with their new rulers, or were forced to do so. Such collaboration ranged from informing on neighbours to fighting for the occupiers.

Others chose to resist, either individually or as part of an organized network. Resistance took many forms, from refusing to work and staging protests to acts of sabotage and attacks on members of the occupying forces. Many countries formed underground resistance movements, which were ready to take up arms against the occupiers when the tide of war began to turn against them.

For many, passive acceptance of occupation was the most logical course of action, as long as they were largely able to

continue with their lives. Harsh reprisals for any resistance activity – suspected or real – discouraged wide-scale opposition to Axis rule, and the unrest that did occur was often the result of localized issues, such as poor working conditions or shortages of food.

ABOVE The Japanese recruited, often forcibly, unknown thousands of men in South East Asia, many from the Dutch East Indies. Known as *heiho* (auxiliary soldiers), they boosted Japan's depleted armed forces. This klewang – a bladed weapon common to the region – and scabbard were used by a member of the *heiho*. *Heiho* did not serve on the front line, but worked in transport, construction and supply. They received lower pay and less food than Japanese servicemen, and were sometimes mistreated.

Unlikely Allies: Britain, the United States and the Soviet Union

As the Axis powers conquered huge swathes of territory in Europe and Asia, an unlikely alliance formed against them. The leaders of the communist Soviet Union, imperial Britain and capitalist America joined forces to fight their common enemies. Following the German invasion of the Soviet Union in June 1941, when Hitler reneged on his non-aggression pact with Stalin, Britain and the USSR became united in their opposition to Nazi Germany. In December that year, when Japan attacked the US Pacific Fleet at Pearl Harbor (discussed above), America was brought into the war first against Japan and then, when Hitler declared war on the United States a few days later, against Germany. The Soviet Union did not, however, join its allies in fighting against Japan, as the two countries had concluded a neutrality pact in April 1941.

⊕ The 'Big Three'

The leaders of the alliance – Winston Churchill, Joseph Stalin and Franklin D. Roosevelt, known collectively as the 'Big Three' – worked together to decide joint strategies for their prosecution of the war. Through regular written communications, telephone calls and in-person meetings, they – along with their teams of political and military advisers – agreed how, when and where they would defeat the Axis powers. Churchill had courted Roosevelt's friendship and support since his early days as prime minister, and the two met several times without Stalin, notably at the Atlantic Conference in August 1941. As we saw in Chapter 3, this meeting produced the Atlantic Charter, which set out a series of international aims for the UK and America that largely reflected Roosevelt's hopes for a union of nations and his opposition to Britain's and other countries' colonialism.

In August 1942 Churchill also met with Stalin, in Moscow, where the Soviet leader berated him for not coming to his country's aid in fighting the Germans by opening a 'second front' in Europe. This issue was one of the main points of contention between the three leaders, with Stalin repeatedly demanding that his allies invade mainland Europe and lift some of the burden from the Soviets in the fight against Germany. But Roosevelt and, in particular, Churchill resisted his demands, knowing that launching an attack against 'fortress Europe' before they were ready was highly risky. They consistently fended off Stalin's calls for action by emphasizing the necessity of thorough preparedness and of building up an effective invasion force. Churchill also stressed his belief that the bombing offensive against Germany was eroding its ability and will to fight. He and Roosevelt sought to appease Stalin with Anglo-American invasions of North Africa in November 1942 (Operation Torch) and of Italy, via Sicily, in the summer of 1943. To Stalin, however, these efforts meant relatively little and he continued to express his disappointment at a lack of action in Western Europe.

This poster was produced by the Communist Party of Great Britain. It echoed Stalin's repeated demands that his allies open a 'second front' by invading mainland Europe. The British Communist Party had previously opposed many aspects of the UK government's prosecution of the war, but, after the invasion of the Soviet Union and Britain's alliance with the Soviets against Germany, it launched a campaign of support for Russia. In October 1942, 50,000 people attended a Communist Party rally in London's Trafalgar Square calling for the opening of a second front.

While it is true that an attack by the Western Allies was needed to alleviate the Soviet Union's military situation – which at times appeared dire – it is also clear that Stalin played on his allies' consciences to some degree, and did so for political expediency. Playing the role of the languishing victim gave him a powerful advantage within the alliance, even after the real danger of Soviet defeat had passed. The issue was finally resolved in Stalin's favour when the three leaders met together for the first time at the Allied conference in Tehran, Iran, in November 1943. The timing of the planned Allied offensive was the most important subject discussed. While Churchill advocated an Allied attack in northern France as well as continued operations in the Mediterranean, Stalin argued forcefully that efforts be concentrated on France alone. The Soviet leader got his way, and a date was set: May 1944.

Another outcome of the Tehran Conference was Stalin's commitment to fighting against Japan once the war in Europe had been won against Germany – although this was kept a closely guarded secret between the Soviet Union and America. During the conference, Poland's borders and post-war fate – both of which were further sources of contention among the three leaders – were discussed. Churchill pressed Stalin for an independent, democratic Poland, while Stalin sought to secure Soviet control over the country. Roosevelt had to tread carefully, as he was unwilling to risk the disapproval of US voters of Polish origin. The issue came up again at later conferences, and agreement was reached over changes to Poland's borders.

During the talks, the three leaders posed for the newsreel cameras at the top of the steps of the Soviet Union's embassy building, where the conference was held. But this public show of unity hid the mistrust, disagreement and fundamental differences between them. As Churchill lamented, 'There is only one thing worse than fighting with allies, and that is fighting without them.' The Allied leaders had contrasting characters, different ways of working and polarized political outlooks, all of which were in evidence at Tehran. Stalin was a blunt-talking, dominant figure during the talks. As the outright leader of his country, he had the advantage of making decisions then and there, without having to take into account the opinions of political and military advisers, or those of the people he ruled over. Neither Churchill nor Roosevelt could act with similar autocracy.

Roosevelt had a shrewd mind and a persuasive charm, characteristics that had won over American voters. However, he did not always get his way with the other leaders. Having already established strong ties with Churchill, Roosevelt arrived at Tehran keen to build a connection with Stalin and assuage his concerns about an Anglo-American power bloc that ran contrary to Soviet interests. This he managed, to a degree, although Stalin was ever wary of his allies and never veered from pursuing his own priorities, conceding little. As Roosevelt observed, 'Gets things done, that man. He really keeps his eye on the ball he's aiming at.' Stalin was also able to manipulate the other two leaders in order to push through his own agenda, driving a wedge between them and undoing Churchill's careful groundwork in building up a relationship with Roosevelt.

The vast reserves of manpower at Stalin's and Roosevelt's command gave them a powerful advantage over the talkative, energetic and strong-willed Churchill. His country's weaker position meant he increasingly had to accept his allies' decisions. Of the three, Churchill was distinct in focusing primarily on the immediate demands of the war; by contrast, both Roosevelt and Stalin had their eyes on the post-war world and, crucially, their respective country's position within it. They both out-manoeuvred Churchill – and each other –

Joseph Stalin, Franklin D. Roosevelt and Winston Churchill – the 'Big Three' – at the Tehran Conference, 1943.

in striving for these ambitions, and, in so doing, ensured that their nations emerged from the war in a stronger position than did Britain.

The Big Three also worked with other Allied leaders and governments in exile, including the leader of Free France, Charles de Gaulle. Although Churchill was annoyed by de Gaulle's arrogant attitude, he recognized his value and potential as a symbolic figurehead of French resistance. However, de Gaulle was excluded from key decision-making. Roosevelt disliked him, and both he and Stalin were dismissive of de Gaulle's claims to the leadership of France while in exile in London. The Americans, meanwhile, hoped that China's nationalist leader, Chiang Kai-shek, would contribute to the fight against Japan. Roosevelt envisaged a post-war world in which the United States, Soviet Union, Great Britain and China would act as the 'Four Policemen' of the peace, leading a union of nations that would ensure an end to global conflict. But both Stalin and Churchill were unconvinced. Stalin refused even to meet with Chiang, who was at war with Japan, for fear of upsetting the Soviet-Japanese neutrality agreement. In November 1943 – prior to the Tehran Conference – Roosevelt and Churchill talked with Chiang in Cairo, where strategy against Japan was discussed. Chiang made various demands for US financial and military aid, while US and British chiefs of staff struggled to reach an agreement on future plans with their Chinese counterparts. Over time, Chiang was sidelined by the Americans, who became increasingly frustrated at his requests for help and inability to deliver results.

In contrast to the Allies, the Axis leaders – Hitler, Mussolini and Japan's Hideki Tojo – never had meetings at which all three were present. The Axis powers had little in common, other than their empire-building aims, and tended to act independently of one another. They neither coordinated strategy nor shared resources. Outwardly, the countries were aligned, but privately their leaders sometimes spoke critically of each other. In June 1941, Mussolini said, 'I've had my fill of Hitler ... For five hours I am forced to listen to a monologue which is quite fruitless and boring,' while Hitler called Japan's emperor, Hirohito, 'weak, cowardly and irresolute'.

⊕ Allies at war

ABOVE A British sailor, Able Seaman Thomas Day, on board an ice-covered HMS *Belfast* during an Arctic convoy. His specially issued clothing was inadequate for the extreme weather conditions.

BELOW This wing section from a US-made Bell P-39 Airacobra fighter aircraft has both British and Russian markings – an RAF roundel and a Soviet star. It was one of a batch of Airacobras sent as part of the Lend-Lease programme, first from the United States to Britain and then by the British to the Soviet Union. The aircraft were found to be unsatisfactory by the RAF when trialled by No. 601 Squadron at RAF Duxford and were sent on to the Soviets. The Airacobras were then used to great effect by the Soviet Air Force in operations at the front in Eastern Europe.

'The United States ... is a country of machines. Without the use of those machines, through Lend-Lease, we would lose this war.' So stated Stalin at the Allied conference in Tehran. Indeed, the Allied war effort was based predominantly on America's wealth and massive industrial output. During the war, America's Ford Company manufactured more army equipment than did Italy as a whole. Under the terms of Lend-Lease, the United States supplied significant amounts of war materiel to its allies. American money funded vitally needed weapons, vehicles and equipment to more than forty Allied nations; some 400,000 US trucks were delivered to the Soviet Union alone. Lend-Lease dated from before America joined the war and was a means by which Roosevelt could aid those countries fighting against the Axis powers while maintaining – officially – US neutrality. The Lend-Lease Act, which came into effect in early 1941, gave the US president unprecedented power to allow American products and property to be leased or lent to foreign countries, thereby delaying payment for these assets by countries under financial strain. Over the course of the war, America provided around $50 billion of goods under Lend-Lease.

The embattled Soviet Union was a principal recipient of US aid. From August 1941, Allied merchant ships with British Royal Navy escorts carried much-needed supplies across the Arctic Ocean to the Soviet Union. These convoys carried trucks, tractors, telephone wire, railway engines, boots and more. The convoy route was highly dangerous, and Churchill called the crossing 'the worst journey in the world'. Sailors battled bitterly freezing weather and heavy seas, as well as German submarines, ships and aircraft. More than 3,000 of them died and 104 merchant ships were lost. Weather conditions were so severe that ships could sometimes arrive at their destination carrying up to 150 tons of extra weight in ice. The Arctic convoys ran up until May 1945, although they were paused on several occasions owing to competing demands for resources. Despite the hostile conditions and hazardous route, they succeeded in delivering more than 4 million tons of supplies to the Soviet Union. They also demonstrated Britain's commitment to its ally and were an important display of unity and action, particularly in the years before the 'second front' was opened.

ARTHUR BAILEY

Arthur served on the Arctic convoys. He was wounded when his ship, HMS *Edinburgh*, was torpedoed by a German U-boat while returning to Britain from the Soviet Union in April 1942.

Arthur was rescued and spent months recovering from his injuries at Vaenga Military Hospital, near Murmansk in the Soviet Union. He was given this Soviet sailor's uniform to wear and this wooden spoon to use. During his convalescence, Arthur developed great respect for the Soviet people, who gave him and other British sailors whatever they could, despite having little of their own.

Lend-Lease

A MATERIAL CONTRIBUTION TO THE ALLIED VICTORY

Under the Lend-Lease programme, the United States supplied more than 40 Allied nations with food, vehicles, weapons and other goods between 1941 and 1945. The Soviet Union was a principal recipient of this aid.

US GOODS SENT TO THE SOVIET UNION
1941–45

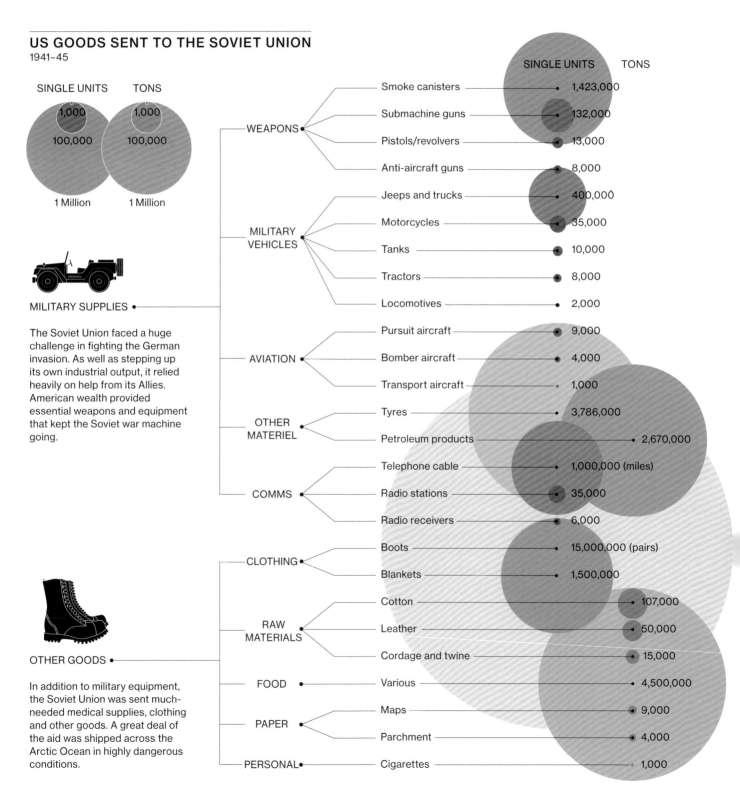

SINGLE UNITS · TONS

SINGLE UNITS · TONS

1,000 · 100,000 · 1 Million

1,000 · 100,000 · 1 Million

MILITARY SUPPLIES

The Soviet Union faced a huge challenge in fighting the German invasion. As well as stepping up its own industrial output, it relied heavily on help from its Allies. American wealth provided essential weapons and equipment that kept the Soviet war machine going.

OTHER GOODS

In addition to military equipment, the Soviet Union was sent much-needed medical supplies, clothing and other goods. A great deal of the aid was shipped across the Arctic Ocean in highly dangerous conditions.

WEAPONS
- Smoke canisters — 1,423,000
- Submachine guns — 132,000
- Pistols/revolvers — 13,000
- Anti-aircraft guns — 8,000

MILITARY VEHICLES
- Jeeps and trucks — 400,000
- Motorcycles — 35,000
- Tanks — 10,000
- Tractors — 8,000
- Locomotives — 2,000

AVIATION
- Pursuit aircraft — 9,000
- Bomber aircraft — 4,000
- Transport aircraft — 1,000

OTHER MATERIEL
- Tyres — 3,786,000
- Petroleum products — 2,670,000

COMMS
- Telephone cable — 1,000,000 (miles)
- Radio stations — 35,000
- Radio receivers — 6,000

CLOTHING
- Boots — 15,000,000 (pairs)
- Blankets — 1,500,000

RAW MATERIALS
- Cotton — 107,000
- Leather — 50,000
- Cordage and twine — 15,000

FOOD
- Various — 4,500,000

PAPER
- Maps — 9,000
- Parchment — 4,000

PERSONAL
- Cigarettes — 1,000

Winston Churchill buys an 'Aid to Russia' flag from his wife, Clementine. Among her other roles, Clementine was chair of the Joint War Organisation's Aid to Russia Fund.

ABOVE This object is a type E1189 cavity magnetron, a key British innovation in radar technology. Although they were highly valuable, the British scientist Henry Tizard took one with him when he travelled to the United States in August 1940. It was an essential part of what Tizard showcased to American scientists and initiated ongoing wartime collaboration between the two nations. Cavity magnetrons enabled radar devices to shrink in size, thereby optimizing their use by aircraft and ships.

RIGHT This 1941 painting, *Loading Tanks for Russia* by Leslie Cole, shows a British Matilda tank being lowered on to the deck of a merchant ship bound for the Soviet Union. Cole was appointed an official war artist in 1942 and travelled extensively to capture various scenes of war and its impact on people.

In addition to the war materiel provided by America and Britain for the Soviet Union's fight against Germany, a significant amount of money was raised by members of the public to buy essential medical supplies and clothing for the USSR. Across the British Empire, there was huge sympathy for the Soviet people's suffering, and many were moved to give what they could to help them. In October 1941 an 'Aid to Russia' fund was set up, chaired by the prime minister's wife, Clementine Churchill. By the time it closed, the fund had raised more than £7 million through fund-raising drives, penny-a-week schemes, collections in workplaces, flag days and sporting events. The proceeds bought 11,600 tons of medical supplies and clothing for the Soviet Union, including medicines and surgical equipment.

As well as resources, the Allies shared knowledge in achieving their mutual aim of victory over the Axis powers. In 1940, before the United States had entered the war, Britain initiated a programme of technological and scientific collaboration between the two nations. Britain had some vital innovations – including the cavity magnetron, a key component in radar technology – but lacked the means to develop them on a large enough scale. A British mission, headed by a leading UK scientist, Henry Tizard, travelled to neutral America to showcase these inventions in a bid to secure US interest in putting them into production. The American scientists, recognizing the importance of what they had been shown, agreed to collaborate. This continued after the United States joined the war and resulted in various technologies that gave the Allies the edge in their fight against Germany and Japan. But not everything was shared between Britain and America, and some useful inventions and important pieces of intelligence – including US bomb-aiming technology and British codebreaking activity – were jealously guarded by the nation they belonged to. Furthermore, Stalin, ever wary and distrustful of his allies, divulged little of what his web of spies and informants reported and played his cards close to his chest.

VICTORY IN THE BALANCE

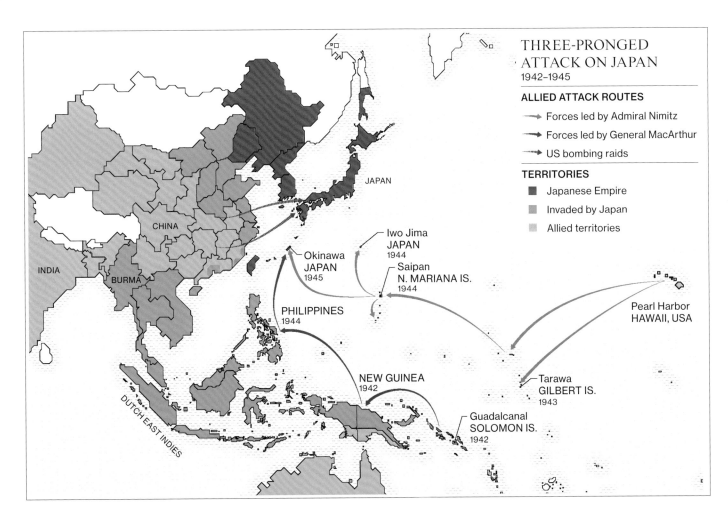

THREE-PRONGED
ATTACK ON JAPAN
1942–1945

ALLIED ATTACK ROUTES

→ Forces led by Admiral Nimitz

→ Forces led by General MacArthur

⤍ US bombing raids

TERRITORIES

■ Japanese Empire

■ Invaded by Japan

□ Allied territories

JAPAN

CHINA

INDIA

BURMA

Okinawa
JAPAN
1945

Iwo Jima
JAPAN
1944

Saipan
N. MARIANA IS.
1944

Pearl Harbor
HAWAII, USA

PHILIPPINES
1944

NEW GUINEA
1942

DUTCH EAST INDIES

Tarawa
GILBERT IS.
1943

Guadalcanal
SOLOMON IS.
1942

Bombing Germany

On the night of 30/31 May 1942, the German city of Cologne became the target of Operation Millennium, an attempt to concentrate a thousand bombers on a single target. This was the brainchild of RAF Bomber Command's new commander-in-chief, Sir Arthur Harris. The future of Bomber Command was in the balance, owing to its failure – despite suffering heavy casualties – to do serious damage to Germany's war effort, or even to find its targets. Harris believed that a large fleet of heavy bombers could devastate Germany to such an extent that it would be forced to give up the fight. He planned an attention-grabbing raid to prove the potential of this strategy. From a publicity perspective, the raid fulfilled Harris's hopes. Reports of it dominated newspaper front pages. Under the headline 'The Vengeance Begins', the *Daily Express* hailed 'the most gigantic air raid the world has ever seen'.

⊕ Cities targeted

Harris's hand was strengthened by the cold reality that strategic bombing was Britain's only means of striking directly at the Nazi homeland. Winston Churchill, under pressure from Stalin to aid the Soviet Union by creating a 'second front', was able to cite Britain's bomber offensive as an example of direct help to his ally. But to sustain such a claim, Bomber Command needed to be hitting its targets, and hitting them hard. During 1942 it began to acquire the capability to do just that. The twin-engine bombers used since the outbreak of war were gradually superseded by new, four-engine types: the Stirling, the Halifax and the Lancaster. These had a longer range and could carry a much greater bomb load. Almost 300 of these heavy bombers took part in the Cologne raid, which also saw the first use of a concentrated 'bomber stream' to swamp the German defences. Furthermore, the attackers were able to use a new navigational device, known as Gee. Using a Gee receiver, a navigator could work out the position of his bomber by interpreting radio signals transmitted by ground stations in Britain. However, Gee signals could not reach beyond north-western Germany.

Even with Gee, accuracy remained a problem. The response of Bomber Command was to attack the targets that were easiest to find, and to bomb city centres, rather than industrial targets that required greater precision. In early 1942 these considerations had combined to prompt the destruction of the medieval hearts of two coastal cities, Lübeck and Rostock. The damage was done with incendiary bombs, because the cities, in Harris's words, were 'constructed more like a fire lighter than a human habitation'. From this point onwards Bomber Command would use increasing quantities of incendiary bombs to destroy cities. This policy was rationalized in terms of the effect it was presumed to have on civilians. It was claimed that their morale and support for the war effort would be fatally weakened, and that 'de-housing' workers would undermine production in German factories. But the words 'morale' and 'de-housing' were euphemistic admissions that the only way of bringing the war on to German soil was to indiscriminately bomb its civilian population.

The continuing difficulty of finding a given target forced Harris to create an elite group of 'Pathfinder' squadrons to locate and mark objectives for the main bomber stream. These squadrons benefited from new technology. Oboe, another radio-pulse navigation system, saw the bombing attack controlled from two home stations, with sound signals telling the bomb-aimer when to release the bombs. January 1943 saw the introduction of H2S, which generated a radar image of the ground below the bomber to which it was fitted. While the image it produced was not always easy to decipher, H2S did not have a limited range like Gee or Oboe. The Pathfinders also made use of newly available Mosquito bombers. These twin-engine aircraft could fly at high altitudes, which maximized the range at which they could use Gee and Oboe. They were also fast enough to outrun German night-fighters. From July 1943, yet another new technology was deployed – Window. This consisted of bundles of reflective strips dropped from attacking aircraft to confuse German radar. Its first use was in a major attack on Hamburg – the deadliest British bomber raid of the war. Between 24 July and 3 August, multiple raids on the city destroyed 250,000 homes and killed more than 40,000 people. The climax came on the night of 27/28 July, when unusually low humidity allowed fires to amalgamate into a huge firestorm, which fed on air drawn in by the intense heat it created. It melted or burned asphalt, hurled people into the flames or asphyxiated them as it sucked the oxygen out of their shelters. The local police chief recorded that 'the streets were covered with hundreds of corpses. Mothers with their children, youths, old men, burnt, charred, untouched and unclothed, naked with waxen pallor like dummies in a shop window.'

On 16 May 1943, Lancaster bombers from the RAF's No. 617 Squadron attacked three dams feeding water to Germany's chief industrial centre in the Ruhr Valley. They dropped special 'bouncing bombs' at low level. This photograph shows some of the fifty-seven 'Dambuster' crew who returned. Fifty-six of their comrades were lost. Although the mission fascinated the public, the attacks, which drowned 4,000 people, did not lead to the long-term disruption of the Ruhr water supply as hoped.

HEINZ-WOLFGANG SCHNAUFER

The son of a family of Württemberg wine merchants, Heinz-Wolfgang became Germany's leading night-fighter pilot. The British nicknamed him the 'Ghost of St Trond', after the location of his base in occupied Belgium and his stealth in attacking bombers.

Night fighters were the deadliest threat faced by Bomber Command aircrew. The markings on Heinz-Wolfgang's Messerschmitt Bf 110 tail fin record his destruction of 121 British bomber aircraft. This equates to around 850 British airmen killed, wounded or taken prisoner.

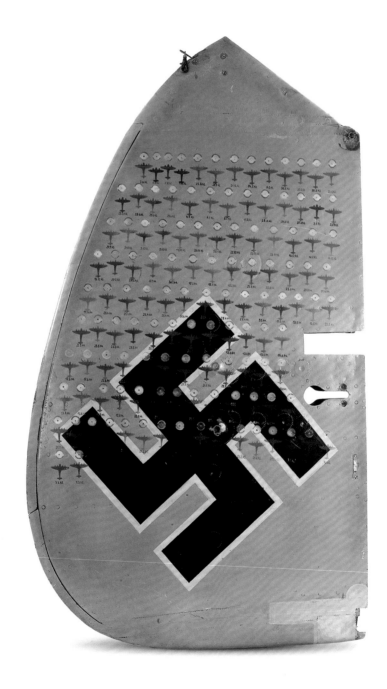

⊕ Airmen under stress

For Harris, the Hamburg attack was proof that, with sufficient bombers, he could knock Germany out of the war. However, given that an attack of this kind required an easily located target and favourable weather conditions, he was not able to repeat it. From late 1943 until the spring of 1944, Bomber Command focused on what was called the 'Battle of Berlin'. Despite its great size, the German capital was difficult to bomb. Beyond the range of Gee and Oboe, its lack of prominent topographical features made it hard to see with H2S. And the German defences were strong. Night-fighters now carried airborne radar to locate their targets, as well as other devices that homed in on H2S and similar electronic transmitters in British bombers. They could also deliver devastating attacks on bombers from their undefended blind spot, below, with twin, upward-firing cannon known as 'Jazz Music'. Over four months, sixteen major attacks on Berlin caused heavy damage and killed around 4,000 people. But almost 500 RAF bombers were destroyed, with the loss of nearly 4,000 valuable aircrew – most of them killed. This casualty rate could not be sustained, and the Battle of Berlin ended in defeat.

For the personnel of Bomber Command, the long-range raids against the 'Big City', as they called Berlin, marked the most arduous period of a difficult war. Bomber crews had to fly a 'tour' of thirty missions before being posted to different duties – usually the training of other flyers. Following a six-month break, most were expected to fly a second tour (of twenty missions from mid-1943). The psychological pressure on these young men – aged largely between nineteen and twenty-five – was immense. At one point in 1943 it was estimated that a member of a bomber crew had a 33 per cent chance of

Bomber crews decorated their aircraft with nose art to boost morale or to bring them luck. This panel from a Handley Page Halifax aircraft shows Disney characters from the 1945 film *The Three Caballeros*, plus a few friends. Crews were expected to complete a tour of thirty operations. In 1943, only one in six men survived their first tour, and one in forty their second.

surviving one tour and a 16 per cent chance of surviving two. This dire situation improved from mid-1944 onwards but, overall, 44 per cent of RAF bomber crews were killed in the course of the war – a total of 55,573 men. Among those who survived hits to their aircraft, hundreds were severely burned. Pioneering reconstructive surgery was available for such casualties, but the painful process could take years. Unsurprisingly, many aircrew suffered from neuroses or exhibited the behavioural symptoms of chronic stress. Up to 6,000 of the worst-affected men underwent psychiatric assessment. An unfortunate minority of them were stigmatized by being classified as 'lacking in moral fibre' (LMF). Stripped of their rank and coveted flyer's badges, they were removed from active operations, and often from the RAF itself, for fear that they might undermine the morale of others.

Bomber Command's aircrew were volunteers, coming from all over the British Empire as well as from European countries under German occupation. One in four came from Britain's Dominions – Australia, Canada, New Zealand and South Africa. So numerous were the Canadians that they were able to completely man one of the seven Groups that made up Bomber Command. Aircrew were just the tip of a manpower iceberg. Two squadrons of bombers would operate from a standard heavy bomber base, with around 200 aircrew, but they required the support of 1,000 ground staff. These men and women kept the base running; armed, serviced and repaired the bombers; and briefed and de-briefed the aircrew before and after missions.

The dead crew of a Halifax bomber laid out by the wreckage of their aircraft. Bomber Command aircrew knew that they faced such a fate every time they took off on a mission, which, if they survived, they might do more than fifty times over the course of the war.

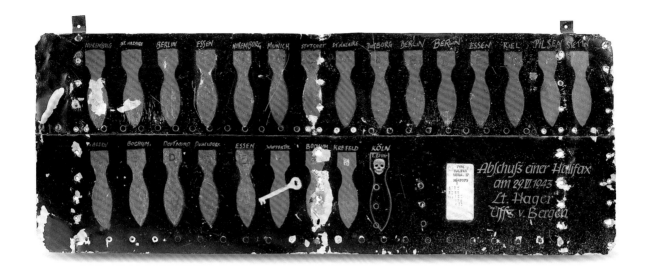

ABOVE This panel from a Halifax bomber records twenty-three successful operations. On the night of 28/29 June 1943, however, the aircraft was shot down over Cologne by a night fighter. The crew were killed. The German night-fighter crew who took the panel as a trophy added a skull to it. The Halifax was one of 169 aircraft shot down in the raid that night, which killed 4,300 Germans, injured 10,000 and made 230,000 homeless.

RIGHT Ground crew were vital to the success of every bombing raid. In this photograph, ground crew push a 4,000-pound bomb towards a Vickers Wellington bomber in Mildenhall, Suffolk. Ground crew serviced, repaired and armed the bombers, frequently joking that they 'owned' the aircraft and would 'lend' them to aircrew only if they promised to bring them back in one piece.

BILLY STRACHAN

Eager to fight, eighteen-year-old Billy sold his beloved bicycle and saxophone to pay for a voyage from Jamaica to Britain. Joining the RAF, he became an air gunner in Bomber Command. After completing his first tour of thirty missions, Billy asked to retrain as a pilot. Wearing this flying helmet and goggles, he flew Lancaster bombers. Unlike the other services, the RAF did not operate a 'colour bar' and Billy attained the rank of flight lieutenant. More than 7,000 West Indian men and women served with the wartime RAF.

US bombers were equipped with the Norden bombsight which, its makers claimed, was capable of directing a bomb into a 'pickle barrel'. US authorities kept the workings of the Norden secret, even from their allies. US bomb aimers took an oath not to reveal how it operated if they were captured. Yet statistics showed that in operational use, the Norden sight failed to live up to its reputation.

⊕ The Combined Bomber Offensive

From mid-1942, the US Army Air Forces (USAAF) began to mount operations from airbases in England. In January 1943 it mounted its first raid on Germany, initiating what Allied planners called the Combined Bomber Offensive. But the USAAF had very different ideas from the RAF on how bombing should be conducted. It hoped to mount precision attacks on vital industrial targets by daylight, using heavily armed bombers flying in defensive formation. Consequently, the joint offensive ostensibly followed two separate paths, with the Americans bombing industrial targets by day, and the RAF pounding Germany's cities by night. The reality proved to be less clear-cut. As Bomber Command had already discovered, weather conditions frequently prevented anything but area bombing, which the USAAF undertook using its own version of H2S.

The airmen of the US Eighth Air Force, part of the USAAF, were the vanguard of a 'friendly invasion' of Britain by its transatlantic ally that grew in strength as forces were built up for the planned liberation of Europe. The USAAF as a whole formed the longest-standing element of this new addition to British society and, at its peak in 1944, numbered more than 450,000 personnel. Just like their counterparts in Bomber Command, USAAF men lived alongside the local people who dwelt in the vicinity of their airbases. The resulting collision of British and American culture provoked a range of responses on both sides: friendly curiosity and amusement, bemusement, or even resentment. But both British and US authorities were on the alert to curb any problems that might harm relationships between the two allies. A senior USAAF commander wryly suggested that of the three most serious crimes that his men might commit – 'murder, rape and interference with Anglo-American relations' – the first two might possibly be pardoned, but 'the third one never'.

The confidence of the Eighth Air Force in its ability to strike Germany by day was soon dented by heavy casualties. The chief threat to the US bombers came from German fighters. The heavy machine-gun defences of

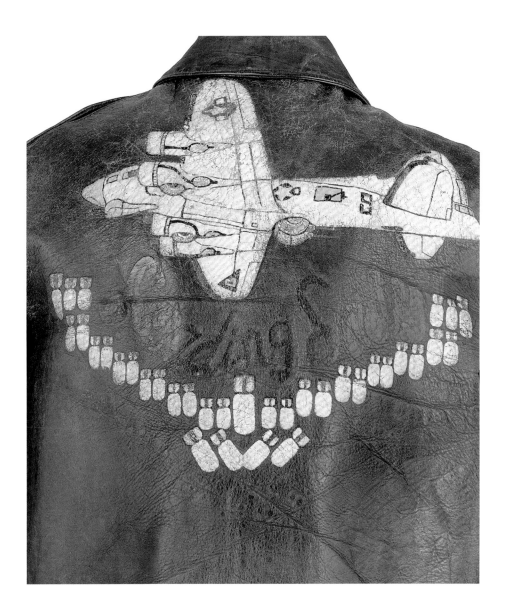

ABOVE AND RIGHT Temperatures in aircraft flying at 25,000 feet could drop as low as minus 50 degrees Celsius. US airmen often wore a padded bomber jacket over their flying suit for warmth. Their helmets and boots were lined with fur. Some aircrew also wore protective body armour to prevent injuries from the metal fragments that would rip through an aircraft when it was blasted with gunfire. Such armour was cumbersome but proved highly effective.

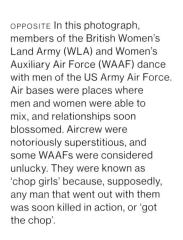

OPPOSITE In this photograph, members of the British Women's Land Army (WLA) and Women's Auxiliary Air Force (WAAF) dance with men of the US Army Air Force. Air bases were places where men and women were able to mix, and relationships soon blossomed. Aircrew were notoriously superstitious, and some WAAFs were considered unlucky. They were known as 'chop girls' because, supposedly, any man that went out with them was soon killed in action, or 'got the chop'.

the bombers did not deter their attacks. The only effective defence was the provision of fighter escorts, but there was a lack of suitable fighters capable of accompanying the bombers deep into Germany. During the summer and autumn of 1943, US bombers on raids over Germany suffered rates of loss that frequently approached 30 per cent. Indeed, in that year alone, the Eighth Air Force lost 9,497 men. This was unsustainable, and attacks became restricted to those areas of north-west Germany to which escort could be provided by the Eighth Air Force's P47 fighters. In early 1944 the tactics of the Eighth were analysed by the newly appointed commander of US Strategic Air Forces, General Carl Spaatz. Spaatz decided to prioritize the destruction of the German fighter force. Fitting a large disposable fuel tank to the P47 gave it greater range, but the real advance was made when the P51 'Mustang' fighter became available from early 1944. The P51 had extremely efficient flying characteristics and, fitted with a 'drop tank', could fly beyond Berlin or Munich. The Eighth Air Force's fighters could now work in relays to provide comprehensive protection for its bombers. Their effectiveness was further enhanced when, instead of closely escorting the bombers, the fighters were encouraged to sweep ahead of them, hunting down the German fighters. Meanwhile, the bombers concentrated their attacks on German fighter production.

VERNON 'GAYLE' ALEXANDER

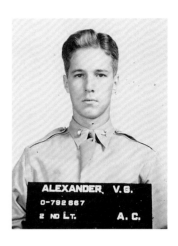

Gayle was twenty-three years old when, as a US pilot flying his nineteenth mission, his bomber was shot down near Merseberg in Germany. Wounded in the leg, he found himself falling head-first from 28,000 feet but managed to deploy his parachute. He landed in a field and was taken prisoner by a farmer brandishing a shotgun. A fellow crew member was not so lucky, being stabbed to death with a pitchfork.

This telegram, dated 17 November 1944, was sent to Gayle's mother. It stated that Captain Vernon Alexander was missing in action. However, Gayle had been picked up by German soldiers and was marched to Stalag Luft III camp at Zagan, now in Poland. After several weeks, the camp was liberated and Gayle once again survived a gruelling trek as the prisoners were marched 880 kilometres to Munich. When he arrived, Gayle ate white bread, had a hot bath and slept in a bed for the first time in months. He was eventually sent home on a hospital ship.

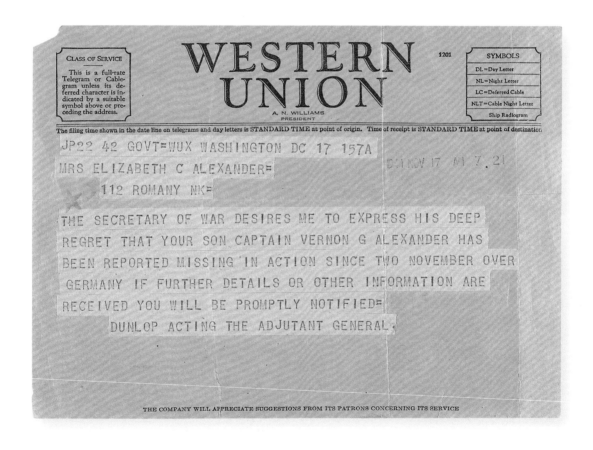

JOHN WHITE

John worked as a clerk with the Westminster Bank before volunteering to join the RAF in 1940. By 1944 he was piloting a Lancaster bomber on operations in support of the Allied liberation of France. He wore this blouse.

Concerned that he might be shot down over German-occupied territory, John kept photographs of himself in civilian clothing inside his blouse pocket. If necessary, they could form the basis of false identification documents. He also sewed a St Christopher charm into his pocket for good luck.

🌐 Air superiority

ABOVE, TOP Victims of a bombing raid are laid out for identification (and eventual burial) in a gymnasium in Berlin decorated with Christmas trees, December 1943. During the war, more than 300,000 Germans died as a result of Allied strategic bombing.

ABOVE 'The enemy sees your light – blackout!' warns this German poster.

During the spring and summer of 1944 both Bomber Command and the Eighth Air Force focused on bombing in support of the invasion of Europe. Only in September were they able to return to a full-scale attack on Germany. This time the dominant role was played by the Eighth Air Force (along with the US Fifteenth Air Force, based in Allied-controlled Italy). Together they could deploy 5,000 bombers and 5,000 fighters. By contrast, Bomber Command could send around 1,400 bombers into action – far short of the 4,000 that its commander considered necessary to force Germany into surrender. The US flyers focused their efforts on two vulnerable elements of the German war effort: production of synthetic fuel and transport infrastructure. They received only limited assistance from Bomber Command. Sir Arthur Harris, wedded to his strategy of shattering cities, avoided diverting his aircraft to attacks on what he dismissed as 'panacea targets'. Nevertheless, the USAAF's policy paid dividends from which the whole Allied cause benefited. German air defences were worn down, with Luftwaffe pilots being sent into battle hopelessly under-trained because of fuel shortages.

In the last seven months of the war, the Allies held air superiority over their foe. The quantity of bombs dropped on Germany rose exponentially; indeed, some three-quarters of the total tonnage of bombs dropped on the country during the war were dropped in this period. Germany's ability to manufacture weapons was never completely destroyed, but its ability to transport them to the front and to fuel its tanks and planes was

ABOVE German civilians search for survivors in Hamburg following RAF raids, 1943.

BELOW Germany had to mobilize hundreds of thousands of civilians to deal with the consequences of Allied air raids. The jacket belonged to a fireman, while the helmet was worn by a member of the *Reichsluftschutzbund*, an air-raid precautions organization. Women and children joined the organization as well, and also manned anti-aircraft guns. Concentration-camp prisoners were brought in to bombed cities to clear rubble and recover dead bodies.

fatally compromised. Defending Germany against air attacks required a massive redirection of resources. Manufacture of fighter aircraft and heavy anti-aircraft guns was maximized at the expense of other vital war production. Extraordinary efforts and vast quantities of steel and concrete were invested in protecting major cities with huge 'flak towers' and creating underground factories. Life for many German city dwellers became almost unbearable. Around half of Germany's deaths from bombing were sustained during the last eight months of the war. Contrary to the wishful predictions of some Allied leaders, civilian morale did not crack. The Nazi Party carefully monitored the responses of civilians in bombed towns. Their discontent most commonly manifested itself in bitter jokes against leading Party members; but they were also heard to speculate that they were being punished for the deportation of their Jewish neighbours to – as few Germans by this time doubted – their probable death.

The bombing of civilians and the indiscriminate destruction of historic city centres in Germany did not pass unquestioned in Britain. Protests were made on moral grounds by politicians and such public figures as Bishop George Bell of Chichester. The general public could be equivocal in their views, with one person in 1943 recorded as saying: 'we appreciate the need for the liquidation of Hamburg, but for heaven's sake don't remind us of what we're doing.' Nevertheless, if Nazi Germany was to be defeated, it was seen as vital that Britain should be striking it directly. Furthermore, friendly populations in France and Italy were also suffering from bombing, because it was seen as crucial to winning the war. Some, chief among them Sir Arthur Harris, saw the campaign as an alternative to a potential slaughter of British troops on European soil. Only in the early months of 1945 did Harris's superiors seek to rein in his ambition to destroy Germany from the air. They were stung into action by the Anglo-American bombing of Dresden on 13/14 February, which created a firestorm that killed 25,000. The bombing of Dresden was conducted for military reasons – to aid the advancing Red Army. But ten days later, Bomber Command attacked the militarily insignificant town of Pforzheim, killing almost 18,000 of its inhabitants and destroying 83 per cent of the town itself. It was not until 16 April 1945 that Bomber Command received an operational directive that did not include the destruction of 'morale' as an objective. By this time, 350,000 Germans, mostly civilians, had been killed in the Allied bombing campaign.

War in Eastern Europe 1943–1945

🌐 The Soviet Union liberated

'Whenever I think of this attack, my stomach turns over.' Thus spoke Adolf Hitler in anticipation of the planned German offensive at Kursk, western Russia, in July 1943. Its aim was to put Germany back in control of the war in the Soviet Union, following the terrible defeat suffered at the turn of the year at Stalingrad. Hitler's nerves proved well founded. The massive offensive on either side of a bulge of Soviet-held territory failed to break through multiple Soviet defensive lines. Soon the attackers were hit by Soviet counter-attacks. They were thrown into retreat and, by the year's end, were pushed out of eastern Ukraine. In the north, the siege of Leningrad was finally broken that winter. Never again would Germany be able to mount a major attack in the east. But how had this transformation in the situation come about? The answer lay chiefly in the response of the Soviet Union to the military disasters it had suffered during 1941 and 1942.

The German advance had robbed the Soviet Union of two thirds of its coal, iron and aluminium production. Also lost to enemy occupation were 40 per cent of its population and 32 per cent of the industrial workforce. Incredibly, despite these losses, by 1943 the Soviet Union was actually out-producing Germany in war materiel. Soviet technicians performed near miracles in relocating factories and re-establishing production in regions safe from attack. But the chief reasons for this dramatic recovery lay in the nature of the Soviet state. First, the centralized control that already existed was put to good effect in directing industry, manpower and transport. Bottlenecks in production and anything else that hampered the war effort were reported upwards and dealt with at the highest level of government. Secondly, unlike other Allied leaders, or even his fellow dictators Hitler and Mussolini, Stalin felt able to demand extraordinary levels of sacrifice from the Soviet people.

Everyone was expected to contribute. Those who did not work did not qualify for a ration card. Long hours were worked in often harsh conditions. During the winter of 1941/42, in some of the relocated factories, production had commenced even before the buildings had roofs. Anyone over sixteen might also be liable for 'labour service', which meant extra

The Soviet Union's solution to the need to produce vast quantities of weapons was to keep them simple. Production was focused on a limited number of reliable types. But new designs had a good chance of being adopted if they could be made more speedily. Of these submachine guns, the pre-war PPD 40 (top) took almost fourteen machine-hours to produce. The PPSh 41 (centre, shown without its magazine) could be made in just over seven hours, and the PPS 43 (bottom) in fewer than three. The brutally simple PPS was designed by Alexey Sudayev in the besieged city of Leningrad.

ОКНО ТАСС № 699
САЛЮТ ГЕРОЯМ!

Вперед, вперед!.. Как близки нам названья
Отбитых сел, и рек, и городов!
И тот, кто знал всю горечь расставанья,
Теперь запеть от радости готов.

И сил как-будто сразу больше стало.
Готов работать, не смыкая глаз,
Чтоб завтра вновь, как песня, прозвучал он,
Победный, гордый, Сталинский Приказ.

художник — В. ИВАНОВ   текст — В. ЛЕБЕДЕВ-КУМАЧ

MOBILIZING SOCIETIES

Total war meant that governments around the world needed to direct and control industry and agriculture far more than they had in peacetime.

Britain centralized control of industry, agriculture and the workforce. In America, massive state investment in industry helped generate a huge volume of war production. Japan relied on the patriotic self-sacrifice of its people to keep its factories and farms going. Expecting a short war, Germany was slower to achieve such a level of effort.

The most intense mobilization of society took place in the Soviet Union, where Stalin's regime exerted complete control. Every able-bodied person, even teenagers and political prisoners, had to work or fight. Their lives were harsh. Unlike its allies and enemies, the Soviet Union did not care about keeping its citizens comfortable or happy.

ABOVE This poster, 'Salute the Heroes', was created for the Soviet news agency, TASS, by the artist Victor Ivanov and the poet Vasily Lebedev-Kumach. It pays tribute to factory workers and miners.

The most startling outward sign of Stalin's reform of the Red Army was the reintroduction of 'shoulder boards' bearing rank insignia. These *pogony* had long been seen as emblematic of the tsarist regime that had been overthrown by the Russian revolution of 1917. Stalin himself wore this pair, proclaiming his rank of Marshal of the Soviet Union. Civilians paid a price for their reintroduction, as their manufacture was only possible after cutting the production of already scarce underwear.

hours of working directly for the war effort in addition to the standard ten-hour working day. Women supplemented a workforce weakened by the army's need for manpower, providing 50 per cent of factory labour and 85 per cent of workers on the land. Children worked too, especially in agriculture.

Soviet industry was focused on the manufacture of weaponry – small arms, tanks, aeroplanes and artillery. In these key categories it greatly out-produced its foe. Unlike in other countries, little production capacity was wasted on consumer products: civilians were expected to make do with the little they had. Soviet weapons production was greatly helped by the fact that many other vital necessities were supplied by the Western Allies. From Britain and – in particular – the United States came army boots, clothing, tinned food, military radios and railway locomotives. America also supplied aluminium, one of the few raw materials in short supply in the Soviet Union. Arguably the greatest Allied contribution to Soviet military effectiveness came in the form of American-made trucks. The United States supplied two-thirds of the 'soft-skinned' vehicles used by the Red Army, giving it a mobility that was superior to that of its enemy.

Many of the American trucks were all-wheel drive, enabling them to operate off-road. By using these trucks, the Red Army was able to achieve its most dramatic victory of the war, when it overwhelmed and destroyed the German Army Group Centre in the summer of 1944. The Germans, deployed to block roads and hold urban centres, found themselves outmanoeuvred as their opponents advanced through the roadless forests and marshes of the region. The Russian war correspondent Vasily Grossman described the result at the fallen German stronghold of Bobruisk: 'Corpses, hundreds and thousands of them, pave the road, lie in ditches, under the pines, in the green barley … A cauldron of death was boiling here, where the revenge was carried out – a ruthless, terrible revenge over those who hadn't surrendered their arms and tried to break out to the west.' As this tactical triumph suggests, the Red Army had changed greatly from the clumsy and unresponsive force that had struggled in the face of the German invasion of 1941. Major changes had been made in the army's structure and command system. Communist Party control over the military command was relaxed. Officers no longer had to fear interference from political commissars.

Stalin began to trust his generals. Although, like Hitler, he made himself supreme commander, he proved increasingly willing to listen to the opinions of his senior generals and to endorse their plans. And with ineffective leaders weeded out during the defeats of 1941 and 1942, he could rely on a growing band of efficient, sometimes brilliant, commanders. The Red Army outnumbered its enemies (it fielded around 6.5 million troops in 1944 compared to the 2.5 million of Germany and its allies), but the huge losses suffered earlier in the war meant that Stalin could no longer call on unlimited reserves of manpower. Soviet units were almost constantly under-strength, despite their ranks being bolstered by a million women. As the Red Army advanced, it kept its numbers up by pressing male citizens of military age (this definition included teenagers) into service. They received their training in the field.

LYUDMILA PAVLICHENKO

When Germany invaded the Soviet Union, Lyudmila, a historian, abandoned her university career to join the army. Rejecting the chance to be a nurse, she became one of the Red Army's first female snipers. By mid-1942, Lyudmila had been credited with killing 309 enemy soldiers. After being wounded, she was sent on a propaganda tour of the United States, Canada and Britain. In America she met President Roosevelt and even inspired a song, 'Miss Pavlichenko', by the folk singer Woody Guthrie. In Britain, Lyudmila's achievements reinforced popular admiration for the fighting spirit of the Soviet people. She features on the cover of this Soviet book produced for an English-language readership.

SOVIET WOMEN
IN THE WAR
AGAINST HITLERISM

Poland's agony

This French-language poster makes anti-Soviet propaganda out of the German discovery of the bodies of 10,000 murdered Polish officers at Katyn in Russia. The massacre, carried out in 1940 by the Soviet security service, had resulted in the deaths of 22,000 Poles. The killings were organized with more sinister efficiency than the poster suggests. Most victims were individually shot in the back of the neck during overnight killing sessions in specially prepared buildings. The burials took place later.

The fate of Poland was a source of conflict between the Allies. Stalin made little secret of his desire to restore the Soviet Union's borders to where they had stood after his carve-up of Eastern Europe with Hitler in 1939. This meant that he intended to keep the eastern portion of pre-war Poland. Naturally, such an intention was strongly opposed by the British-based Polish government-in-exile. But in order to maintain Allied unity, Polish wishes were largely ignored. In the spring of 1943, tensions between Poland and its allies were heightened when the Germans revealed their discovery – on Soviet territory – of the bodies of 10,000 murdered Polish officers. Stalin affected outrage at the Polish government's support for an International Red Cross investigation into the matter. In reality, this was just one of the burial sites used to inter 22,000 captured Poles murdered on Stalin's orders in 1940.

By August 1944, the success of the Red Army's summer offensives had brought it to the gates of Warsaw. The Polish resistance, known as the Home Army, saw an opportunity to rise up and ensure that they, and not the Soviets, liberated their capital. A tragedy ensued. After a savage struggle from 1 August to 2 October, in which 15,000 of its members were killed, the Home

DEPORTATION

The enforced movement of people was a major feature of the Second World War. Stalin exiled millions of people he considered to be traitors to distant regions of the Soviet Union. Among them were ethnic Germans, Chechens, Poles and Crimean Tartars. Unknown thousands of them died. Germany forced more than 400,000 Poles from their land, replacing them with German-speaking settlers. At the war's end, millions of ethnic Germans were expelled from Central and Eastern Europe. Approximately 600,000 of them perished.

TOP After taking control of eastern Poland in 1939, Stalin deported an estimated 350,000 Poles to Soviet Central Asia. In 1942, after the Soviet Union had joined the Allies, many Poles were allowed to walk south into British-controlled Iran. This badge was worn by members of the exiled Polish government's II Corps, which later recruited soldiers from among these displaced Poles.

ABOVE Polish women and children walk into British-controlled Iran after leaving Soviet captivity.

Soldiers of the Polish resistance, the Home Army, during the Warsaw Uprising of 1944. Much of their arms and equipment had been captured from the Germans.

Army was forced to surrender. The Red Army, exhausted after its long advance, did not help, and was certainly not encouraged to do so by Stalin. He dismissed the Home Army as 'a handful of power-seeking criminals' and obstructed attempts by the Western Allies to send aid by air. The main victims of the Warsaw Uprising were the civilians caught up in the fighting. More than 150,000 were killed – many of them in massacres carried out by the Germans. When the fighting was over, Germany attempted to wipe Warsaw from the map. Most of the remaining inhabitants were deported or sent to labour or concentration camps.

ANNA DE LAVEAUX

Anna, the twenty-one-year-old daughter of a Polish general, was a member of Poland's Home Army. In August 1944 she and her brother both joined the struggle to liberate Warsaw from German occupation.

Like other Home Army personnel, Anna fought under a *nom de guerre*, in her case 'Dot'. She wore this armband instead of a uniform. Identifying her as a legitimate combatant, it had the potential to save her from being executed if captured. In fact, the terms of the Home Army's surrender granted its fighters full prisoner-of-war status, and Anna was sent to a prison camp in Germany. At the end of the war, she walked across western Germany to find her father, who had been held as a prisoner since the German conquest of Poland in 1939.

The Attempt to Annihilate Europe's Jews

Germany's invasion of the Soviet Union in 1941 had seen the Nazi persecution of Jews cross a threshold of violence. The *Einsatzgruppen*, encouraged by the head of the SS, Heinrich Himmler, had initiated a campaign of mass murder. By late 1941 it was clear that there would be no swift victory for Germany. This put an end to such vague German ideas as deporting Jews to Madagascar or expelling them into Siberia. On 11 December, in the wake of Japan's entry into the war, Hitler declared war on the United States while simultaneously blaming Jewish influence for American hostility towards Germany. On the following day, his propaganda supremo, Goebbels, found Hitler expressing the view that 'The World War is here ... the extermination of the Jews must be the necessary consequence.' This was not the first time that Hitler had expressed such a wish, and his henchmen were already working to make it a reality.

⊕ Mass murder in occupied Poland

On 8 December 1941 at Chelmno, in the part of Poland annexed to Germany, the SS began using the carbon monoxide in vehicle exhaust to murder Jews and Roma rounded up in the local region. Soon, Jews from the nearby Lodz ghetto were being murdered at Chelmno – to eliminate 'useless eaters' and make room for Jews deported from Germany. Meanwhile, in the *Generalgouvernement* – the Nazi-controlled rump of Poland – plans were being made to annihilate the large Jewish population that, since 1940, had been forced into ghettos there. This would be carried out at killing centres equipped with permanent gas chambers. These killing centres, at Belzec, Sobibor and Treblinka, were not concentration camps. Virtually everyone who was sent to them was killed shortly after arrival. Only a few, deemed necessary to help bury or cremate the bodies, or to process the personal belongings taken from those murdered, were kept temporarily alive. At the three sites mentioned above – plus the Majdanek concentration camp at Lublin, which had its own gas chamber – more than 1.25 million people were murdered in less than ten months. The ghastly work of these sites was wound down during 1943; but by the end of that year, the number of people killed, either at the sites themselves or in the brutal process of deportation to them, approached 2 million.

The Germans were able to carry out this mass murder by cynically manipulating the inhabitants of their ghettos. They kept them in a constant state of disorientation and terror, which they coupled with deception – especially through the offering of false hopes of survival. Jewish ghetto administrators, appointed by the SS, were forced to use their own makeshift Jewish police to round up people for deportation. They cooperated in the hope of saving themselves and their families, or because they believed that the suffering would be worse if the SS themselves felt the need to intervene. Some ghetto dwellers resisted, especially when word reached them of what was going on at the killing centres. In January 1943 poorly armed Jewish fighters in the Warsaw ghetto fired on members of the SS attempting to carry out a round-up. In April, full-scale fighting broke out as the SS sought to finally clear the ghetto. The Germans began to burn the ghetto down, block by block, but still took a month to end Jewish resistance. The last letter written by the uprising's leader, twenty-three-year-old Mordechai Anielewicz, reveals something of the spirit that inspired it: 'the fact that we are remembered beyond the ghetto walls encourages us in our struggle ... Self-defence in the ghetto will have been a reality. Jewish armed resistance and revenge are facts.' Fighting also erupted when the SS cleared the Vilnius ghetto in Lithuania in September 1943. Here, many resisters escaped into the nearby forests, joining existing bands of Jewish partisans.

⊕ Extermination through work

Some Jews in Poland managed to prolong their lives through their involvement in work that fed the German war effort. Until well into 1943, however, the Nazi leadership proved reluctant to fully exploit this potential source of forced labour. But captive people, whether Soviet prisoners of war or Jews, or concentration-camp prisoners in general, turned out to be a labour force that could not be ignored as the war turned against Germany. An ever growing number of captives were used as slaves in German factories. They worked alongside labourers forcibly recruited in occupied countries, particularly the Soviet Union. In 1942 only some 25,000 concentration-camp prisoners were working for the German war economy; by 1944, however, this figure had risen to 400,000. The SS profited directly, by leasing the labour of their prisoners to manufacturers and industrial concerns. Concentration camps spawned networks of sub-camps, sited near the factories or plants where their prisoners were forced to work. For Jews, work might offer a reprieve from the gas chamber, but not from terrible maltreatment and risk of death. They became victims of a policy of 'extermination through work', from which only an end to the war could save them.

RIGHT The red triangle on this concentration-camp prisoner's jacket indicates that it was worn by a political prisoner. Concentration camps provided slave labour for German industries. As the war turned against Germany, Jewish prisoners who had not already been killed were also enslaved. Working conditions were appalling, with little food or medical care. Jews received the harshest treatment of all: the intention was to work them to death.

BELOW These parts from a V-1 flying bomb – a compass housing (left) and a tail-fin former – were made in the underground factory that produced Germany's secret 'revenge' weapons, the V-1 and the rocket-powered V-2. The factory's workers came from the adjacent Mittelbau-Dora concentration camp. An estimated 20,000 of them died or were killed there – more than the number of people killed by the V-weapons they were forced to produce.

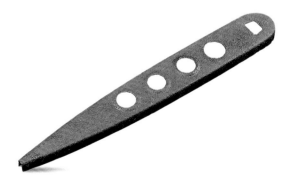

The Holocaust

NAZI GERMANY ATTEMPTS TO ANNIHILATE EUROPE'S JEWS

Hitler's desire to exterminate Europe's Jewish population resulted in the death of millions. What began in 1939 with the rounding-up of Jews into ghettos would eventually lead to the 'final solution' and mass murder across a network of death camps.

Nazi camps, ghettos and massacre sites stretched from France in the west to Estonia in the east. At the height of the Holocaust, Jews from all over Europe were being deported to concentration or extermination camps.

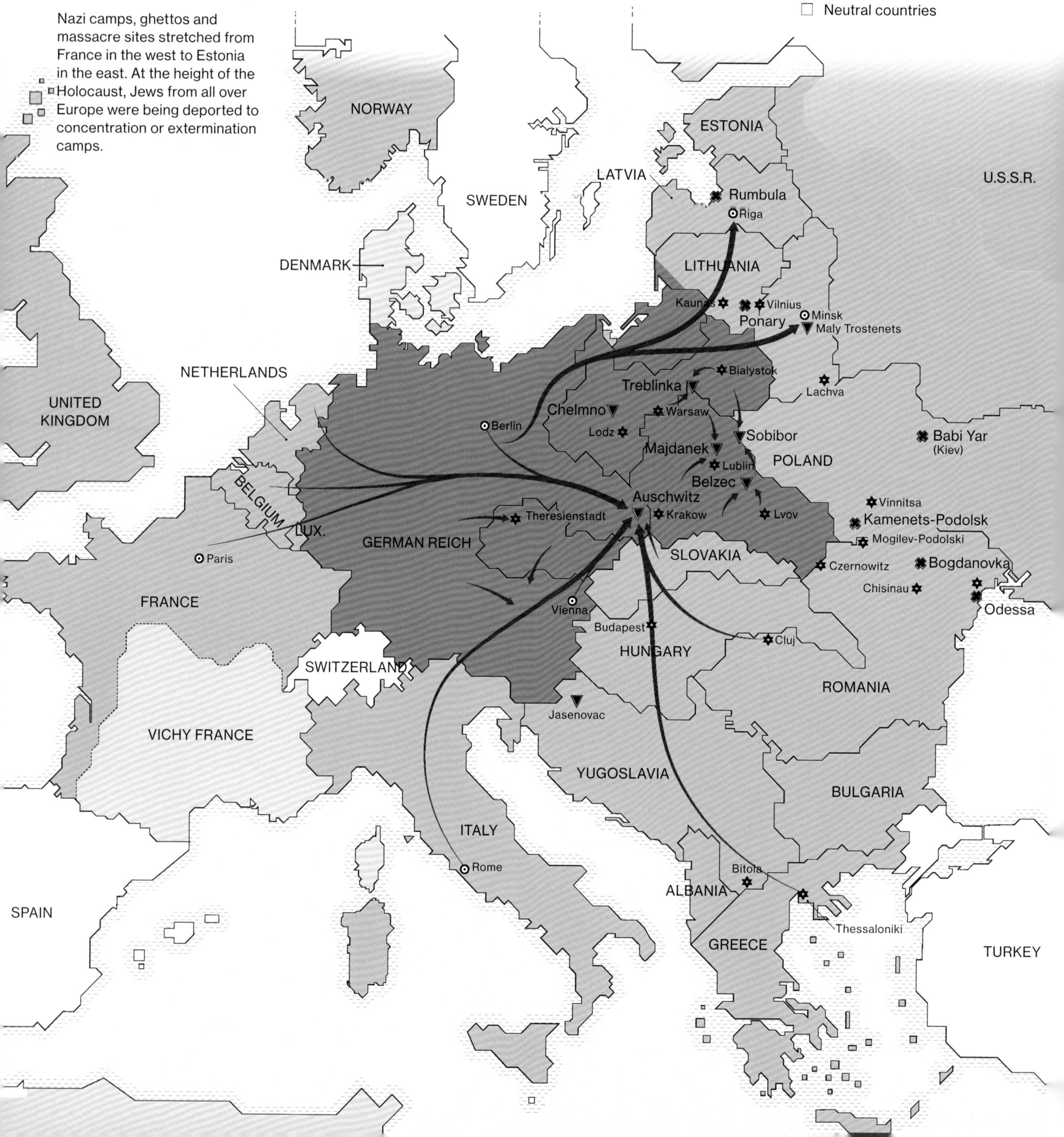

→ Main deportation routes

TYPE OF SITE
✿ Ghetto
▼ Extermination camp
✸ Large-scale massacre
⊙ Transit city

TERRITORIES, 1941–42
German Reich
Axis territories
Nominally unoccupied
Allied territories
Neutral countries

NORWAY

SWEDEN

DENMARK

ESTONIA

LATVIA

U.S.S.R.

Rumbula
⊙ Riga

LITHUANIA

Kaunas ✸ ✸ Vilnius
Ponary ⊙ Minsk
▼ Maly Trostenets

✿ Bialystok
Lachva

Treblinka ▼
Chelmno ▼
✸ Warsaw
Lodz ✿
Sobibor
Majdanek ▼
✿ Lublin
POLAND
Belzec ▼
✿ Babi Yar
(Kiev)

NETHERLANDS

UNITED KINGDOM

⊙ Berlin

✿ Vinnitsa
Kamenets-Podolsk
Mogilev-Podolski
✿ Czernowitz
✸ Bogdanovka
Chisinau ✿
Odessa

BELGIUM
LUX.

⊙ Paris

GERMAN REICH

Theresienstadt
Auschwitz ▼ ✿ Krakow
✸ Lvov
SLOVAKIA

FRANCE

Vienna ⊙
Budapest ✿
Cluj
HUNGARY

SWITZERLAND

VICHY FRANCE

ROMANIA

Jasenovac ▼

YUGOSLAVIA

BULGARIA

ITALY

⊙ Rome

Bitola ✿

ALBANIA

Thessaloniki

SPAIN

GREECE

TURKEY

PHASES OF THE HOLOCAUST

Starting in July 1941, German forces engaged in the systematic killing of Jews and other persecuted groups. By the end of the war, almost 6 million Jews had been killed in the Holocaust.

ESTIMATED NUMBER KILLED

 1,000 deaths (Jews only)

TYPE OF SITE

▼ Extermination camp

✹ Large-scale massacre

1. JULY 1941 ONWARDS
'HOLOCAUST BY BULLET'

The shooting of Jewish Soviet citizens by *Einsatzgruppen*, German Order Police and local collaborators (and also Romanian forces). At least 1.5 million victims. Shown here are the principal massacre sites.

27–29 Aug 1941
KAMENETS-PODOLSK
23,600

July–Sept 1941
PONARY FOREST
21,000

29–30 Sept 1941
BABI YAR RAVINE
33,761

22–24 Oct 1941
ODESSA
27,000

30 Nov–8 Dec 1941
RUMBULA
26,000

21–31 Dec 1941
BOGDANOVKA
40,000

2. DEC 1941–MAR 1943
KILLING BY CARBON MONOXIDE

The creation of the death camps represented a shift in Nazi policy. At Chelmno, the first of the extermination camps, where gassing began on 8 December 1941, the carbon monoxide in vehicle exhaust was used to murder Jews and Roma from the local region.

CHELMNO
150,000

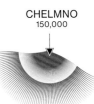

3. MAR 1942–OCT 1943
OPERATION REINHARD

Most of Poland's Jews and some from further afield are murdered at specially constructed sites in the *Generalgouvernement*, notably Belzec, Sobibor, Treblinka and Majdanek. At least 1.7 million killed.

SOBIBOR
167,000

TREBLINKA
925,000

BELZEC
430,000

MAJDANEK
60,000   18,400

Nov 1942
OPERATION 'HARVEST FESTIVAL'

Polish Jews formerly retained for labour in the *Generalgouvernement* are murdered, the majority at Majdanek. At least 18,400 victims in total.

AUSCHWITZ-BIRKENAU
960,000

4. FEB 1942–NOV 1944
KILLING BY ZYKLON B AT AUSCHWITZ-BIRKENAU

The killing of Jews using Zyklon B – a cyanide-based pesticide – was first carried out at Auschwitz-Birkenau, part of the Auschwitz camp complex. By 1944, more than a million people had been murdered at Auschwitz, the vast majority of them Jews. Victims came from as far afield as Norway and Greece.

⊕ The final solution

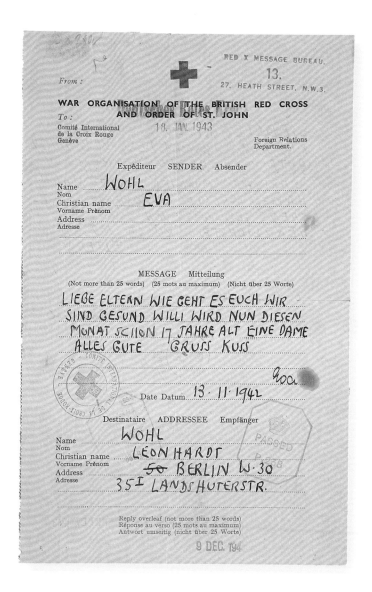

This is the last telegram sent by German-Jewish refugee Eva Wohl to her father, Leonhardt. Eva had fled to Britain in 1938. Her parents, trapped in Berlin, communicated with her through the Red Cross. The reply to this telegram is dated 16 January 1943; by the time it reached Eva, however, both her father and her mother, Clara, had been deported to their deaths.

Even before the death camps of the *Generalgouvernement* had been built, the Nazi leadership was formulating an even more unthinkable plan for a 'final solution' to its self-imposed 'Jewish question'. This plan was made explicit at a meeting held in January 1942, at a villa on the banks of the Wannsee lake in Berlin. The Nazi Party and government officials who attended were told that the SS would take charge of the annihilation of the entire Jewish population of German-controlled Europe. Himmler knew that bringing Hitler's murderous ideas to fruition would cement not only the power of the SS but also his own position in the Nazi hierarchy. Centralized control of the mass murder – euphemistically termed 'resettlement' – would put an end to competitive attempts by local Nazi leaders to rid their areas of Jews. At the same time, it allowed less eager officials to distance themselves from the process.

From the summer of 1942 onwards, Jewish people from across Western Europe found themselves corralled into transit camps from which they were then forced to endure terrible rail journeys ending in either death or slave labour. Many would pass through the gates of the camp complex at

RIGHT This photograph, taken at the Auschwitz-Birkenau death camp in the summer of 1944, shows Jewish people deported from Hungary shortly before their murder in one of Birkenau's gas chambers. At this, the most lethal phase of Birkenau's existence, the numbers killed overwhelmed the capacity of the crematoria, and bodies had to be burned in pits.

BELOW These drawings were made by the Jewish cartoonist and political activist Wilhelm Spira. Spira was made to work at the Blechhammer synthetic-oil plant in eastern Germany, a sub-camp of the Auschwitz concentration-camp complex. The drawings show various groups of forced and slave labourers marching to work, including French, British and Soviet prisoners of war, Jews, and German 'work education' camp prisoners.

Auschwitz, situated in the industrial region of Lower Silesia. Auschwitz was already the site of a concentration camp, but Himmler had ordered the construction of a new killing centre nearby in late 1941. It was there, at Auschwitz-Birkenau, that the first experiments were made in killing prisoners with Zyklon B – a cyanide-based pesticide. As the deportation of Jews intensified, the facilities at Auschwitz were expanded, ultimately comprising four large gas chambers with associated crematoria for the disposal of the bodies of their victims. Between February 1942 and November 1944, more than a million people were murdered at Auschwitz. Those not killed immediately became slave workers – either in a third Auschwitz camp, built to serve a proposed synthetic rubber factory, or in a network of sub-camps that provided labour for industry, mines and agriculture.

The deportation of Jews to Auschwitz required the cooperation of local administrations and police forces in German-dominated Europe. This generally proved disturbingly straightforward for the Nazis in Western Europe, but more complicated in the case of Germany's allies in the east. Romania had independently persecuted its own Jewish population and had murdered thousands of Soviet Jews. But, as the war turned against Germany, it refused to allow deportations from Romania. Bulgaria refused to give up Jews who were Bulgarian citizens. Hungary persecuted its many Jewish citizens, but resisted their deportation until 1944, when Hitler intervened in Hungarian politics. In a massive operation, 440,000 Jewish people were deported from Hungary to Auschwitz-Birkenau in a matter of months, with the majority being gassed immediately. With this, the murder of Europe's Jews reached a frightful climax.

⊕ News gets out

In the autumn of 1942 a member of the Polish Home Army, Jan Karski, made a perilous journey across occupied Europe and fascist Spain, to make contact with the British authorities in Gibraltar. His mission was to bring news of the murder of Poland's Jews. Unlike earlier rumours of Nazi persecution that had been circulating, Karski's was an eyewitness account. He had covertly visited the Warsaw ghetto and had gained access to a hideous ghetto at Izbica, where Jews en route to their deaths at Belzec were held. As a result of Karski's intelligence, Britain's foreign secretary, Anthony Eden, made a statement in the House of Commons on 17 December, condemning this 'bestial policy of cold-blooded extermination'. Karski conveyed his dreadful news to the United States as well. By this time, however, most of the victims of the killing centres in occupied Poland had already gone to their deaths.

In April 1944 two Slovakian Jews, Alfred Wetzler and Rudolf Vrba, escaped from Auschwitz and clandestinely published a report that detailed the killing process at Auschwitz-Birkenau. Via Switzerland, its contents became known in Britain and America during the summer of 1944. Then, on 22 July that year, Soviet troops liberated the city of Lublin and, with it, Majdanek concentration camp. Here they found gas chambers and a crematorium that had seen recent use, along with survivors who could bear witness to what had gone on there. Stacks of clothing taken from victims testified to the scale of the killings throughout Poland. A visiting Soviet journalist, Konstantin Simonov, described the scene as 'too gruesome to be fully taken in'. The nature of Hitler's war against Europe's Jews was now clear for all to see, but the grim truth was that most of the killing had already taken place.

A crematorium at Majdanek concentration camp, as it was found by the Soviet Army.

These shoes were found
when Majdanek concentration
camp, near Lublin in Poland,
was liberated by the Red Army
in 1944. Lublin had been the
administrative centre for the
mass murder of Jews at purpose-
built killing centres in occupied
Poland between 1942 and 1943.
Hundreds of thousands of shoes
were among the stores of personal
belongings taken from murdered
people that were discovered at
the camp.

⊕ Germany under pressure

German soldiers taken prisoner by the Red Army. About 14 per cent of the 3 million German prisoners held by the Soviet Union died in captivity.

The huge scale of Hitler's war with the Soviet Union stretched Germany to its limits. Of the 13.5 million military casualties suffered by Germany in the entire war, nearly 11 million were inflicted by the Soviet Union. In 1944 these losses hit a peak, with 1.2 million Germans killed in the east. But manpower was not the only area in which Germany was overstretched. Bombing by the Western Allies hit its war industry and severely restricted the amount of air support available to front-line troops, as the Luftwaffe focused on defending the Reich itself. Furthermore, only Germany's elite armoured formations were fully mechanized. The infantry still relied on horse-drawn transport, with 1.5 million horses in service by 1945.

As the Germans were forced out of the Soviet Union, it became clear to all that Germany was losing the war. In August 1944, Hitler's chief ally in the east, Romania, changed sides. Romania had enthusiastically participated in the invasion of the Soviet Union but now, as the Red Army advanced into Romania, its dictator, Marshal Ion Antonescu, was deposed in a coup. More than a million Romanian troops now turned from fighting for Germany to fighting against it. Finland too had been fighting alongside Germany, hoping to recover what it had lost to the Soviet Union in 1940. By the summer of 1944, however, it found itself under heavy Soviet attack and was relieved to be able to make peace with Stalin on terms that preserved its independence. Hungary was also looking for a way out of the war.

To pre-empt its surrender, Germany launched a coup of its own, overthrowing the Hungarian leader, Admiral Horthy, and putting local fascists in charge to keep the country fighting. Despite these German efforts, most of Hungary was under Soviet control by the year's end, with Budapest under siege. More alarmingly for the German people, further to the north, the Red Army actually stood on pre-war German territory on the borders of East Prussia.

With an invasion of the Reich looming, the Nazi Party prepared the German people to resist. A home defence force, the *Volkssturm*, was created, in which all males from sixteen to sixty not already in uniform were liable to serve. Propaganda, while hinting at new secret weapons, exhorted German men to save their women and children from the 'Asiatic barbarism' of the Red Army. Huge publicity was given to exaggerated reports of a massacre of German civilians in the East Prussian village of Nemmersdorf, with newsreels purporting to show the gruesome evidence. Fear of Soviet retribution sustained the will of Germans to fight on, with many expressing the view that, 'If the Russians don't come here, we could bear anything else'. In the January snows of 1945 their fears were realized, as the Red Army launched another major attack. Liberating the remainder of Poland, it struck deep into eastern Germany. Its leading elements came to a halt just 60 kilometres short of Berlin. As winter turned to spring, the end of Nazi Germany was at hand.

ABOVE, TOP Germany's leaders aimed to create a home defence force of 6 million men – the *Volkssturm*. By January 1945, however, it had access to only 40,000 rifles and 2,900 machine guns. The former consisted mostly of a hotchpotch of foreign weapons captured earlier in the war. Emergency weapons, such as this *Volkskarabiner*, were put into production. It combines simple stamped metal parts with existing components from other weapons, including an obsolete machine-gun barrel.

ABOVE In June 1944 the Red Army launched an offensive to knock Finland out of the war. Finnish forces managed to hold out, but at a price that confirmed that Finland must make peace at almost any cost. This Finnish submachine gun was designed to be fired from inside defensive bunkers. It was made compact by replacing the butt with a pistol grip, and the barrel jacket was flattened at the muzzle to enable it to be fired through a narrow aperture.

RIGHT This Soviet propaganda leaflet was dropped over German lines in February 1945. It shows a terror-stricken German soldier crying, 'Enough!' Despite the near hopelessness of their situation, most German soldiers fought on. Many were inspired by the desire to defend their homeland from Soviet invasion. But they also knew that, if they deserted, they faced execution after a perfunctory trial by 'flying courts martial'.

War in Asia 1943–1945

⊕ A three-pronged attack on Japan

In 1942 Japan's rapid conquest of territory in Asia and the Pacific appeared unstoppable. Yet within a few short months the tide of the war had changed, with Japanese forces reeling from losses at Guadalcanal, Midway and New Guinea. The Japanese were now on the defensive, and the Allies began to strike Japanese outposts in the Pacific. The Pacific theatre was too large for one person to oversee, so responsibility was divided between two American commanders, one from the army and one from the navy. General Douglas MacArthur commanded Allied ground and air forces in Australia, New Guinea, the Dutch East Indies and the Philippines. Admiral Chester Nimitz, commander of the Pacific Fleet, targeted Japanese-occupied islands in the central Pacific. The simultaneous assault by Nimitz and MacArthur would force the Japanese to fight in two places at once. Meanwhile, China was locked in a struggle against Japanese troops. Despite internal political conflict, famine and defeats on the battlefield, China fought on. As long as China stayed in the war, millions of Imperial Japanese Army soldiers would be tied up in the fighting there, instead of being used to fortify the Pacific islands. The United States sent supplies to China over land and air, knowing that a victory for the country would also allow America to build airfields on Chinese soil from which it could bomb Japan. This three-pronged attack – MacArthur, Nimitz and bombing raids from China – focused on getting close enough to Japan to launch a full-scale assault on the mainland and win a decisive victory in Asia.

⊕ Island-hopping across the Pacific

Using a combination of land, sea and air power, US forces hopped from island to island in the Pacific. Strategically selecting islands that would enable them to close in on Japan, US forces were able to bypass and isolate other islands, cutting off Japanese troops from their supply lines. The Japanese garrisons defending the Pacific islands were small. On Tarawa, one of the first islands targeted by Nimitz, there were some 4,600 men. But the Japanese had constructed impressive defences, digging into the sand to conceal heavy coastal-defence guns, laying beach mines, and placing machine guns on the beaches directed at every angle of approach. Prior to Nimitz's landing on 21 November 1943, American battleships and aircraft bombarded Tarawa in an attempt to destroy the Japanese defences. However, the machine guns and beach mines remained intact, as did a camouflaged concrete wall. Tarawa's shallow coral reef prevented boats from

ABOVE Japanese civilians hid in caves in Saipan, one of the Mariana Islands. Many leapt off cliffs in fear as the Americans drew near.

BELOW US casualties on the beach at Tarawa, November 1943.

getting close to the shore. The US Marines were therefore forced to crawl forward under heavy fire, taking out Japanese defensive positions one by one with grenades, portable flamethrowers and machine guns. Over the course of 76 hours, 3,300 Americans were killed or wounded. The United States had won the battle, and learned valuable tactical lessons about amphibious assaults, but the American public were shocked at the price of capturing such a tiny and seemingly insignificant island.

To avoid another public disaster like Tarawa, Nimitz's landing forces were equipped with more firepower. When they launched an attack on the Mariana Islands – Saipan, Tinian and Guam – in June 1944, the islands were subjected to longer and more concentrated bombardments from sea and air. As on Tarawa, the Japanese defenders hid in bunkers or built networks of underground caves, and the only way to attack these positions was through hand-to-hand combat using hand grenades and flamethrowers. Faced with defeat, the Japanese on Guam charged at the US Marines in mass suicide attacks. On Saipan, Japanese civilians leapt off the cliffs in fear as the Americans drew near. While the US Navy was supporting the landings on the Mariana Islands, its ships were vulnerable to strikes from Japanese aircraft carriers. However, American submarines torpedoed the large Japanese carriers. They pursued the fleeing Japanese fleet, while US pilots shot down more than 400 Japanese aircraft in only eight hours in what the pilots nicknamed the 'Great Marianas Turkey Shoot'. With an overwhelming victory, the United States was now able to build airfields on the Mariana Islands, and US B-29 bombers soon began to unleash a bombing campaign on Japanese cities.

🌐 Taking back New Guinea and the Philippines

While Nimitz pursued an eastern approach towards Japan across open ocean, General MacArthur and his combined force of US and Australian troops faced a heavily fortified route across land through New Guinea to reach the Philippines. The Japanese were unwilling to sacrifice New Guinea, which protected their main air and naval base at Rabaul on the island of New Britain. They therefore reinforced the area by establishing strong positions to defend Rabaul against attack. Soldiers from both sides endured hot, humid days, freezing nights and torrential rain in the jungle. Weapons failed because of the moisture, and soldiers hauled 25-pounder guns through the muddy and mountainous terrain. MacArthur's forces captured key airfields on New Guinea, utilizing aircraft fitted with external fuel tanks to support his long-range attacks and isolating Japanese ground forces. American aircraft soon dominated the skies, reinforcing troops inland and forcing the Japanese to retreat.

MacArthur turned his attention to the Philippines and began an attack on Leyte, a small, narrow island in the central Philippines. As before, MacArthur moved the infantry forward under the protection of American air cover. On 20 October 1944, MacArthur walked from his landing craft to

This machete was issued to Australian soldiers fighting in the Pacific Theatre to help them cut through dense jungle undergrowth.

the beach at Leyte, declaring, 'I have returned.' It was a significant moment after the devastating losses MacArthur and the US Army had endured in the Philippines two years earlier. The Japanese flooded the island with troops and resources but suffered terrible losses owing to the Allies' dominance of the air, which allowed the Americans to land troops anywhere on the island and bring reinforcements to isolated areas. The landing at Leyte was a key moment, but it was clear that the final fight for the Philippines would take place on Luzon, the country's largest island. MacArthur's troops began their attack on 9 January 1945. They headed for Manila, the Philippine capital, and fought for each building and street. Many innocent Filipinos were killed and wounded by Japanese and American artillery attacks. It took more than a week to bring the city under US control. Further American attacks on Bataan and the island of Corregidor faced strong Japanese resistance, and the attempts to clear Luzon continued for several months.

⊕ Targeting Tokyo

On 10 March 1945, American B-29 bomber aircraft destroyed 41 square kilometres of Tokyo. Almost 100,000 Japanese civilians were killed, and fires destroyed wooden buildings. This 'extinguish' flag showed where Japanese fire fighters could access water.

In the midst of the Philippines campaign, Nimitz and the American fleet set their sights on the volcanic island of Iwo Jima, which was only 1,200 kilometres from Tokyo. It was ideally situated between Japan and the US bomber airbases on the Mariana Islands, and therefore a perfect site for emergency landings by bomber crews. But the Japanese intended to hold off the attackers for as long as possible, and were prepared to fight to the last man. Three weeks of bloody hand-to-hand fighting ensued before the Americans claimed victory. While the battle for Iwo Jima came to a close, another US attack, this time on the island of Okinawa, began. Okinawa was located only 530 kilometres to the south-west of Japan, and its air bases and harbours were an ideal supply base to support an American attack on the Japanese mainland. Hundreds of kamikaze planes, launched from a base in Formosa (now Taiwan), targeted the American fleet stationed to support the Okinawa landings. While no major warships were lost, several carriers were damaged. The British Pacific Fleet (BPF), established in November 1944, and comprised of British Commonwealth vessels, was able to support the Okinawa operations by neutralizing Japanese airfields on Formosa. Meanwhile, on land, a bloody battle raged. While many of the islands that became battlefields in the Pacific campaign had been evacuated or were uninhabited, Okinawa had a large civilian population, who were now caught in the crossfire. Reports surfaced of Japanese soldiers drafting Okinawans to fight, using them as human shields, stealing their food or forcing them out of their shelters. Urged on by the Japanese, who claimed that victorious American soldiers would murder or rape any survivors, some civilians committed suicide.

Following the capture of the Mariana Islands, American B-29 bombers targeted Japanese cities with incendiary bombs. Japan was close to economic collapse. Homes made of wood were quickly destroyed in the fires, and the government had not built sufficient air-raid shelters. Almost a million Japanese civilians were killed in the raids, while millions more were left homeless. Japanese industries were in ruin. By 1945, women, prisoners of war, the elderly and children were being drafted to help in factories or civilian defence. Japan depended on its merchant fleet to supply the Japanese people with food, and for the raw materials needed to sustain its war effort. But the constant movement of troops between Japan and Pacific islands required the use of merchant ships and oil tankers, as well as troop ships. American submarine attacks proved to be a key weapon against these vessels, sinking Japanese ships faster than the country could build them. Through the use of unrestricted submarine warfare, America had cut off Japan from the supplies and raw materials it desperately needed to feed its people and continue fighting. Having to defend against both MacArthur and Nimitz simultaneously, as well as continued fighting in China, had forced Japan to spread its troops thinly.

The beaches of Iwo Jima were made up of steep dunes and volcanic ash, causing great difficulties for the US Marines as they unloaded supplies from landing craft in 1945.

GORDON POINDEXTER

Gordon joined the US Marine Corps on his seventeenth birthday, in September 1943. After being sent to fight in the Pacific, Gordon wrote to his family: 'I wish I could tell you all the things I've seen.' He took photographs of his experiences and kept them in his kit bag. On 17 October 1944, the first day of the Battle of Leyte in the Philippines, Gordon landed on the beaches. He remained on Leyte for more than a month before being sent to Guam, where the Marines were preparing to launch an invasion of the Japanese mainland. At the end of the war, Gordon returned home to the United States.

SIDNEY HAGERLING

Sidney, a member of the US Marine Corps, took part in the battle for the Japanese island of Okinawa, April–June 1945. Sidney's unit used flamethrowers to flush out Japanese soldiers from their heavily defended caves. Almost 150,000 Okinawan civilians were killed, went missing or committed suicide. The Japanese had told them that US troops would torture, rape or murder civilians if they were captured.

⊕ The war in China

Indian and Burmese labourers help build a road between Ledo in India and Kunming in China. Flying US supplies to China over the Himalayas was highly dangerous, so construction on an alternative, overground route was started in December 1942. Chinese civilians and US soldiers, most of them African Americans, also helped to build the road. Many labourers died.

The third strategic prong of the Allied attack on the Japanese mainland focused on keeping China in the war. Chinese troops were fighting hard to defend the country, tying down Japanese troops that could otherwise have been used as reinforcements in the Pacific campaigns. The political rivals Chiang Kai-shek, leader of the Chinese nationalists, and Mao Zedong, who led the Chinese communists, had united against Japan. While the nationalists fought battles in China and alongside the Allies in Burma, the Communist Eighth Route Army engaged in guerrilla warfare, working with local people to attack behind Japanese lines. But to continue fighting, China relied on support and supplies from the United States. In April 1942, because of the Allies' defeat in Burma, access to the Burma Road, a direct supply route to China, had been cut. The US opened up an air-transport route from Assam in India across the Himalayas to Kunming in China, known as the Hump. Ferrying supplies across the Hump was dangerous: violent winds and lack of navigational aids, as well as attacks from Japanese

YANG ZIRONG

Zirong was born in Muping (now Yantai), in the Chinese province of Shandong. During Japan's occupation of the area, Zirong was arrested by the Japanese Army and forced to work in a mine.

In 1943, twenty-six-year-old Zirong managed to escape by beating the Japanese foreman. He fled to his home village, and secretly joined the local militia force, infiltrating and attacking areas of Japanese-occupied China. In 1945 Zirong joined the Communist Eighth Route Army.

fighter aircraft, resulted in many losses. The construction of an overground route from Ledo in Assam to Kunming began in December 1942. The road was built by hand with pickaxes by American soldiers and local labourers from India, China and Burma. The work was hard and medical treatment was not given, resulting in the deaths of thousands of men, women and children. For most of 1943, the Chinese Army engaged in conflicts with its Japanese counterpart while defending the construction of the Ledo Road. On 24 January 1945 the first convoy departed from Ledo, reaching Kunming on 4 February. Over the following six months, approximately 129,000 tons of supplies were transported along the route and delivered to China.

Before the capture of the Marianas in November 1944, China was the closest landmass to Japan on which the Allies could build airbases for an aerial attack on the Japanese. The United States established several airfields in southern China, threatening the Japanese mainland with bombing raids. In retaliation, in April 1944 the Japanese launched Operation Ichi-Go, with the intention of destroying American airbases, controlling the railroads between Beijing and Hong Kong, and establishing a rail link between forces in China and Indochina. Chiang Kai-shek and the Chinese government dismissed intelligence reports predicting the large-scale offensive. They believed that the fighting in Burma was a priority for the Japanese, and assumed that Japanese troops in China would continue to maintain the relatively defensive position they had held since 1940. In the first phase of the attack, the Japanese secured railways between Beijing and Wuhan. In the second, they destroyed US airbases in Hunan province as they made their way to the border with Japanese-occupied Indochina. Despite Japan achieving its objectives, US air forces were able to move further inland to re-establish their bases. Additionally, the new bases built in the Marianas in early 1945 enabled B-29 bombers to get closer to Japan than ever before, thereby ending the limited protection that the Japanese mainland had received from the success of Operation Ichi-Go.

RYOJI UEHARA

Ryoji was studying economics at Keio University in Tokyo when he was called up to the Japanese Army. On 11 May 1945, he was ordered to undertake a suicide mission. Shown here is an Allied recognition model of an Ohka aircraft, the type that kamikaze pilots often flew.

As Ryoji waited for his order to attack, he wrote a final letter, trying to understand why he had to die: 'A pilot in our special aerial attack force is nothing more than a piece of the machine which holds the plane's controls – endowed with no personal qualities, no emotions, certainly no rationality – simply just an iron filament tucked inside a magnet itself designed to be sucked into an enemy aircraft carrier ... but I find that I am a complete human being after all, complete with human emotions and passions too.' The next morning, Ryoji flew directly into US ships at Katena Bay, Okinawa, and was killed.

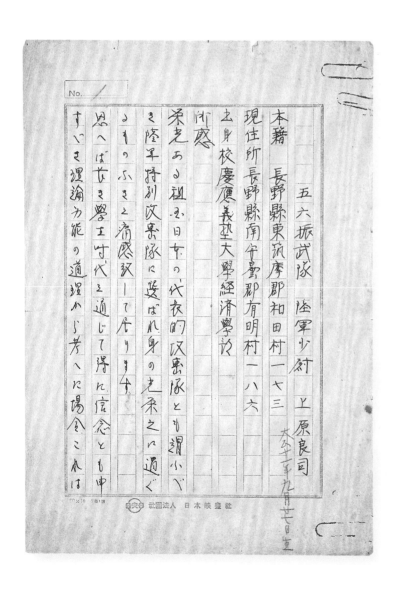

PARK YOUNG-SHIM

Young-shim was born in 1921 in Japanese-ruled Nampo, Korea (now North Korea). When she was in her early twenties, the Japanese military forced Young-shim to become a sex slave. She was taken from her home and transported, along with countless other 'comfort women', to Japanese combat zones – first to Nanjing and Songshan in China, and later to Lashio in Burma.

In September 1944, Japanese troops in Burma retreated. Young-shim was pregnant. The Japanese left her behind and she was found by Allied forces.

⊕ British troops in Burma and the defence of India

Following Japan's rapid conquest of Burma in 1942, the Allies engaged in fierce fighting to retake the country. Britain's army consisted of 340,000 Indian soldiers, 100,000 from the UK, and 80,000 soldiers from western and eastern Africa. Special-operations units known as the 'Chindits' conducted raids against the Japanese Army, attacking troops, facilities and lines of communication deep behind enemy lines. Although they had limited success, the Chindits proved that British troops could take on the Japanese, and their exploits boosted morale. A similar American task force, named 'Merrill's Marauders', embarked on long-range penetration missions in the Burmese jungle through harsh jungle terrain, battling Japanese troops and disrupting Japanese forces.

In March 1944 the Japanese decided to break through into India at the cities of Imphal and Kohima, along India's eastern border with Burma. They reasoned that Indian soldiers and civilians seeking independence would rebel against the British, and that the British Empire in Asia would fall. Capturing Imphal and Kohima would also enable the Japanese to

Soldiers from a regiment composed of men from Nyasaland (now Malawi), East Africa, with a captured Japanese flag in Burma, 1945.

interrupt air supplies to China, and would provide them with a base for aerial attacks on India. At Kohima, bitter close combat saw armies separated only by the length of a tennis court. In April 1944 the monsoons began and turned the battlefields into a swamp. The RAF was able to support the British troops, flying in supplies and evacuating the wounded; the Japanese, weakened by losses and starvation, were forced to retreat.

The battles of Imphal and Kohima were a crucial turning point. Allied troops could now begin removing the Japanese forces from northern Burma and push towards the south, clearing the banks of the Irrawaddy River to retake the cities of Meiktila and Mandalay before finally liberating the capital at Rangoon. Air support was crucial for delivering supplies, reinforcements and evacuating the wounded. The RAF and the Indian Air Force engaged in bombing sorties, fighter cover and photo-reconnaissance. The Royal Navy and the Royal Indian Navy supported coastal offensives, providing landing craft, gunfire and minesweeping operations. The Allies were able to deploy large armoured and mechanized forces throughout these battles in central Burma, taking advantage of the depleted Japanese military and its lack of anti-tank weapons to reoccupy the country.

This poster, in Swahili, encouraged women to write to their husbands in the army. Contact with home was vital for morale because African soldiers serving overseas rarely received leave. Concerns about adultery, children, property and land were frequently mentioned in the letters.

The 11th East
Africa Division's rhinoceros badge
was worn in Burma by troops
from Kenya, Uganda, Nyasaland,
Tanganyika (now Tanzania) and
Northern Rhodesia (Zambia).

The 81st West African Division's
spider badge represents Anansi,
the half-man, half-spider trickster
and hero of West African folklore.
The badge was worn on the sleeve,
and when a soldier pointed his
weapon, Anansi appeared to be
scuttling down his arm to attack.

The 81st – and later the 82nd West
African Division, which wore this
badge featuring spears – recruited
soldiers from the Gambia, Nigeria,
Sierra Leone and the Gold Coast
(now Ghana).

Sherman tanks and trucks of the 62nd Motorised Brigade advance on the road between Myaungyu on the Irrawaddy bridgehead and Meiktila, Burma, March 1945.

SETH ANTHONY

Before the war, Seth was a Latin, English and Mathematics teacher in his hometown of Adafienu, Gold Coast. After enlisting, Seth served with the Royal West African Frontier Force. He was the first black African to become an officer in the British Army.

Seth was awarded the Order of the British Empire for his 'outstanding ability as a patrol leader' in Burma, and for his 'greatest courage and determination'. In later years, Seth joined the diplomatic service, and was attached to the British embassy in Washington DC. When Gold Coast gained independence from Britain and was renamed Ghana, Seth became the country's first permanent representative at the UN in New York.

ARTHUR WILLSHAW

Arthur volunteered to serve as a radio operator with the Chindits – units of British, Burmese and Gurkha troops fighting behind Japanese lines in Burma. Their badge is shown below.

Following a gruelling expedition, Operation Longcloth, Arthur and his comrades withdrew to India. However, the River Chindwin barred their way. Arthur used this airman's life jacket to help get himself and his exhausted comrades across the river. It saved not only his own life but also that of Aung Thin, a Burmese liaison officer.

⊕ Indian political consequences

Britain's reputation as a protector of its empire had been damaged. Indian refugees fleeing from Burma brought back tales of British losses, and Indian independence groups used such stories as evidence against the supposed invincibility of British rule. Anti-war sentiments in India grew. The leader of the National Congress Party, Mohandas Gandhi, demanded an end to British rule in India. In August 1942 he launched the 'Quit India' movement. Gandhi and other Indian nationalist leaders, including Jawaharlal Nehru, were arrested and imprisoned by the British government. Mass demonstrations erupted throughout India, and the British swiftly imprisoned 60,000 political protestors. The Indian nationalist Subhas Chandra Bose also wanted to rid India of British rule, but, rather than political protest, Bose sought the support of the Axis powers – Germany and Japan. Bose created the Indian National Army (INA), enlisting Indian soldiers who had been captured as prisoners of war, as well as members of the Indian population in South East Asia, to fight alongside Japan. The INA fought in key battles against the British Army in Burma, including at Imphal, Kohima, Meiktila and Mandalay.

Britain relied heavily on the support of India to keep fighting. By the end of 1941, there were approximately 900,000 Indian men in the British Army, reaching a peak of about 2.6 million in 1945. Furthermore, between 1941 and 1946, India supplied the British with materials worth £286.4 million, and by 1945 Britain owed India £1.3 billion. Across the Indian home front, civilians volunteered to work for the war effort. They trained as doctors or nurses to treat the mass casualties coming to India from Burma, and thousands of Indians worked on the land to provide food for the troops. The Women's Auxiliary Corps (India) started in April 1942 and had 10,000 members by 1944. Almost a million Indians were engaged in the construction of airfields, railways, hospitals, roads and pipelines. Despite this huge contribution, when famine struck Bengal in eastern India in 1943, Winston Churchill refused to use valuable shipping resources for the delivery of food to India. The Japanese occupation of Burma had cut off Bengal's vital source of rice. Price increases, panic buying, hoarding and inflation followed. Between two and three million Bengalis died of starvation and disease.

LAKSHMI SAHGAL

Lakshmi, an Indian Nationalist, was nursing prisoners of war in Singapore when she joined the Indian National Army (INA), the epaulettes of which are shown below. Lakshmi created a regiment of women called the Rani of Jhansi Regiment with the support of the Japanese Army. The female volunteers were trained in the same way as men, preparing to fight the British in Burma. However, before this could happen, the INA and Japanese troops were defeated. Lakshmi was arrested and imprisoned by the British.

CHITTOPRASAD BHATTACHARYA

In the towns and cities of Bengal, India, the political artist Chittoprasad Bhattacharya sketched people who had lost their livelihoods and loved ones in the famine that had struck the region in 1943. The medicine man shown with his wife in this sketch told Chittoprasad, 'The only medicine needed today is a full stomach, and I do not know how and from where to get it.'

Chittoprasad published some of his sketches in a book, *Hungry Bengal*. The British authorities saw the book as a political attack on their rule and burned it. Very few copies survive.

War in Italy

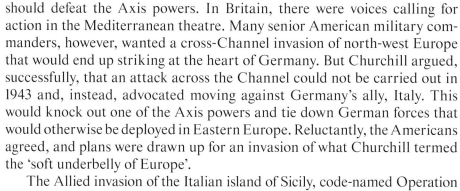

⊕ From Sicily to victory

During 1942, Allied political and military leaders disagreed over how they should defeat the Axis powers. In Britain, there were voices calling for action in the Mediterranean theatre. Many senior American military commanders, however, wanted a cross-Channel invasion of north-west Europe that would end up striking at the heart of Germany. But Churchill argued, successfully, that an attack across the Channel could not be carried out in 1943 and, instead, advocated moving against Germany's ally, Italy. This would knock out one of the Axis powers and tie down German forces that would otherwise be deployed in Eastern Europe. Reluctantly, the Americans agreed, and plans were drawn up for an invasion of what Churchill termed the 'soft underbelly of Europe'.

The Allied invasion of the Italian island of Sicily, code-named Operation Husky, began on the night of 9/10 July 1943. In a large-scale attack, Allied troops were sent in by both air and sea. Although the defending forces were caught off guard, they soon put up a strong resistance and made the Allies battle for control of the island. Sicily was captured after six weeks of fighting, although around 100,000 German and Italian troops managed to escape to the mainland.

On 25 July Benito Mussolini, Italy's fascist dictator, was overthrown, and in early September a new Italian government surrendered to the Allies. Once the armistice had been agreed, the Allies knew they could continue their campaign on the Italian mainland without any danger of resistance from Italian forces. Two Allied armies, one British and one American, landed in southern Italy in September 1943. The two armies linked up as the defenders fell back. Instead of abandoning Italy now that Germany's alliance with it had ended, Hitler ordered his forces to occupy, fortify and hold it. Germany poured in troops to fight the Allied advance northwards, and bitter fighting followed as the Germans retreated to the mountainous terrain of central Italy, ideal for defensive warfare. Conditions were tough for all combatants: mechanized vehicles were often of no use on small, hilly roads, making it difficult to keep men regularly supplied, while frequent rain and cold nights made life uncomfortable and miserable.

The Allied forces in Italy consisted of soldiers from a particularly high number of countries. There were units from Algeria, Australia, Belgium, Brazil, Britain, Canada, Czechoslovakia, France, Greece, India, Italy, Morocco, Nepal, New Zealand, Poland, South Africa and the United States. Allied commanders were hampered by reductions in manpower over time, as divisions were withdrawn for service elsewhere. German forces were commanded by Field Marshal Albert Kesselring, who conducted a robust defensive campaign, but also suffered from depleted numbers of men as it progressed.

By early 1944, the Allied advance through Italy was being frustrated by stubborn German defence and difficult terrain. It ground to a halt at the Gustav Line, one of the Germans' defensive barriers stretching across Italy. The ancient abbey of Monte Cassino stood atop a mountain that formed part of the line. It took the Allies four costly attacks between January and May 1944 to capture it. On 15 February, 1,400 tons of high explosives were dropped in a huge bombardment that destroyed the abbey. The Germans were able to

This badge was worn by members of the only African American infantry division that fought in Europe. The 92nd Infantry Division, known as the 'Buffalo Division', served in Italy from August 1944. Its members were racially segregated from white soldiers, poorly trained, and badly led by their white officers. The division took part in heavy fighting in Italy and suffered nearly 3,000 casualties.

take up defensive positions in the rubble and both sides suffered high casualties as the battle wore on. On 18 May, after some of the bloodiest fighting in Italy, Polish troops raised their country's flag in the ruins of the abbey.

While the struggle to breach the Gustav Line wore on, a plan was devised to break the deadlock in Italy. In January 1944 the Allies landed a large force behind German lines at Anzio, on Italy's west coast near Rome, to draw German forces from their defences further south. The landing was a success but, instead of then quickly moving inland, the Allies' cautious commander, US General John Lucas, opted to dig in. The result was months of stalemate. Lucas was replaced in February, and in May 1944 the Allies finally struck out of the Anzio bridgehead, threatening to overwhelm the Germans. But, against orders and eager to gain a high-profile personal coup, US General Mark Clark

This propaganda poster, made in German-occupied Vichy France, ridicules the slow progress of Allied forces in Italy. The mountainous terrain and dogged German defence resulted in a lengthier and bloodier struggle than the Allies had envisaged.

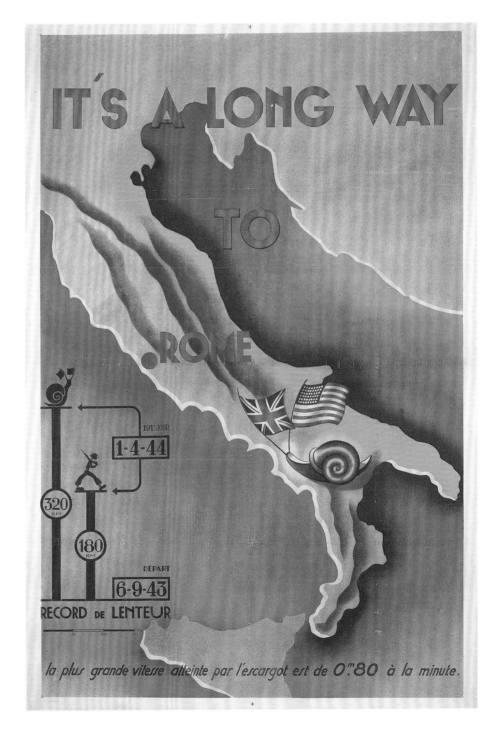

told the troops under his command to head for Rome instead, which allowed a sizeable German force to escape. His men entered Rome on 4 June, although the bulk of the German forces in the city had already been withdrawn further north. Clark's triumph was soon eclipsed by D-Day, the great invasion of northern France on 6 June.

After Rome was captured, the Germans withdrew to their defences north of Florence, known as the Gothic Line, which ran from coast to coast through the Apennine mountains. Allied attacks breached the line but failed to break through decisively and ground to a halt as winter set in. The mountainous terrain of the Apennines, muddy conditions and river-crossed land restricted mobility, and little progress could be made by the attacking armies. In the spring of 1945, once the weather had improved, the Allies renewed their offensive and captured the city of Bologna on 21 April. The Germans surrendered soon after, and fighting in Italy officially ceased on 2 May.

In the end, while the Italian campaign did not deliver the knock-out blow that some Allied planners had hoped for, it did tie down fairly significant numbers of German forces and demonstrate to the Soviet Union – and Germany – that the Allies were still in the fight. But it also used up valuable Allied resources of men, equipment and weapons, all of which could have been conserved and better used elsewhere. Furthermore, the campaign resulted in several hundred thousand deaths, a significant number of which were civilian.

Indian troops on the outskirts of Monte Cassino, Italy, 16 March 1944.

NERALTINO FLORES DOS SANTOS

When he was twenty years old, Neraltino enlisted as a gunner in the Brazilian Expeditionary Force (Força Expedicionária Brasileira, FEB). Brazil joined the war on the Allied side in 1942. However, there was a delay before the 25,000-strong FEB was sent to fight in Italy.

This delay led to a popular saying: 'It is more likely for snakes to smoke than it is for the Brazilian Expeditionary Force to set out.' The FEB called themselves *Cobras Fumantes* (Smoking Snakes). Neraltino wore this divisional patch showing a smoking cobra. He later received an FEB Cross for fighting in Italy.

Italian Campaign

ALLIED FORCES FIGHT A LENGTHY CAMPAIGN IN ITALY

Between July 1943 and May 1945, a multinational Allied army fought a gruelling battle against Axis forces in Italy. Troops from 17 countries, Italy included, contributed to the Allied force.

FRANCE

The French Expeditionary Corps (FEC), totalling 112,000 men, fought in the Italian Campaign. The FEC was commanded by General Alphonse Juin, and comprised two Moroccan divisions, one Algerian division and one Free French division. Each division was commanded by a French officer.

POLAND

The Polish force that fought in Italy, Polish II Corps, numbered around 55,780 men, and more than 1,000 women in auxiliary roles. The Corps' 22nd Transport Artillery Supply Company had a pet mascot – a Syrian brown bear named Wojtek. During heavy fighting at Monte Cassino, Wojtek carried ammunition to front-line troops.

GREECE

The 3rd Greek Mountain Brigade arrived in Italy in August 1944. It was formed of men loyal to the Greek government in exile. Attached to the 1st Canadian Division, the Greek soldiers went into combat in September near Rimini. The unit occupied the town on 21 September, earning it the honorary title 'Rimini Brigade'.

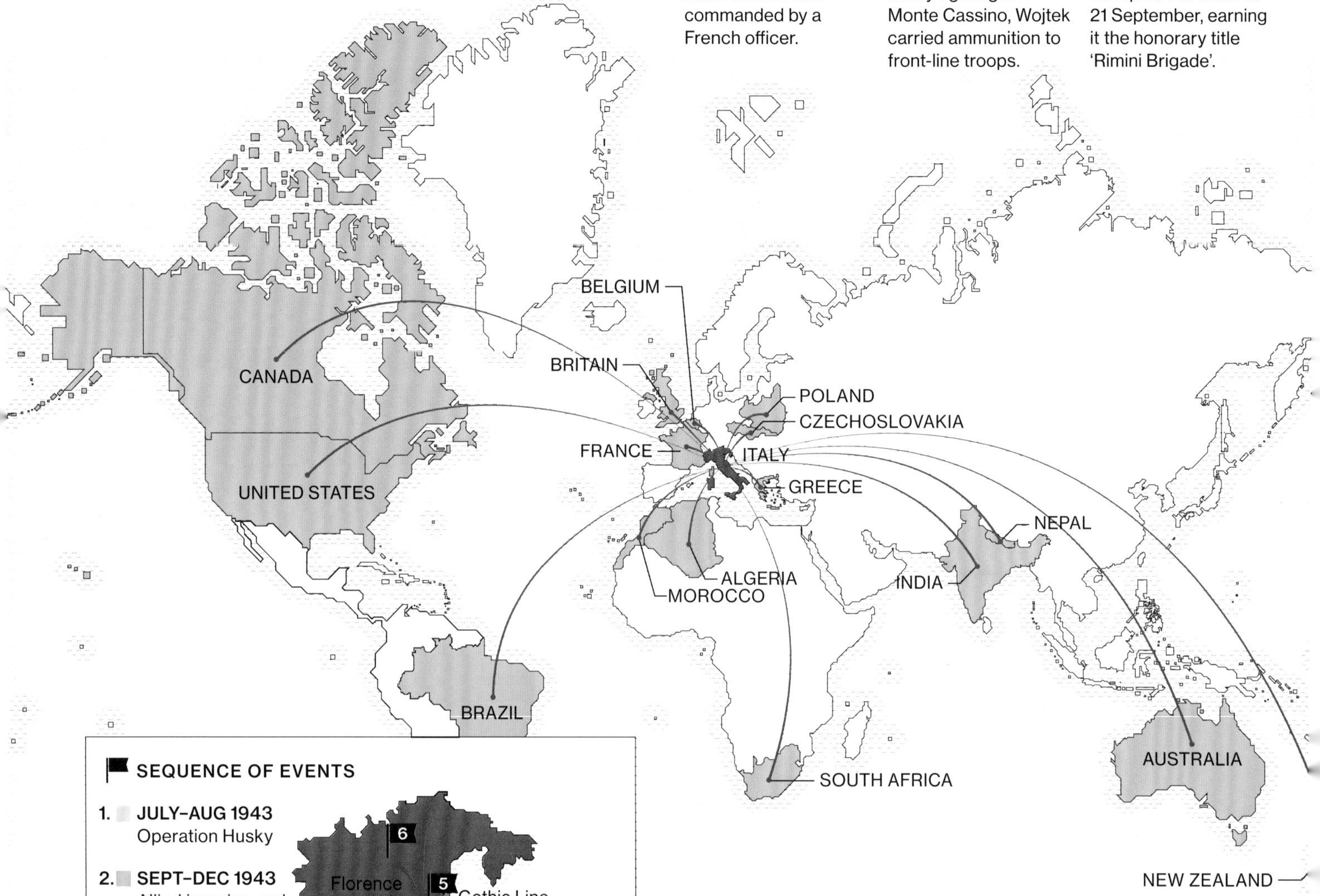

BELGIUM
BRITAIN
CANADA
POLAND
CZECHOSLOVAKIA
FRANCE
ITALY
UNITED STATES
GREECE
NEPAL
ALGERIA
MOROCCO
INDIA
BRAZIL
SOUTH AFRICA
AUSTRALIA
NEW ZEALAND

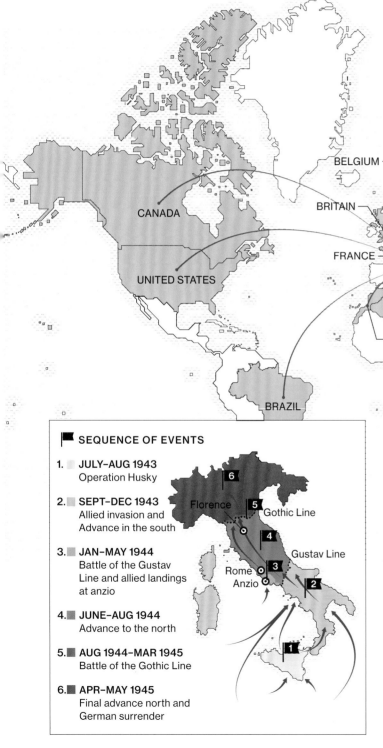

SEQUENCE OF EVENTS

1. JULY–AUG 1943
Operation Husky
2. SEPT–DEC 1943
Allied invasion and Advance in the south
3. JAN–MAY 1944
Battle of the Gustav Line and allied landings at anzio
4. JUNE–AUG 1944
Advance to the north
5. AUG 1944–MAR 1945
Battle of the Gothic Line
6. APR–MAY 1945
Final advance north and German surrender

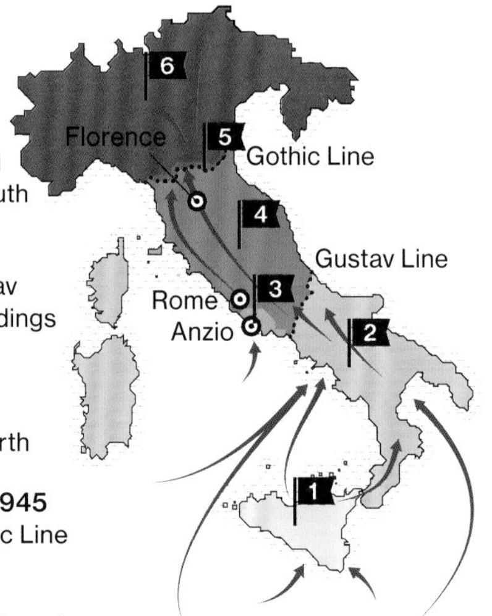

6
Florence
5
Gothic Line
4
Gustav Line
Rome
3
Anzio
2
1

BRAZIL

The Brazilian Expeditionary Force (Força Expedicionária Brasileira, FEB) was formed after Brazil entered the war on the Allied side in 1942. Composed of 25,334 men, the FEB captured more than 20,000 enemy prisoners during the campaign.

INDIA

Nearly 50,000 Indian troops served in Italy. They were drawn from the 4th, 8th and 10th Indian infantry divisions and the 43rd Independent Gurkha Infantry Brigade. Most of these soldiers were aged between 19 and 22, and 5,782 lost their lives in the campaign.

NEW ZEALAND

New Zealand troops of the 2nd New Zealand Division arrived in Italy in October 1943. The division joined the Eighth Army, a multinational force under British command. Around 2,100 New Zealand soldiers were killed and 6,700 were wounded during the campaign.

⊕ Italy at war

The war brought devastation to Italy and its people. While Allied and Axis armies battled one another, a bitter civil war raged between Mussolini-supporting fascist forces and pro-Allied, anti-fascist resistance groups known as partisans. After he was deposed and arrested in July 1943, Mussolini was liberated by the Germans, who installed him in a fascist regime in northern Italy. Various groups opposed this German puppet state and formed a partisan movement. Out of 300,000 partisans – an estimated 40,000 of whom were women – around 45,000 were killed. Fewer fascists were killed during the civil war, although the exact figure is not known. In April 1945 partisans captured and killed Mussolini. They put his body on public display in Milan, where it was attacked by a mob.

For nearly two years the whole country became a battleground. Almost all Italians were affected as fighting erupted around them. As the Germans staged a fighting retreat through central and northern Italy, towns and cities became the sites of heavy battle. Civilians' homes were requisitioned, plundered and destroyed as the various armies moved through the country. Italy's agriculture and infrastructure suffered and food became scarce, reducing many to hunger and causing widespread malnutrition. Around 64,000 Italian civilians were killed in Allied bombing raids on German-occupied territory, and many cities were badly hit. In areas that came under Germany's control as its forces occupied the country following Italy's surrender, civilians were exploited for labour, and some were massacred for real or suspected support of the resistance. The Germans acted with increasing brutality towards their former allies, as thousands of men were rounded up to work for Germany, food and supplies were requisitioned, and partisan activity was strongly repressed.

Italian partisans during an awards ceremony in Ravenna, Italy, 1945.

ROSA BABINI

Rosa lived with her parents and siblings in Faenza in northern Italy, an area devastated by war. In late 1944 German troops invaded her home. They took over the bedrooms and made Rosa and her family sleep on the floor downstairs.

   The soldiers seized most of the food and left the family with very little to eat. Rosa's mother, Celeste, made cheese in this dish, but only when there was any milk to spare. During heavy bombardments, the family hid in a haystack to remain safe.

War in Western Europe
🌐 Operation Overlord

This painting, *Preparations for D-Day* (1944), is by the British artist Richard Eurich. It shows some of the intense activity along England's south coast in the build-up to Operation Overlord.

During their discussions at the Tehran Conference in late 1943, the leaders of the United States, Britain and the Soviet Union agreed that a 'second front' would be opened in north-west Europe in May 1944. This would both take some of the pressure off the Soviet Union and provide the means to attack Germany from east and west. As preparations for the invasion took shape, huge numbers of men and supplies crossed the Atlantic. By early 1944, with the bombing war against Germany delivering results, the Allies felt secure in attacking German-occupied Europe.

On 6 June 1944 – D-Day – the Allies unleashed their much-anticipated attack, with amphibious landings on the northern French coast. Starting in the early light and continuing throughout the day, thousands of Allied troops poured on to the beaches of Normandy. Finally, the long-awaited second front in Europe had been opened, and the invasion of German-occupied France had begun. D-Day had been many years in the planning. The Western Allies had worked meticulously to coordinate the largest sea and land invasion in history. Code-named Operation Overlord, it was vast in scale, involving more than 150,000 troops, nearly 12,000 aircraft and 7,000 naval vessels. The Supreme Allied Commander of the Allied invasion force, General Dwight D. Eisenhower of the US Army, had a heavy responsibility. He prepared a statement to be issued if the invasion failed, saying: 'if any blame or fault attaches to the attempt it is mine alone.'

Field Marshal Erwin Rommel (holding a baton), commander of the German anti-invasion forces, inspects the German 'Atlantic Wall' defences, spring 1944.

Field Marshal Erwin Rommel was in command of the German defences in north-west Europe. The Germans anticipated an invasion but had no way of knowing for certain where it would be. Their principal form of defence was the more than 3,200-kilometre-long 'Atlantic Wall', which stretched from Norway to Spain. The wall had weak points, however, and Rommel ordered it to be strengthened. His defensive force was also hardly ideal: many units were under-strength or contained older men and those on rest from Eastern Europe.

Allied planners, having learned from the disastrous Dieppe Raid of August 1942 that the element of surprise was paramount in any cross-Channel attack, enacted an elaborate deception campaign. It worked – even after the landings in Normandy. Crucially, the Germans were convinced for several weeks that there would be another, bigger invasion at Calais. This gave the Allies an advantage, as the Germans held back troops in anticipation of a second attack that never came. The Allies also had vast air superiority over the Germans. In the lead up to D-Day, Allied bomber aircraft attacked key road and rail networks around the planned invasion area. On the night of 5/6 June, 18,000 airborne troops were dropped into Normandy on either side of the invasion zone. Their objectives were to seize key roads and bridges to prevent the Germans from moving troops to meet the invasion. Despite many men landing far from their targets, they achieved most of their aims.

From early on 6 June, Allied ships bombarded German defences along the Normandy coast in preparation for the assault troops' landings. Almost 5,000 ships carried 132,000 men across the Channel. The landings took place at five points along the Normandy coast. US troops landed at the western-most beaches, code-named 'Utah' and 'Omaha'. British troops went ashore at 'Gold' and 'Sword' beaches, and Canadian troops at 'Juno'. Four of the beaches were secured fairly quickly, with relatively few casualties; but Omaha was more heavily defended, and it was there that the greatest loss of Allied life occurred. Using machine guns positioned on the cliffs that rise high above the beach, the German defenders inflicted concentrated fire on the attacking troops. Despite the heavier losses at Omaha, by the end of the day it was clear that the landings had been an overall success. Believing the attack to be a distracting cover for the real invasion, the Germans reacted slowly to it, holding back nearby reserves. They missed their chance to repel the Allies while they were at their most vulnerable, during the beach landings. By the time they were ordered to counter-attack, it was too late. The Allies had managed to get significant numbers of men ashore, although they failed to reach some of their key objectives. Over the following days, they consolidated their position while sustaining the invasion's momentum by bringing in increasing supplies. By 30 June, over 850,000 men had been landed in Normandy.

HAZEL PERKIN

Hazel was a twelve-year-old British schoolgirl living on the Isle of Wight at the time of the Normandy invasion. On 3 June 1944, Hazel went out with friends. Hurrying back home before darkness fell, she realized she had left her skipping rope behind. Three Allied soldiers, who were waiting for D-Day, overheard Hazel and her friends discussing her loss. The next evening, the soldiers turned up at Hazel's house. They had been unable to find her original rope, so they gave her a replacement one they had made out of parts of a landing craft. Hazel was thrilled. As she watched the invasion force leave for France a couple of days later, Hazel hoped the soldiers would survive.

Troops of the 9th Canadian Infantry Brigade, some of them carrying bicycles, wade on to Juno Beach during the D-Day landings, 6 June 1944.

HENRY OAKES

US naval officer Henry Oakes wore this wet-weather parka and trousers and carried this canvas bag when he landed on Omaha Beach on D-Day. Henry was an experienced naval officer and oversaw operations at the Normandy beachhead. Prior to D-Day, he had trained the US Naval Construction Battalions, the 'Seabees'. These specialized troops built a port and docks that kept supplies coming in during and after the landings. Shortly after D-Day, Henry said of the Seabees: 'They caught hell, but they did the job.'

Henry was wounded after the landings. He spent time in hospital in July 1944 and was back home in the United States in August.

HUGH COLLINSON

'We were up to our waists in water with bullets whistling round our ears,' wrote Hugh Collinson shortly after D-Day. Hugh and his fellow soldiers waded on to Sword Beach on 6 June under heavy fire. As they crossed the beach, a shell exploded nearby and a splinter from it hit Hugh's water bottle. It saved his hip from shattering. Hugh's friend, however, was killed beside him in the blast. The next day, Hugh was seriously wounded by mortar bombs. He was taken to hospital and evacuated back to Britain. Hugh's Army Service Book records the three days he spent in Normandy.

RECORD OF SERVICE (including Extra-Regimental Employment).

UNIT. (N.B.—The unit in which the officer is at present serving must not be shown.)	HOME.		ABROAD.			
			With Expeditionary Force.		Elsewhere.	
	From	To	From	To	From	To
*In the ranks. Enlisted T.A. 87th Fd Regt. R.A. as Gnr	April 1939	June 1939				
Posted as 2/Lt to 136th Fd Regt. R.A. on formation	June 1939	March 1941				
Posted to 55 Div as M.L.O	March 1941					
Appointed G III L 55 Div	March 14th 1942	19.10.42	*		*	*
Posted 178 Fd Regt RA.	19.11.42	15.12.42				
Posted 109 Field Regt.	15.12.42	7.9.43.				
Posted	8.9.43		6.6.44	9.6.44		

* Enter first any service in the ranks.

10

11

⊕ Normandy Campaign

After the success of D-Day, the Allies faced a huge struggle to clear Normandy and northern France of German forces. Hitler ordered his troops not to give up ground and they fought tenaciously. The Allies needed to seize key Normandy towns and ports to tip the balance. The Americans captured the port of Cherbourg on 26 June, providing a means to build up supplies and reinforcements. The city of Caen was an important objective for the British and Canadian troops led by General Montgomery, who we last saw, as a lieutenant general, in the deserts of North Africa. Multiple attempts to take Caen were met with stiff German resistance. Finally, after Allied bombardments had reduced much of it to ruins, the city was captured on 19 July. While Montgomery's forces were locked in the fight for Caen, General Omar Bradley's US First Army launched Operation Cobra, which broke through German defences and made the battle more mobile. The Americans had an overwhelming advantage in terms of mechanized vehicles compared with the Germans, who still

British infantry hitch a ride on Sherman tanks, 18 July 1944. Armoured vehicles played a key role in Normandy.

A group of German prisoners at Maltot, Normandy, 23 July 1944.

relied on horse-powered transport. The Germans also suffered from shortages of manpower, supplies and ammunition, and were now at breaking point. Having established air superiority, the Allies could use their greater numbers of men and resources to wear down remaining German resistance. The Germans soon found themselves trapped between separate Allied forces at Falaise, under a devastating artillery and aerial barrage. Around 60,000 Germans were killed or captured, while many managed to escape eastwards. Coupled with a successful Allied invasion of southern France, the loss of Normandy convinced the Germans to abandon hope of holding on to the country. The battle for Normandy resulted in many thousands of military and civilian deaths. Around 20,000 French civilians were killed between D-Day and the end of the Normandy Campaign, mostly caused by Allied aerial bombing in support of ground operations.

After the breakout from Normandy, Allied forces pressed eastwards in pursuit of the retreating Germans. They now faced the task of liberating north-west Europe from German occupation. Members of resistance groups played a key part in this activity, by supporting the Allied invasion and undermining German defences through acts of sabotage. In August 1944 members of the French Resistance rose up against the German garrison in Paris. After fighting broke out on the streets, the Germans surrendered.

Infantry soldiers bore the brunt of the fighting in Normandy. German mortar bombs, such as those fired from this *Nebelwerfer* rocket launcher, accounted for 75 per cent of all British casualties. Allied troops came to fear their distinctive, moaning sound.

Dutch children during celebrations in Eindhoven, September 1944. Eindhoven was the first major town in the Netherlands to be liberated.

⊕ Battle of the Scheldt and Operation Market Garden

By September 1944, the Germans were in full retreat. Following the liberation of Paris, the Allies' advance slowed as they regrouped. They pressed on, and by the end of September had liberated parts of France, Belgium and the Netherlands. But they had overstretched their supply lines. Allied troops captured the large port of Antwerp in Belgium on 4 September; however, before they could use it to bring in supplies, they needed to clear German forces from the surrounding area, the Scheldt estuary. German troops had been told to fight to the last man to defend the Scheldt peninsula. Throughout the cold, wet autumn months, Canadian, British, Polish and other forces carried out a series of attacks that eventually overpowered German resistance. It was a hard-won victory, spearheaded by the Canadians, who suffered high casualties and battle fatigue.

In the late summer of 1944, Allied commanders disagreed over the best way to defeat Germany. Eisenhower favoured a broad-front advance on the German border, but this would require a more robust supply line than the Allies had in place. After extensive lobbying, Montgomery's idea won the argument. It was a bold plan to cut through the Netherlands into Germany on a narrow front. Code-named Operation Market Garden, it involved airborne troops seizing key bridges over the Rhine, at Eindhoven, Nijmegen and Arnhem, before ground troops advanced to meet them. On 17 September a vast air fleet dropped 35,000 airborne troops into the Netherlands. The landings were largely successful, but the airborne troops soon ran into difficulties as they tried to secure the bridges. The Germans swiftly deployed SS tank units, which airborne troops were ill-equipped to deal with. Meanwhile, Allied ground troops struggled to reach their objectives over waterlogged ground that hindered rapid movement. Although Eindhoven and Nijmegen both fell into Allied hands, Arnhem proved to be 'a bridge too far'. The Allied gamble to invade Germany quickly had failed.

ABOVE This beret was worn by George Baylis, a member of the British Glider Pilot Regiment. Airborne troops fought tenaciously during Operation Market Garden but suffered heavy losses. George was taken prisoner near Arnhem in the Netherlands.

RIGHT US paratroopers receive a final briefing before Operation Market Garden, 17 September 1944.

The Siegfried Line and the Battle of the Bulge

Hitler chose troops of the Waffen SS to spearhead the attack in the Ardennes. The troops wore camouflage clothing, such as this jacket, over their uniforms.

In the autumn of 1944, German forces had fallen back to the Siegfried Line, a stretch of fortifications that protected Germany's western border. From mid-September, US forces fought a lengthy, costly campaign against the Siegfried Line. The attacks were soon paused in favour of Operation Market Garden, and the Germans were able to build up their defences. When Market Garden failed, the US offensive resumed. After street-to-street fighting and heavy bombardments, Aachen fell to the Americans on 21 October: the first German city captured by Allied forces, and a symbolic blow to German morale. South of Aachen, US forces faced the dense, heavily defended Hürtgen Forest. They fought a long-running battle for the forest, suffering heavy casualties in winter conditions. The battles for the Siegfried Line slowed down the overall Allied advance at a high price, in terms of both casualties and combat fatigue among the troops.

On 16 December 1944, German forces launched a large-scale counter-attack in the Ardennes Forest in Belgium and Luxembourg. The attack, ordered by Hitler, was a complete shock. US forces, thinly spread across the Ardennes sector, were caught off guard. The Germans made swift advances, which soon created the 'bulge' that gave the battle its name. But US troops rallied and fought back with tenacity, slowing the Germans down. When the weather cleared, air support was brought in to help Allied ground forces. At Bastogne, an important crossroads, besieged American troops held out in below-freezing temperatures and with dwindling supplies for a week until they were relieved. By the end of December, the German attack had ground to a halt. Fighting continued until 25 January as Allied forces pushed the Germans back to where they had started from. Hitler's dream of inflicting a decisive defeat on the Allies in the west was over.

BEN RUGG

Ben wore this steel helmet during the fighting in the Ardennes in December 1944. Like many American soldiers, he fought strongly in the harsh winter conditions. The US forces' determined resistance slowed, then halted, the German advance.

An officer in the US 2nd Infantry Regiment, Ben was twice wounded during the fighting, the first time on Christmas Day. Originally from Brooklyn, New York, he was decorated for his bravery in action. Ben later married Edith, a British woman he had met before D-Day, and returned to New York with his new bride.

⊕ The advance towards Germany and the crossing of the Rhine

Allied forces now faced the final push towards Germany in the early months of 1945. US forces battled to take the cities of Koblenz and Cologne in early March. In Operation Veritable, British and Canadian troops fought hard against ferocious German defences and suffered heavy casualties. Intense fighting took place in the Reichswald Forest. The Allies eventually cleared it of German forces, with heavy casualties on both sides. The Germans fell back as the Allied advance continued towards the Rhine – a major barrier they needed to cross to reach the German heartland. The Germans had destroyed most bridges across the river, and the Allies knew that they would defend it to the last. By the spring of 1945, a vast Allied army stood poised at this symbolic frontier. On 7 March, infantry of the US First Army crossed an intact bridge at Remagen and took the town, despite repeated German counter-attacks. Although the bridge collapsed on 17 March, significant numbers of American troops had managed to get across and create a secure bridgehead. To the south, men of the US Third Army crossed at Oppenheim, near Mainz, on 22 March. North of Remagen, the British 21st Army Group staged a large-scale attack across the Rhine. Following a huge air and artillery bombardment, British and American troops crossed on 24 March. Although some Germans fought hard to defend their country, they were outnumbered and outgunned. More Allied forces soon crossed the Rhine, encircled the Ruhr and quickly advanced into Germany. The series of breaches across the Rhine and subsequent overpowering of German resistance ensured that the final defeat of Germany was now only a matter of time.

Troops of the US Seventh Army board assault craft on the western bank of the Rhine, 26 March 1945.

CHAPTER 6

THE END AND AFTER

THE FINAL ADVANCE
SPRING 1945

■ Areas under German control

■ Allied powers, Dec 1944

☐ Neutral countries

ALLIED ADVANCES

■ Up to 18 Apr 1945

■ Up to 1 May 1945

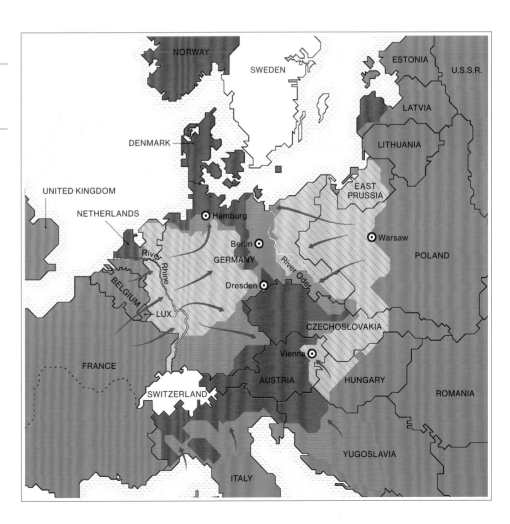

Germany Surrenders

By April 1945, the Allies were closing in on the heart of Germany from east and west. Hundreds of thousands of German soldiers were taken prisoner, most preferring to surrender to western Allied forces rather than members of the Red Army. Following the campaign of murder and terror Germany had waged in the Soviet Union, they knew they would be treated more favourably by the Western armies than by Russians bent on revenge. While this was largely true, the overwhelming numbers of German POWs that fell into American, British and French hands in the closing weeks of the war resulted in overcrowded makeshift camps where prisoners lacked enough food, water or shelter, and in which thousands died.

Germany was broken and defeated. Refugees crowded the roads and civilians were caught in the crossfire as German soldiers put up a last desperate defence of their homeland. During January and February 1945, Soviet forces advanced deep into eastern Germany, coming to a halt just 60 kilometres to the east of Berlin. After crossing the Rhine into Germany in March 1945, British and US troops advanced on a broad front. British and Canadian forces moved northwards, through the Netherlands, towards Hamburg and then on to Denmark and the Baltic, while the Americans progressed through southern and central Germany, reaching Austria and racing the Soviets to Berlin. Even as the country fell rapidly to Allied forces, the Nazi leadership continued to resist, with Hitler – completely unrealistically – demanding that the Western Allies be pushed back; any deserters faced severe punishment. Elderly German men were conscripted into the *Volkssturm*, and members of the Hitler Youth were also called on to fight. Most Germans realized the war was lost, although some of the more fanatical followers of Nazism still hoped for a final miracle that would deliver them from defeat. Others put up resistance,

having been told by Nazi propaganda that enemy troops would treat them harshly. Major G. Ritchie, a British officer serving in Germany in the spring of 1945, wrote home to his wife: 'The people are very docile and polite, and in most cases seem very pleased the war is for them over ... There is no doubt though that they are fully aware now that they are beaten.'

While Allied forces converged on Germany on land, the aerial bombing of German cities, industry and communications continued – with devastating results. Large-scale British and American bombing raids destroyed around 50 per cent of the habitable spaces in the country's major cities and sought to hammer home to the German people that they were truly defeated. Berlin, Hamburg and Dresden suffered particularly badly, the last of these in a number of controversial raids in February 1945 that ruined the city.

On 16 April the Red Army launched a two-pronged attack to capture the German capital. Adolf Hitler had decided to stay in Berlin, where he and his entourage had taken up residence in a bunker near the Reich Chancellery. On 20 April the dictator marked his fifty-sixth birthday. On the same day, Berlin came under Soviet artillery fire for the first time. It would take another twelve days of bitter fighting before the city fell. By this time, Hitler was dead, having committed suicide on 30 April. The capture of Berlin was the moment of supreme victory for Stalin, but it came at a heavy cost. More than 80,000 Soviet personnel were killed in the operation. German military losses approached 100,000, with 22,000 civilian Berliners also losing their lives.

The fall of the German capital was accompanied by a wave of sexual violence perpetrated by soldiers of the Red Army. Thousands of women were raped, often on multiple occasions. Officers lost control of their men, who were frequently drunk, or, conscious of similar exploitation of Soviet women by the German invaders over the previous four years, simply did not try to stop them. Many women felt forced to enter into relationships with Soviet officers, simply to protect themselves from worse abuse. But for others, the end of Nazism meant liberation. An estimated 1,500 Jewish Berliners could emerge from their existence as so-called U-boats, living in hiding or under false identities.

As well as Hitler, other high-ranking Nazis and large numbers of civilians and military leaders took their own lives in the closing days of the war. In some instances, whole German families committed suicide to avoid the vengeance they were sure would come with Allied victory.

With certain defeat in sight, Germany's military leaders negotiated an end to the war while also seeking to save as many Germans as possible from falling into Soviet hands. Hitler's named successor, Grand Admiral Karl Dönitz, surrendered to the Allies. In the end, three separate surrender ceremonies took place, each along national lines. On 4 May a delegation representing German forces in the Netherlands, north-west Germany and Denmark surrendered to Field Marshal Montgomery (a rank he had held since September 1944), while on 7 May General Eisenhower, as the Supreme Allied Commander, accepted the unconditional surrender of all German forces. This armistice was signed by the German general Alfred Jodl at Eisenhower's headquarters in Reims, France, and came into effect the following day. Stalin, however, wanted his own surrender ceremony, so, on 8 May, a further document was signed in Berlin – this time by the German field marshal Wilhelm Keitel.

As news of Germany's unconditional surrender was announced by radio and newspapers, people in the Allied nations – across Europe, North America and British Empire countries – rejoiced. In Britain, it was declared that 8 May

ABOVE, TOP This battle-scarred street sign from Berlin's most famous thoroughfare, Unter den Linden, is a souvenir of the city's fall. It was wrenched from its post by a visiting British officer, with the aid of some Red Army soldiers.

ABOVE Max Bock was defined as a half-Jew by Nazi race laws. He had been hidden by friends in Berlin after his Jewish wife was deported to her death from the sanatorium in which she was a patient.

The arrival of the Red Army meant liberation for Max, but his relief was balanced by his concern for his friends and for Germany, for which he was proud to have fought in the Great War. In a diary that he kept during this momentous period, he recorded a woman returning to his apartment block with 'a young Red Army soldier ... He comes into the flats, gives a brief military salute, shakes each of us by the hand and says, "voyna kaput, voyna kaput!" – "the war is over!" I cannot believe my ears on hearing this wonderful, incredible news.'

would be a national holiday: Victory in Europe Day, or VE Day. Many people, however, did not want to wait and began the festivities as soon as they heard the news. Flags and bunting lined streets, bonfires were lit, and pubs filled up as the celebrations began. In the victorious nations, various events were organized to mark the occasion, including parades, thanksgiving services and street parties. In New Zealand, the national holiday was delayed until peace in Europe had been announced by Winston Churchill. Its people, therefore, had to go to work on 8 May and wait until the following day to celebrate. The Soviet Union's celebrations also occurred on 9 May, or 'Victory Day', as the country's surrender document was signed the day before. In the United States, the victory was tempered by the recent death of President Roosevelt, whose successor, Harry S. Truman, ordered that flags be kept at half-mast. But there was still country-wide rejoicing, and in New York, 15,000 police were mobilized to control the huge crowds that had massed in Times Square. In Paris, people packed the centre of the city, while looting and riots broke out in Halifax, Canada, in the charged atmosphere. But not everyone was in the mood to celebrate, and for those who had lost loved ones in the conflict, it was a time to reflect. Amid the street parties and rejoicing, many people mourned the death of a friend or relative, or worried about those who were still serving overseas. The war was not yet over in East Asia and the Pacific.

On 4 May 1945, a German delegation arrived at the headquarters of Field Marshal Bernard Montgomery at Lüneburg Heath, to the east of Hamburg. There, Montgomery accepted the unconditional surrender of German forces in the Netherlands, north-west Germany and Denmark. Surrender documents were also signed at General Eisenhower's headquarters at Reims, France, on 7 May, and in Berlin the following day.

Liberating the Camps

Hala Lichtenstein was a Polish-Jewish prisoner at Auschwitz-Birkenau from August 1943. While there, she worked as a forced labourer in one of the storage warehouses that held prisoners' belongings. Hala took this scarf while sorting clothing. When Auschwitz was evacuated, she was forced to take part in the 'death march' from the site. Hala survived the march and ended up at Zwodau concentration camp, in the modern Czech Republic, where she was saved by US soldiers.

As Allied forces converged on Germany from east and west, they uncovered evidence of Nazi Germany's attempted annihilation of Europe's Jews. Across Eastern Europe, Soviet forces discovered sites of atrocity and murder committed against Jewish people. The first concentration camp they encountered, in July 1944, was at Majdanek in Poland, where, as we saw in Chapter 5, they found gas chambers and human remains. Although the Nazis were careful to destroy evidence of their crimes, they had not had time to erase all such evidence at Majdanek, and the Soviet media publicized what had been found. The Germans had managed to dismantle the killing centres of Sobibor, Treblinka and Belzec before the Soviets could discover them. In January 1945 the Red Army was approaching the concentration camp complex of Auschwitz. The camp's guards hurriedly evacuated most of the remaining 60,000 prisoners, forcing their captives to flee with them. Thousands died during this and other so-called death marches. Survivors of the marches ended up in overcrowded, disease-ridden camps in Germany. As the Western Allies also fought their way into the German Reich, they overran a number of concentration camps where Nazi-perpetrated atrocities were more clearly in evidence. American forces liberated Buchenwald, Dora-Mittelbau, Flossenbürg, Dachau and Mauthausen in April and May 1945. Eisenhower visited Ohrdruf, a subcamp of Buchenwald, with other senior American commanders, and was filmed as he observed the corpses and burial pit there. He was shaken by what he saw, writing to his wife soon after: 'I never dreamed that such cruelty, bestiality and savagery could exist in this world.'

On 15 April British troops arrived at Bergen-Belsen and discovered an overcrowded, disease-ridden camp that was full of sick, emaciated people and littered with unburied bodies. Newsreel footage captured the horrific scenes at the camp as British soldiers and medical personnel sought to organize what relief they could, burying the dead and administering food and medicine to the surviving prisoners. When footage from the liberated camps was shown, first in America and Britain and then in other countries, the images shocked the world. For many who encountered the evidence of what became known as the Holocaust first-hand, a natural reaction was anger towards the perpetrators and a desire to exact vengeance not only on those in charge but also on the citizens of Germany. There were instances of violence towards camp guards, who were also made to bury decomposing bodies at Belsen. In some cases, German and Austrian civilians were also brought into the camps and forced to view the victims of the Nazi regime.

DORIS ZINKEISEN

Doris was a British war artist who was commissioned by the Joint War Organisation to record the work of the British Red Cross and the Order of St John in north-west Europe. She arrived at Bergen-Belsen concentration camp after it had been liberated by British forces in April 1945. It was full of unburied corpses and 60,000 starving, diseased people – most of whom were Jews.

Doris based this painting, *Human Laundry,* on what she saw at Belsen. It shows former prisoners being washed and cleansed of lice in an ad hoc decontamination centre. She contrasted the healthy, well-fed medical staff with the dangerously thin people they were forced to care for. Doris never forgot the shock of Belsen and all she witnessed there.

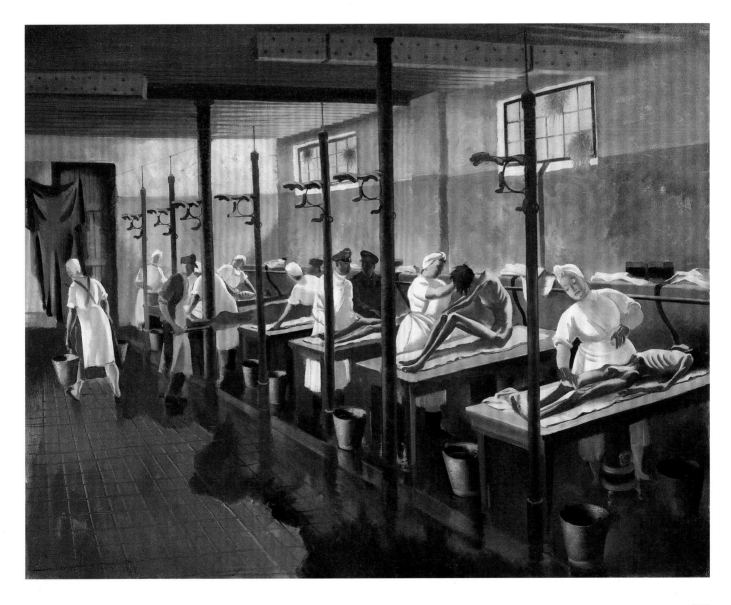

Japan Surrenders

OPPOSITE The ruins of the Hiroshima Prefectural Industrial Promotion Hall following the dropping of an atomic bomb on the city on 6 August 1945.

BELOW This photograph shows Soviet soldiers at Harbin railway station in Manchuria – now named in the Russian alphabet.

During the battle of Okinawa in April–June 1945, the island had been heavily defended. Japanese troops had fought to the last man with suicidal determination, with many preferring to die rather than surrender. In planning for the Allied invasion of the Japanese mainland, it was clear that defensive preparations would be even more extensive, and that the number of deaths would be considerable. President Truman considered an alternative option. He had been briefed on the Manhattan Project, a collaboration between the United States, Canada and Britain to produce an atomic bomb. Two bombs were available, and several cities were discussed as targets. The list came down to Hiroshima, Kokura, Nagasaki and Niigata. On 6 August 1945, the US dropped the first of their two atomic bombs on the Japanese city of Hiroshima. On 9 August, they targeted Nagasaki. The atomic bombs dropped over Japan killed approximately 66,000 people in Hiroshima, and 39,000 people in Nagasaki. Exact numbers of casualties are unclear, with tens of thousands more dying from radiation sickness, burns and malnutrition in the months that followed. Yet Japan did not surrender.

On 8 August, the Soviet Union broke its non-aggression pact with Japan by invading Japanese-occupied Manchuria. The pact had been signed in 1941 to avoid overstretching resources. But now the Soviet Union saw its opportunity to take advantage of a seriously weakened Japan. The hopes of Japanese leaders that the Soviet Union would help negotiate a peace deal with the Allies were dashed, and Japan surrendered.

At noon on 15 August 1945, Emperor Hirohito addressed the Japanese people over the radio to tell them the news. Unlike many of the world leaders at the time, Hirohito had never spoken to his citizens before. During his speech, he spoke in a court dialect that many Japanese people struggled to understand. Despite the emperor's announcement, some members of the Japanese military wanted to continue fighting. When ordered to surrender, some chose to commit suicide instead. In Manchuria, the Japanese Army fought on until 22 August. Soviet troops took thousands of Japanese soldiers into captivity as forced labourers.

On 2 September 1945 a Japanese delegation arrived on the USS *Missouri* moored in Tokyo Bay to sign the formal surrender. General MacArthur and Admiral Nimitz also signed the document, along with representatives of the other Allied nations. The Allied occupation of Japan was led by MacArthur. On his insistence, Emperor Hirohito remained on the imperial throne. However, Japan's wartime cabinet was replaced, and the country became a parliamentary democracy. Under MacArthur and the Allies' guidance, the new government introduced numerous social and economic reforms.

ABOVE, TOP A Soviet tank unit crosses the Great Khingan Mountain in Japanese-occupied Manchuria, China.

ABOVE Raisuke Shirabe with his mother, Iso; his wife, Sumiko; his three daughters, Choko, Reiko and Junko; and his sons, Seiichi and Koji.

TSUKIMI YAMAMOTO

Tsukimi was a Japanese soldier fighting in Manchuria in August 1945 when the Soviet Army invaded. Tsukimi feared he would be captured and killed. The other men in his unit called him *hikokumin* – an unpatriotic traitor. However, two of them listened to Tsukimi and together they escaped through Korea and on to Japan. If they had been caught, they would have been shot for desertion.

By the time Tsukimi arrived in Japan, the war was over. He went unnoticed among the other Japanese soldiers returning from the fighting.

The Aftermath of War

The significant and lasting impact of the Second World War has shaped the world we live in. It caused human suffering and physical destruction on an unprecedented scale. An estimated 60 million people lost their lives, 27 million of whom were from the Soviet Union. For the almost six years of the conflict, a death occurred on average every five seconds – the majority of which were civilian. Many cities, including Tokyo, Berlin, Manila and Warsaw, were all but wiped out. The conflict also precipitated huge logistical and humanitarian crises in which millions of displaced people – civilians, refugees, prisoners and combat personnel – needed to be fed, cared for, and housed or returned home. Some had been away for years, been imprisoned, suffered torture or seen horrific sights. Sometimes their homes were gone. It was difficult for many to readjust to civilian life in a changed world. Parents were often strangers to children they had hardly seen, and the divorce rate soared in Europe as couples who had been through separate experiences struggled to cope. While many servicemen received a hero's welcome, those who had been captured or fought for the defeated nations usually did not.

The war's immediate aftermath was chaotic and uncertain. Although the global fighting had stopped, violence continued as people took revenge or started up new conflicts, which often ran along nationalistic or racial lines. Peace had returned, but so much had changed, and more upheaval was yet to come. Some wanted a return to normality, but others felt the need for reform. Many hoped for a world free of war, but ideological divisions, racial tensions and growing opposition to imperialism meant that conflict continued. Infrastructure, communications and economies had been heavily damaged, and the long process of rebuilding countries, societies and communities began. Amid the destruction and after all they had sacrificed and lost, people looked for someone to blame. As the Allied powers put German and Japanese leaders on trial for war crimes, many took the law into their own hands and meted out swift reprisals against those who had wronged them – or who had found themselves on the losing side at war's end.

The victorious Allied powers agreed to punish those who had committed crimes and atrocities during the war in Europe. Just months after the war ended, legal representatives from Britain, the United States, the Soviet Union and France held ground-breaking trials to bring Nazi Germany's leaders and officials to justice. The accused were charged with war crimes, crimes against peace and crimes against humanity, as well as conspiring to commit these acts. Held before the International Military Tribunal for Germany, the most high-profile of the trials took place in the ruined German city of Nuremberg from November 1945 until October 1946. In total, twenty-two German political and military leaders were indicted and tried in the long-running proceedings, during which the enormity of Nazi Germany's crimes against peace and humanity were laid bare. The defendants included Albert Speer, the armaments minister; Rudolf Hess, the deputy leader of the Nazi Party; and Hermann Goering, whom Hitler had named his successor until he branded him a traitor shortly before his suicide. Martin Bormann, Hitler's powerful private secretary, was tried in absentia. Prosecutors drew on copious documents written by the Nazis themselves, and presented as

ALLAN WILMOT

Allan returned to Jamaica after serving in Britain's Royal Navy and RAF during the war. Good jobs were scarce, so he decided to make Britain his new home. Allan had visited England during the war, when he was mostly treated well as a man in military uniform, fighting for Britain.

Allan travelled to Britain by ship, arriving on 21 December 1947. He brought this suitcase and Stetson hat with him, wanting to look smart for potential employers. But he faced racial discrimination and struggled to find work. He occasionally earned money washing dishes, and sometimes had to sleep in London Underground train carriages.

British artist Dame Laura Knight based this painting, *The Nuremberg Trial*, on sketches she made during the trial of German leaders accused of war crimes that opened in Nuremberg, Germany in late 1945. Shocked by the ruined state of the city, she included a destroyed landscape above the courtroom. A team of international prosecutors drew on vast amounts of evidence, which included eyewitness testimony, documents and film. Twelve defendants were sentenced to death, seven to imprisonment and three were acquitted. Hermann Goering, the most senior Nazi on trial, committed suicide before his execution.

evidence footage from camps in which Jews had been murdered. The verdicts passed down included twelve death sentences and three acquittals. The remainder went to prison. Smaller trials of further German war criminals took place elsewhere in Europe and the Soviet Union, in which industrialists, judges, doctors and others were tried. However, owing to political and logistical pressures, not all criminals were caught or sentenced, and some senior Nazis managed to escape justice. Allied personnel also committed war crimes, but these largely went unpunished.

Another international military tribunal was convened in East Asia. Between May 1946 and November 1948, former leaders of the Empire of Japan were put on trial in Tokyo. They were charged with waging a war of aggression, crimes against humanity and war crimes. The judges and prosecutors hailed from eleven countries whose people had been victims of Japanese atrocities: Australia, Canada, China, France, India, the Netherlands, New Zealand, the Philippines, the Soviet Union, the United Kingdom and the United States. The defendants included the prime minister, Hideki Tojo; the foreign minister, Koki Hirota; and General Heitarō Kimura, a military commander. As at Nuremberg, the prosecutors drew on written evidence as well as witness testimony. When the verdicts

were handed down, seven of the defendants were sentenced to death, sixteen were given life imprisonment, and two served lesser terms. More than
2,200 Japanese war-crimes trials were held in other countries across the
former Japanese Empire. The charges included torture, maltreatment,
forced labour, mass killings and even cannibalism. But the prosecution of
Japanese war criminals was less comprehensive than in Europe and many
escaped justice.

Following their victories over Germany and Japan, the Allied powers
were left with the huge task of administering and rehabilitating the defeated
nations. They set up military occupations and took over control in both
countries until it was felt that they were ready – and could be trusted – to
move to self-governance. Rebuilding war-torn countries was a slow process,
and societies had to be repaired too. Lost children and bombed-out people
were without homes. In places, law and order had broken down, and many
faced disease and hunger.

A US-led Allied force occupied Japan for six years after it surrendered.
Its members were allowed to mix with the population – unlike in Germany,
where this was initially banned. Most of the troops that were stationed in
Japan were American, but a British Commonwealth Occupation Force
(BCOF), which included men from the UK, India, New Zealand and
Australia, also participated in the occupation. The BCOF was largely
responsible for supervising the demilitarization of Japan. General
MacArthur was supreme commander during the occupation. As we saw
earlier, he allowed Emperor Hirohito to remain in power, in order to avoid
public outcry in Japan, and his headquarters issued directives to a Japanese
cabinet. Under US supervision, as has been mentioned, some progressive
economic and social reforms were introduced, including, in 1947, women's
suffrage. There was also an attempt to rid Japan of the militarism and
ultra-nationalism that many blamed for starting the war of conquest in East
Asia. Following screening and questionnaires, thousands of military police

and civil servants were dismissed. But many others, including prominent individuals who had supported or benefited from the war, escaped these purges, which were not conducted thoroughly and lacked clarity of purpose.

Japan's economy and bombed-out cities were slowly rebuilt. War had brought great poverty to the country, and there was an acute housing shortage in the capital, Tokyo. Homeless people filled the cellars beneath the city's station, while others did their best to build makeshift shelters amid the twisted ruins of the city's buildings; similar scenes could be found in other Japanese cities, including Nagasaki and Hiroshima. As starvation loomed, many Japanese people managed to obtain US military supplies, often through prostitution or the black market. For surviving Japanese military personnel, the return home and transition from war to peace was difficult. Many former soldiers felt the judgment and disappointment of their compatriots and resented the injustice of being blamed for Japan's defeat.

Across Japan's former empire, people struggled to return to some degree of normality amid the ruins of war and the deprivations it had caused. There were widespread shortages, which resulted in poverty, rationing, inflation and black-market trading. Some places in need, including China, the Philippines and Korea, received supplies from the United Nations relief agency, the UNRRA (see below). In others, including Singapore and Hong Kong, Japanese prisoners of war were put to work to clear the debris as the rebuilding of towns and cities began. Many thousands of people died from dysentery, typhoid and cholera, which spread quickly through places unable to cope with such diseases owing to the breakdown in infrastructure and sanitation. Nations emerging from years of Japanese occupation were unsettled and weakened. Some countries, such as the Philippines, gained independence after the end of the war; in others, such as Vietnam and Singapore, colonial rule was restored. In some regions, the period of occupation had opened up divisions that resulted in civil war and political unrest in the years that followed. China was torn apart by a civil war that had restarted following Japan's defeat. After years of suffering under Japanese rule, millions more were killed or became refugees from the continued fighting.

This pull-along Daschund toy dog was made by Walter Klemenz. Walter was a German prisoner of war who worked on the Duke family's farm in Kent, Britain. He became friends with the family and made the toy for the three children, Chris, Felicity (Phil) and Francis. Walter made it from an old apple crate, fixed together with pieces of scrap metal. He stayed in touch with the family after he returned to Germany, where he was reunited with his wife and daughter.

In Europe, too, the Allied powers occupied the nation they had defeated. Germany was divided, and the United States, Britain, the Soviet Union and France each occupied a zone. Austria was also occupied and split into four zones. The Allies agreed to demilitarize and 'de-Nazify' Germany. Efforts were made to 're-educate' the German people and to rid government and industry of Nazis. But this proved to be an impossibly large task for the Allies, who were overstretched and struggling to feed and house the huge numbers of people under their control. Attempts to rebuild the shattered country were frustrated by shortages and by the Soviet seizure of assets and machinery in the east of the country. Life in Allied-occupied Germany was bleak and harsh, particularly in the Soviet zone. Severe food shortages left many close to starvation, forcing them to sell their possessions or their bodies for food, or to buy it illegally.

These straitened circumstances were to be found across Europe, which, as well as suffering from material insufficiency and physical devastation, was heavily affected by the fallout from the years of oppression and murder wrought by German occupation. As a result, the violence and chaos that had been unleashed during the war did not end in 1945. For years afterwards, Europe was a volatile continent in which racial and national tensions, political instability and vengeful reprisals resulted in thousands more deaths. The racially motivated violence perpetrated during the war, particularly in Eastern Europe by Nazi Germany and its allies, spilled over into its aftermath. Despite all they had endured, Jews continued to be the targets of antisemitic violence, such as the pogrom at Kielce in Poland in July 1946, in which forty-two Jews were killed. Thousands died in the fight over ethnic nationalism between Ukraine and Poland. Greece descended into a viciously fought civil war in which government and communist forces vied for control. Germany was despised for having started the war. In many countries recently liberated from German rule, Germans and German-speaking people were marked with swastikas, driven from their homes, and even killed. In a policy that had been approved by the three Allied leaders – Winston Churchill, Joseph Stalin and Harry S. Truman – at their conference at Potsdam, Germany, in the summer of 1945, around 12 million 'ethnic Germans' were expelled from Eastern Europe into an already over-crowded Germany. They joined the columns of lost people, displaced by war, who trudged along Europe's broken roads. Millions of children lost their parents and their homes. Many were looked after in displaced-persons camps, and a lost-children campaign in East Germany helped thousands find their families. People took revenge against collaborators, traitors and enemies. Women who had been in relationships with German occupying troops were publicly shamed and shunned. In concentration camps, former prisoners attacked the SS guards. A wave of vengeful killing swept through such countries as Italy and Yugoslavia, where opposing factions had clashed while the war was still being fought. Crime levels soared owing to severe shortages of food and other goods and the breakdown in law and order. Theft and looting were widespread, particularly among those who had been displaced or who had been liberated from concentration or forced-labour camps. Europe's cities were in ruins. In Berlin, people could sunbathe in their bomb-hit homes while *Trümmerfrauen* (rubble women) – and even elephants – cleared up the damage. The destruction of transport links, agriculture and industry meant that economic renewal was of paramount importance. Slowly but surely, and with financial aid from the United States under the Marshall Plan, reconstruction took place and countries got back to work again.

DISPLACED PEOPLE

More people were displaced during and after the war than at any other time in human history. Around 40 million people in Europe had been forced from their homes. Up to 100 million Chinese people were displaced, while 6.5 million Japanese people were scattered across Asia and the Pacific. The overstretched Allied occupying forces struggled to help those who wanted to go home.

Among them were refugees, forced labourers, prisoners of war, emigrants, concentration-camp prisoners and victims of deportation. Huge numbers ended up in displaced-persons camps.

ABOVE A Russian couple arrives at the displaced-persons (DP) camp at Hamburg Zoo. During the war, the camp had housed the forced labourers who worked in a nearby factory. The camp was taken over by the British on 5 May 1945 and quickly became an arrivals centre for some of the huge numbers of displaced persons in Germany. Some people were stuck in DP camps for years. Many made their own way back over miles of ruined roads. Some, including Europe's Jews, felt they could no longer return home for fear of further persecution.

The Impact of Total War

THE SECOND WORLD WAR CAUSED DEATH AND DESTRUCTION ON AN UNPRECEDENTED SCALE

The human and material cost of the war is almost beyond measure. In addition to an enormous death toll, the conflict resulted in the destruction of cities and the displacement of millions.

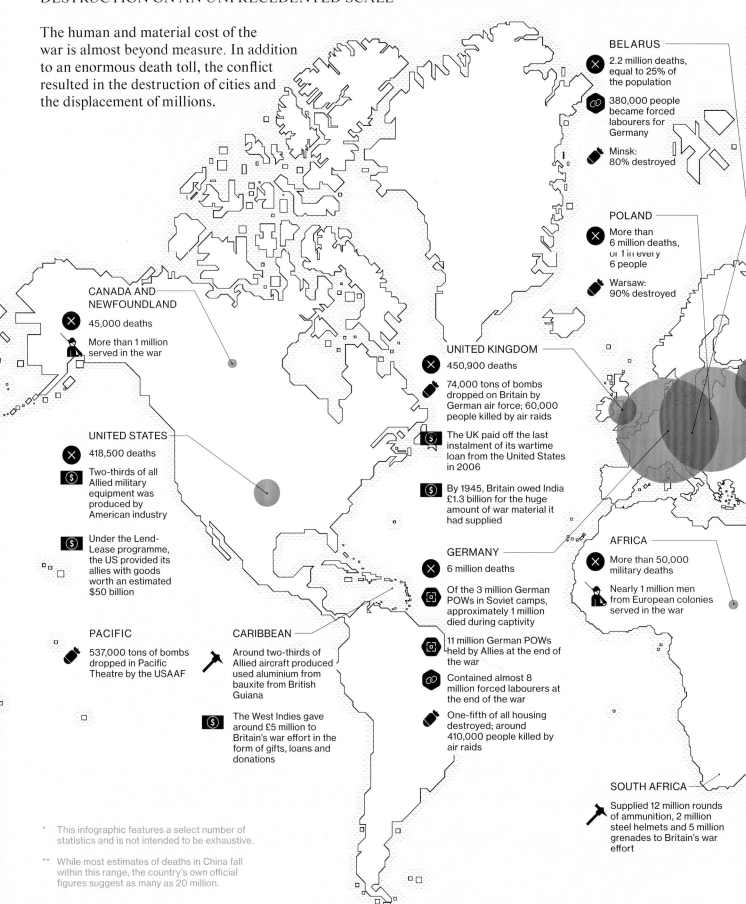

BELARUS
- ✕ 2.2 million deaths, equal to 25% of the population
- ∞ 380,000 people became forced labourers for Germany
- Minsk: 80% destroyed

POLAND
- ✕ More than 6 million deaths, or 1 in every 6 people
- Warsaw: 90% destroyed

CANADA AND NEWFOUNDLAND
- ✕ 45,000 deaths
- More than 1 million served in the war

UNITED KINGDOM
- ✕ 450,900 deaths
- 74,000 tons of bombs dropped on Britain by German air force; 60,000 people killed by air raids
- $ The UK paid off the last instalment of its wartime loan from the United States in 2006
- $ By 1945, Britain owed India £1.3 billion for the huge amount of war material it had supplied

UNITED STATES
- ✕ 418,500 deaths
- $ Two-thirds of all Allied military equipment was produced by American industry
- $ Under the Lend-Lease programme, the US provided its allies with goods worth an estimated $50 billion

AFRICA
- ✕ More than 50,000 military deaths
- Nearly 1 million men from European colonies served in the war

GERMANY
- ✕ 6 million deaths
- ☐ Of the 3 million German POWs in Soviet camps, approximately 1 million died during captivity
- ☐ 11 million German POWs held by Allies at the end of the war
- ∞ Contained almost 8 million forced labourers at the end of the war
- One-fifth of all housing destroyed; around 410,000 people killed by air raids

PACIFIC
- 537,000 tons of bombs dropped in Pacific Theatre by the USAAF

CARIBBEAN
- Around two-thirds of Allied aircraft produced used aluminium from bauxite from British Guiana
- $ The West Indies gave around £5 million to Britain's war effort in the form of gifts, loans and donations

SOUTH AFRICA
- Supplied 12 million rounds of ammunition, 2 million steel helmets and 5 million grenades to Britain's war effort

* This infographic features a select number of statistics and is not intended to be exhaustive.

** While most estimates of deaths in China fall within this range, the country's own official figures suggest as many as 20 million.

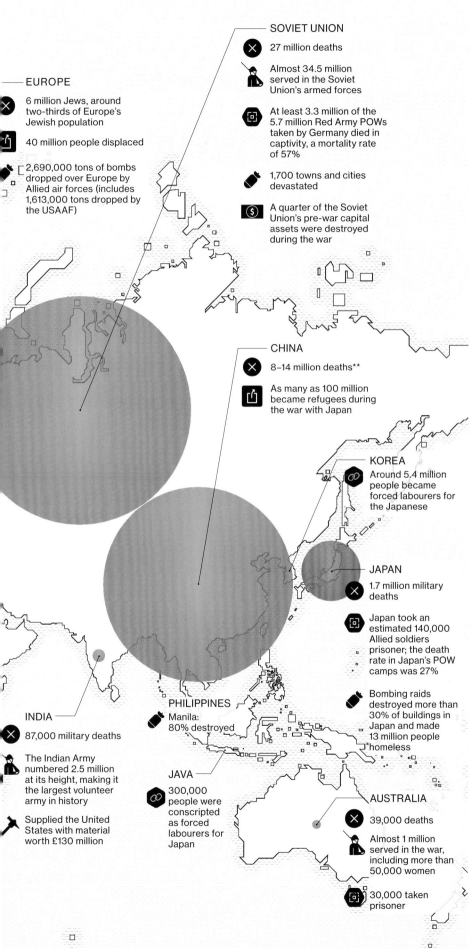

EUROPE

❌ 6 million Jews, around two-thirds of Europe's Jewish population

⬆ 40 million people displaced

💣 2,690,000 tons of bombs dropped over Europe by Allied air forces (includes 1,613,000 tons dropped by the USAAF)

SOVIET UNION

❌ 27 million deaths

👤 Almost 34.5 million served in the Soviet Union's armed forces

🔩 At least 3.3 million of the 5.7 million Red Army POWs taken by Germany died in captivity, a mortality rate of 57%

💣 1,700 towns and cities devastated

💲 A quarter of the Soviet Union's pre-war capital assets were destroyed during the war

CHINA

❌ 8–14 million deaths**

⬆ As many as 100 million became refugees during the war with Japan

KOREA

∞ Around 5.4 million people became forced labourers for the Japanese

JAPAN

❌ 1.7 million military deaths

🔩 Japan took an estimated 140,000 Allied soldiers prisoner; the death rate in Japan's POW camps was 27%

💣 Bombing raids destroyed more than 30% of buildings in Japan and made 13 million people homeless

INDIA

❌ 87,000 military deaths

👤 The Indian Army numbered 2.5 million at its height, making it the largest volunteer army in history

🔨 Supplied the United States with material worth £130 million

PHILIPPINES

💣 Manila: 80% destroyed

JAVA

∞ 300,000 people were conscripted as forced labourers for Japan

AUSTRALIA

❌ 39,000 deaths

👤 Almost 1 million served in the war, including more than 50,000 women

🔩 30,000 taken prisoner

HUMAN COST

An estimated 60 million people died in total, an average of 1 every 5 seconds between 1939 and 1945.

Post-war efforts to arrive at accurate figures for the number of casualties caused by the conflict faced huge logistical challenges. As a result, figures differ widely between sources and, for most countries, are estimates of varying reliability. Yet even the more conservative estimates are a clear reminder of the enormous impact of the war on human life.

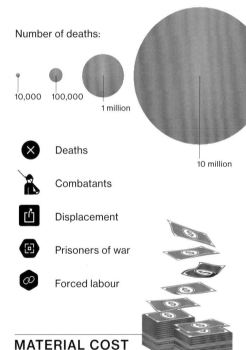

Number of deaths:

10,000   100,000   1 million   10 million

❌ Deaths

👤 Combatants

⬆ Displacement

🔩 Prisoners of war

∞ Forced labour

MATERIAL COST

Estimated total cost of the war in 1945: $1.075 trillion.

While the estimated monetary cost to governments involved in the war is huge, it cannot fully account for the damage caused by the conflict – to people, economies and infrastructure.

🔨 Resources

💣 Destruction and bombing

💲 Financial cost

The Legacy of Total War

The all-encompassing nature of the total war that had engulfed the world from the late 1930s until 1945 ensured that it had a lasting impact on the decades that followed. It gave rise to new ideas, movements, divisions and conflicts that cast long shadows over people's lives. After their wartime sacrifice, many people across the world hoped for a better future and sought to reject the forms of ultra-nationalism and expansionism that had been at the root of much of the fighting. New international organizations, including the United Nations (see below), promised an end to war and greater global collaboration. Meanwhile, having watched the decline of the imperial powers during the war, nationalists throughout Asia and Africa fought for independence from European empires. Perhaps the greatest legacy of the war was the onset of a new, mostly political conflict soon afterwards. After Germany's defeat, the lack of a common enemy in Europe meant that the innate differences between the Grand Alliance were laid bare. Before long, two politically opposed superpowers – the United States and the Soviet Union – emerged. Soviet domination of Eastern Europe and new communist regimes in Asia divided the world into 'East' and 'West'. By 1949, the Cold War had begun.

In response to the magnitude of human suffering and physical destruction that the war had precipitated, a number of international organizations emerged in its wake to foster closer global alliances, keep the peace and support greater financial stability. The United Nations (UN) was created

German women who have been put to work by the Russian occupying forces clear debris and salvage building materials from bomb-damaged buildings in Berlin, July 1945. Elephants from local zoos were also sometimes used to clear the broken ruins of German cities.

This 1943 poster shows the flags of the many countries that joined the United Nations (UN) fighting together. This cooperation continued after victory but there were soon disagreements within the UN, reflecting growing tensions between the Soviet Union and the United States.

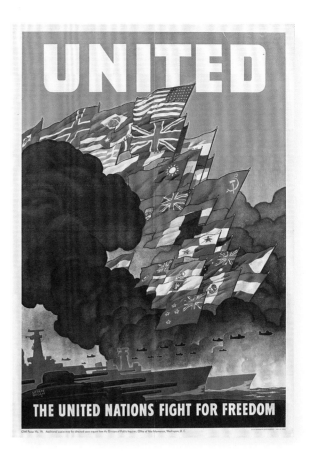

while the war was still being fought. Its founding charter stated that its members were 'determined to save succeeding generations from the scourge of war'. Continuing the spirit of wartime solidarity, UN representatives from fifty countries first met in 1945. Their goal was to make a better world and to preserve the peace that so many had died for. But there were soon disagreements within the organization, reflecting the growing tensions between the Soviet Union and America. The UN, as mentioned earlier, ran the UNRRA, which delivered much-needed food, clothing and medical care to victims of war around the world. The UNRRA also ran camps for some of the millions of people who had been displaced by war. In addition to the UN, the International Monetary Fund (IMF) was founded in 1944 and the World Bank began operating in 1946. The IMF sought to achieve greater monetary cooperation between nations, while the World Bank assisted in the post-war reconstruction of Western Europe.

For many, the physical and psychological effects of the war were far-reaching. Both combatants and civilians were affected by their hugely traumatic experiences, and millions of people were wounded. Owing to the nature of total war, civilians were harmed in vast numbers, either through bombing or as a result of being caught up in the fighting. The impact of the conflict on mental health was impossible to measure, particularly as many people found it difficult to discuss what they had been through. Many were haunted by the widespread violence they had witnessed, suffered from – or carried out. In Britain alone, there were 300,000 disabled ex-servicemen and -women, 600 of whom had been left paralysed. Many of them were treated by Dr Ludwig Guttmann at Stoke Mandeville Hospital in Buckinghamshire.

KATY GARBUTT

Katy wore this gold dress when she married Len Davies in August 1948. The couple had met on their first day at Durham University, two years previously. Like thousands of others in Britain, they both received grants for their university places under a government scheme for ex-servicemen and -women. During the war, Katy had served in the Women's Royal Naval Reserve and Len had been an RAF pilot. Their war service opened up greater opportunities in post-war Britain than they had had before.

Members of the Haganah, a Jewish paramilitary group active in British-controlled Palestine after the war.

Guttmann's pioneering treatments helped his patients to live as fully as possible. He believed that sport was a major method of therapy and organized the first Stoke Mandeville Games for disabled people in 1948. These later became the Paralympic Games.

For Britain, victory came at a cost. Waging the war had stretched the country's finances to their limits. Moreover, the fundamental shifts in people's attitudes and expectations that had occurred during and because of the conflict – both within Britain itself and throughout its empire – shaped British society and the UK's global standing in the post-war era. While the war was still being fought, Britain's coalition government realized that it had to offer a better future to a nation made weary through sacrifice and hardship. It promised post-war welfare reforms that would encompass better schooling, a universal benefits system and a national health service that would provide free medical care for all. Many of these ideas were based on the Beveridge Report. Published in 1942, the report set out ways in which the government could improve people's lives under a 'welfare state'. The delivery of these promises became a major issue during the bitterly fought general election of July 1945. The Conservative Party emphasized Churchill's wartime leadership, while Churchill himself shocked voters by suggesting that Labour's socialist policies would need 'some kind of Gestapo' to be implemented. The Labour Party, with its radical programme of public ownership and welfare reform, won a landslide victory. The heavy defeat of the staunch wartime prime minister Winston Churchill surprised many. But he had not kept pace with the public mood. Labour's campaign was more in tune with

RAMINDER PARKASH SINGH

When Raminder married the Indian war hero Parkash in April 1947, they both held this bright *palla* (headscarf). Just four months later, they had to flee their home when India was partitioned. As Sikhs, they left the newly created Islamic country of Pakistan to avoid religious violence.

Raminder and Parkash barely escaped with their lives, witnessing the bloodshed as millions of people of different religions crossed the new border. They migrated eastwards to a new farm, arriving with this tawa cooking pan and very few other possessions. At their new farmhouse, they found a stone plaque engraved with the name of the Islamic family who had lived there previously, and who had been forced to leave and move westwards to Pakistan. It took several months before they were reunited with other family members who had managed to get across the new border.

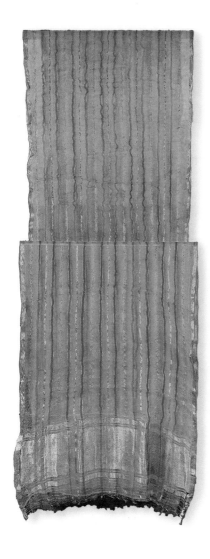

public feeling, promising a fairer Britain under Clement Attlee. In July 1948, the National Health Service came into being. It was created by Attlee's minister of health, Aneurin Bevan, and transformed the lives of millions of people with its provision of free healthcare.

Along with other European colonial powers, Britain found that its prestige had been damaged by its enemies' wartime occupation of its overseas territories. This hampered its ability to retain control of its empire in the post-war years, particularly in a world that was hostile to the types of conquest and exploitation that had been so strongly in evidence during the war. In the decades that followed, Britain lost much of its imperial holdings as people across its empire, who had fought and worked for Britain, claimed their independence. The United States was opposed to the old, colonial world order and supported the rights of countries to self-determination, even as Britain, France and the Netherlands tried to retain, or reclaim, their empires. The French reoccupied Indochina, while the Dutch regained the East Indies, but both nations eventually had to give up their control of these colonies.

In 1947, following decades of pressure and campaigning, India gained independence from Britain. However, as part of the transition to independent rule, and in response to calls from Indian Muslims for a homeland, the British partitioned the vast country along religious lines into separate states: India and Pakistan (today the Islamic Republic of Pakistan, and Bangladesh). This decision caused widespread chaos and religious violence when it came into effect on 14–15 August 1947. In total, an estimated 14 million people were displaced, and as many as 2 million killed, in the bloodshed that accompanied the movement of vast numbers of people of different religions across the new border. Anti-British uprisings undermined British rule in other parts of the world, including Palestine and Malaya. After the war, many Jewish survivors of Nazi persecution hoped to emigrate to British-controlled Palestine. However, fearing renewed Arab–Jewish violence and wary of Palestinian Arab opposition, Britain enforced tight pre-war immigration limits. Some Palestinian Jews turned to armed resistance, and fighting soon broke out between Arabs and Jews. Amid worsening violence, Britain withdrew from Palestine in 1948.

The Western powers were largely unable to stop the spread of communism that had gained ground in parts of Asia in the war's aftermath. In Vietnam, part of French Indochina, the communist leader Ho Chi Minh declared independence from France in the north; the French, however, continued to rule in the south. The struggle for control in Vietnam would last for decades. Korea had been under Japanese rule since 1910, but this came to an end with the Japanese surrender in 1945. Afterwards, the country was divided, with the north joining the communist bloc. In 1950 the two halves went to war in the first military action of the Cold War. After the four years of civil war in China that had followed the surrender of Japan, the communist People's Republic was formed in 1949. By the end of the bitterly fought war, the communist People's Liberation Army had defeated Chiang Kai-shek's Nationalist Party forces. The United States had supported the nationalist forces during the war, but in the end communism prevailed. China's new communist leader, Mao Zedong, marked the start of the new republic in Beijing on 1 October 1949. China's people now looked to Mao for stability, although the years that followed were turbulent and often violent.

Communism also took an increasing hold in parts of Europe in the post-war era. 'From Stettin in the Baltic to Trieste in the Adriatic, an iron curtain has descended across the continent.' This famous phrase, from

Winston Churchill's speech to Westminster College in Fulton, Missouri, on 5 March 1946, gave rise to the term 'Iron Curtain' as a description of the post-war divide across Europe. Decades of Soviet domination of Eastern Europe began in the closing stages of the fighting. As the Red Army surged towards Berlin, clearing territories of German occupying forces, Moscow took advantage of the power vacuum and seized control. Communists gradually gained power in multiple countries, through a range of means that included fixed elections, coercion and physical force, while the Western powers protested ineffectually. For years, people fought this onslaught. Armed resistance movements, in Lithuania, Estonia, Latvia, Poland, Ukraine and elsewhere, were eventually crushed by the all-powerful Soviet Union. Huge numbers of people took part in the anti-Soviet resistance, including an estimated 400,000 in western Ukraine and 100,000 in Lithuania. At great personal risk, they left their homes to live in hiding, often in forests. The resistance fighters battled the Red Army, attacked Soviet officials and killed communist leaders. Despite their defiance, they were too few in number to have any real effect and were vastly outnumbered by the Soviets, who used torture, deportation, forced collectivization, infiltration and murder to break them. The exact number of resistance fighters who were killed is unknown, but they were gradually wiped out until no real opposition was left.

Meanwhile, the spread of communism was exposing the pre-existing fault lines within the alliance that had formed to defeat Nazi Germany. In addition to each occupying a zone of Germany in 1945, the Allied nations of Britain, the Soviet Union, the United States and France had occupied a section of its capital, Berlin, which lay within the Soviet zone. Berlin became a focal point for the growing tensions between the great powers. These tensions came to a head in 1948, when the Soviets cut off land access to West Berlin, which was the only way those who lived there could receive supplies. The Western Allies organized flights carrying food, fuel and provisions to the desperate citizens. The airlift operation ran so successfully that, after nearly a year, the Soviets were forced to lift their blockade, thereby ending the first major confrontation of the Cold War between East and West.

At the Allied conference at Potsdam in July 1945, America's new president, Harry S. Truman, had said to Stalin: 'We have a new weapon of special destructive force.' He was referring to the atomic bombs that the United States had developed, and which it subsequently dropped on Japan the following month. Stalin did not react to Truman's enigmatic statement; his spies had already provided him with information on America's nuclear programme. Privately, however, he called for the Soviet Union to develop atomic weapons of its own. On 29 August 1949, at Semipalatinsk, Kazakhstan, the USSR successfully tested its first atomic weapon. Within days, America had learned of what the Soviets had achieved. It stepped up its nuclear programme and began work on a more destructive, hydrogen 'superbomb'. In the decades that followed, the rival superpowers brought the world to the brink of nuclear war in their race for supremacy. As they entered the 'atomic age', people across the world soon lived in fear of nuclear apocalypse. They had survived the horrors of total war, but were now under threat from an entirely new type of warfare in the Cold War era.

List of Quotations

Further Reading

General Histories

IAN KERSHAW
To Hell and Back: Europe 1914–1949 (2015)
RICHARD OVERY
Why the Allies Won (1996)
GERHARD WEINBERG
A World at Arms (1994)

Context

PIERS BRENDON
*The Dark Valley: A Panorama
of the 1930s* (2000)
MICHAEL BURLEIGH
The Third Reich (2000)
IAN BURUMA
Year Zero: A History of 1945 (2013)
JONATHAN FENBY
*Alliance: The Inside Story of How Roosevelt,
Stalin and Churchill Won One War and
Began Another* (2007)
KEITH LOWE
*Savage Continent: Europe in the
Aftermath of World War II* (2012)
RICHARD OVERY
The Dictators (2004)
DAVID REYNOLDS
*The Long Shadow: The Great War
and the Twentieth Century* (2014)

Theatres and Campaigns

JOHN BUCKLEY
*Monty's Men: The British Army and
the Liberation of Europe* (2014)
DAVID GLANTZ & JONATHAN HOUSE
*When Titans Clashed: How the
Red Army stopped Hitler* (2015)
RICHARD OVERY
The Battle of Britain (2010)
The Bombing War: Europe, 1939–1945 (2013)
MARC MILNER
The Battle of the Atlantic (2003)
RANA MITTER
*China's War with Japan, 1937–1945:
The Struggle for Survival* (2013)
RONALD SPECTOR
*Eagle Against the Sun: The American War
with Japan* (1984)

British Empire

ASHLEY JACKSON
*The British Empire and the Second
World War* (2006)
YASMIN KHAN
*The Raj at War: A People's History
of India's Second World War* (2015)
DANIEL TODMAN
Britain's War: Into Battle, 1937–1941 (2016)
Britain's War: A New World, 1942–1947 (2020)

Holocaust and Occupation

CHRISTOPHER BROWNING
The Origins of the Final Solution (2004)
DAVID CESARANI
Final Solution (2016)
MARK MAZOWER
*Hitler's Empire: Nazi Rule in Occupied
Europe* (2008)
TIMOTHY SNYDER
Bloodlands (2010)
YUKI TANAKA
*Hidden Horrors: Japanese War
Crimes in World War II* (2017)

Acknowledgments

This book is based on the content of IWM London's Second World War Galleries, and on the research conducted by the authors in their roles as members of IWM London's Second World War project team.

The historical content of the galleries – and, by extension, of this book – evolved in consultation with the following advisory board:

SIR HEW STRACHAN
   University of St Andrews (Chair)
TERRY CHARMAN
   Imperial War Museums
PROFESSOR YASMIN KHAN
   Kellogg College, Oxford
PROFESSOR LUCY NOAKES
   University of Essex
PROFESSOR DAVID OLUSOGA
   University of Manchester
PROFESSOR RICHARD OVERY
   University of Exeter
PROFESSOR DAVID REYNOLDS
   Christ's College Cambridge
PROFESSOR DANIEL TODMAN
   Queen Mary University of London

IWM would like to thank those who have kindly provided their advice and assistance, including Professor Rana Mitter, Yukako Ibuki, Dr Diya Gupta, Keith Lowe and Margaret MacMillan.

We would also like to thank those people, and their families, whose objects, images and stories appear in the galleries and this book, as well as the museums and archives that have helped us to tell their stories.

Further thanks are due to Nigel Steel, Anna Ravenscroft, Laura Boon, Madeleine Brady and the curators of the museum's Narrative and Content Department. Finally, thanks to Madeleine James of IWM Publishing.

Picture Credits

All images © IWM unless otherwise stated. The publishers will be glad to correct in future editions any error or omission brought to their attention.

r = right; l = left; t = top; b = bottom; c = centre

Front cover: © IWM B 6794; back cover: © IWM SE 1884; frontispiece: NYF 58682; 8: EA 49925; 11: HU 55639; 12: AUS 1726; 14: HU 53134; 16: CHN 198; 17: UNI 16119; 20: HU 53134; 21: LBY K. 06/1794-1; 22: t UNI 12794, © the rights holder, b HU 41086; 23: Art.IWM ART 15205; 24: t HU 82609, b Art.IWM ART LD 5975; 25: Art.IWM ART LD 6217; 26: t INS 7901, b INS 7906; 27: t LBY 79/52, b MH 11040; 28: t HU 23732, b Art.IWM PST 4105; 32: EPH 1784; 33: t © the rights holder EPH 4776, b Documents.4998/A; 34: EPH 4731; 35: t EPH 3922, b EPH 11668; 36: Documents.9756/G & H © Celia Jane Lee; 35: Documents.26371/AAA & ZZ © Peter & Lesley Urbach; 38: t Documents.20478/D © The Nathan Marsh Pusey Library, b Documents.20478/C © Harriet Crawley; 39 B33; NYP 68075; 43: HU 105680; 44: t, F 3085, b EPH 9751; 47: t EPH 8980, c C 1564. b FIR 9120; 48: HU 5547; 49: t HU 103752, b MUN 39; 50: HU 65336; 51: t EPH 10659, b HU 55639; 52: UNI 13661; 53: t Art.IWM ART LD 232, b UNI 16099; 54-5: RML 257; 56: NYP 68075; 57: t Documents.14398/A, b Documents.14398/C both courtesy of Kelvin Osborne; 58: MAR 556; 59: Art.IWM ART LD 1285; 60: LBY E.J. 5815-1; 61: HU 3266; 62: 9608-01; 63: t LBY E. 47146-1 courtesy Mirrorpix/Reach Licensing, b Art.IWM PST 6421; 64: HU 36162; 66: t A 4815, b Jacques Voyer courtesy Voyer-Vincent Family; 67: t Art.IWM ART LD 2322, b Art.IWM PST 0033; 68: t Art.IWM PST 3158, b CF 166, 69: t SAF 205, bl Art.IWM PST 16290, br Art.IWM PST 15826; 72: t Documents.1071/I, b Art.IWM PST 13879; 73: t George Roberts courtesy Samantha Harding, b Art.IWM PST 13888; 74: Art.IWM PST 14617; 76: t INS 4731, b H 1917; 77: Documents.11929/J; 78: CH 2477; 79: t Art.IWM ART LD 1550, b CH 1533; 80: t UNI 3766, b © the rights holder MOD 597, 81: t CH1550, c OMD 4263, © the rights holder Documents.17351/A, b UNI 13724; 81: t MOD 394, b HU 63827A; 83: Documents.506/C; 84: t D 1516, b EPH 10929; 85: t HU 36162, b MUN 2447; 86: D 2593; 87: Art.IWM PST 3095; 88: t © Estate of Dorothy Davies, b EPH 10662, 89: t © Estate of John Sadler, b EPH 10895; 90: t Art.IWM PST 2893, b D 77; 91: t EPH 4611, b EPH 3195; 92: t LBY K.15/333, b CH 10739; 93: COM 150; 94: © the rights holder (Documents.12716/C); 95: t Art.IWM PST 16883, b WEA 4117; 96: COM 228.1; 97: D 8799; 98: t Documents.12547/G, b Art.IWM PST 6078; 99: t Documents.6503, b Art.IWM PST 2832; 100: t D 8598, b H 36315; 102: CH 8368, 103: 613495892 via Getty images; 104: t © Estate of Louie White, b Art.IWM PST 3645, 105: © Estate of Eva Albu, b Art.IWM PST 8286; 106: t HU 53753, b Art.IWM PST 3096; 107: t 3267608 'Lady Flyer'/Fox Photos via Getty images, b D 21237; 108: t EPH 3545, bl EPH 3546, br © PDSA; 109: t Documents.26385/A, b EQU 15028; 110: K325; 113: FEQ 374; 114: t INS 9785, c INS 8040, INS 28055, INS 8042, bl INS 50705, br INS 50752; 115: t K 325, b E 2182; 116: t E 6135, bl EPH 9799; 117 t E 3285, b Art.IWM ART LD 3518; 118: EPH 2963; 119: ORD 134; 120: t E 15905, b CM 2079; 121: Art.IWM ART LD 3400; 122: BArch RW 19/7388; 123: COL 338; 124: t COL 337, bl COL 173, br COL 341; 125: t UNI 12917, b RUS 1964; 126: t UNI 11104, b HU 130942; 127: HU 86369; 128: HU 89821; 129: Documents.816/B; 130: t HU 86087, bl Documents.26543/F, br Documents.12382/E; 132: t 2629222 'Lost Homes'/Three Lions via Getty images, b Flying Tigers © Estate of Ron Smith; 133: t 514679206 'Madame Chiang Kai-Shek'/Bettmann via Getty images; 135: HU 2783; 138: 295977 courtesy US National Archives at San Francisco; 139: MAR 1281; 140: Documents.11712/A; 141: t FLA 2449b, b HU 2781; 142: KF 102; 143: NYP 60749; 144: t ART23175, b 026851 images courtesy Australian War Memorial; 145: AWM2017.1129.3.1 image courtesy Australian War Memorial; 146: t NY 6397, b image of Shelagh Brown courtesy the daughter of Shelagh Lee (nee Brown); 147: EPH 500; 148: t EPH 1218, b Documents.19584/A; 149 t HU 4659, b EPH 800; 150: Art.IWM PST 8104; 151: CH 16145; 152: Art.IWM ART LD 3055; 153: MUN 3439; 154: HU 140127 & 8; 155: A 21988; 156: t UNI 16062, b UNI 12903; 157: EQU 4412; 158: t HU 40239, b HU 74975; 160: HU 6278; 161: Art.IWM PST 6431; 162: t EPH 9823, b JAR 1230; 163: K 7108; 164: NYP 55903; 165: t Art.IWM ART LD 5620, b KF 199; 166: WEA 892.1, WEA 892.2; 168: © the rights holder Art.IWM PST 8220; 169: E 26615; 170: t A 20689, b AE1067.13; 171: t ACQ1/EXH/L/107, tr UNI 13594, c UNI 13597, b EPH 10030; 173: t H 16020, c COM 933.1, b Art.IWM ART LD 1922; 174: HU 39146; 177: TR 1127; 178: t RRMA78 INTERFOTO/Alamy Stock Photo, b EPH 2961; 179: AIR 436; 180: HU 25782; 181: t EPH 4623, b TR 11; 182: t AE 6145 © the Estate of Billy Strachan, c EQU 15153, b EQU 15154; 183: AIR 35; 184: UNI 12132; 185: D 14124; 186: t SUP 81.1 Courtesy of Vernon Gayle Alexander, b Documents.25800/E; 187: t © the Estate of John White, b UNI 12565; 188: t HU 12143, b Art.IWM PST 3708; 189: t MH 24762, c UNI 12871, b UNI 12872; 191: t FIR 6448, c FIR 6118, b FIR 8577; 192: Art.IWM PST 6150; 193: INS 7087.1, INS 7087.2; 194: LBY K. 173; 195: Art.IWM PST 9274; 196: t INS 8026, b E 19024; 197: HU 39146; 198: t Documents.19686/A © the rights holder, b INS 51348; 201: 201: t UNI 7006, bl MUN 4715 Loaned by the Buchenwald Memorial Collection, br MUN 4718; 204: Documents.26371/F; 205: t HU 90295, bl Art.IWM ART 17130 1, 2 & 3 © the rights holder; 206: NYP 36236; 207: tl TXL 52, tr TXL 54, bl TXL 58, br TXL 67; 208: t MH 12868; 209: t FIR 8574, c FIR 6440, b LBY K Aerial 3802; 211: t 0811181202272 Associated Press, b photo no. 127-GR-113-83266 Courtesy US National Archives; 212: t 441020075 AP Photo/US Army/Shutterstock, b FIR 6162; 213: t WEA 759.1, b FLA 925; 214: NYF 58682; 215: tl Documents.27314, tr UNI 16196, bl Courtesy National Museum of the Marine Corps, br FIR 9430; 216: t RB64PJ Photo 12/Alamy Stock Photo, b Yang Zirong © IWM; 217: t EPH 5425, b 3309788 Battle Of Changteh/Keystone via Getty Images; 218: t, c images courtesy Koichi Uehara, r MOD 849; 219: t (detail) & c photo no. 111-SC-230147 Courtesy US National Archives; 220: K 8631; 221: Art.IWM PST 15379; 222: t INS 4123, c INS 4165, b INS 4929; 223: t SE 3071, b K 9320; 224: t IND 2292 c EQU 15035, r INS 43124; 226: t IWM 22852, b INS 4015; 227: Chittoprasad Bhattacharya images © IWM; 228: INS 24311; 229: Art.IWM PST 3324; 230: NA 12895; 231: t Documents.228472, c INS 302366; 233: NA 22066; 234: t & c 6814.1.2, EPH 11502; 235: Art.IWM ART LD 4587; 236: HU 28594; 237: r ACQ1/EXH/P/181, b EPH 10995; 238: A 23938; 240: t Documents.27224/A, cr UNI 16144, cl UNI 16145, b EQU 15047; 241: t Documents.17931/A, c EPH 10369, b Documents.17931/B; 242: B 7520; 243: t B 7928, b ORD 170; 244: TR 2371; 246: l UNI 3380, r EA 37782; 247: UNI 13133; 248: t HU 140472, b UNI 6169; 249: EA 59880; 250: CL 3214; 252: EA 60386; 253: t Documents.1164/E, b EPH 2576; 254: t FEQ 379, b Documents.10800/B; 255: Documents.5000; 256: EPH 1460; 257 t image x24299 © National Portrait Gallery London, b Art.IWM ART LD 5468; 258: MH 29427; 259: HU 57914; 260: tl B949MT SPUTNIK/Alamy Stock Photo, c image courtesy the estate of Raisuke Shirabi, b HU 140468; 262: t C1.S1.TI, c EPH 11495 & EPH 11493 courtesy of Allan Charles Wilmot; 263: Art.IWM ART LD 5798; 264: SE 6985; 265: EPH 6354; 267: BU 6669; 270: CL 3214; 271: Art.IWM PST 0660; 272: t 8246.2 courtesy Janet Felce, c UNI 16064; 273: © the rights holder HU 54573; 274: t 8313.1.1, cl EPH 11579 courtesy the family of Major Parkash Singh VC and Mrs Raminder Parkash Singh, cr EPH 11578; 277: HU 73010.

Index

Page numbers in *italic*
refer to the illustrations
and their captions

First published in the United Kingdom in 2021 by Thames & Hudson Ltd, 181A High Holborn, London WC1V 7QX

British Library Cataloguing-in-Publication Data
A catalogue record for this book is available from the British Library

ISBN 978-0-500-25248-2

Printed and bound in Italy by Printer Trento SrL

Be the first to know about our new releases, exclusive content and author events by visiting
thamesandhudson.com
thamesandhudsonusa.com
thamesandhudson.com.au

Kate Clements has worked at Imperial War Museums since 2006. She has undertaken curatorial and interpretation work on a number of exhibitions at IWM London, including the Lord Ashcroft Gallery display of Victoria Cross and George Cross awards. She has also delivered a range of historical digital content, including a popular podcast series based on IWM sound recordings for the First World War centenary, as well as online articles covering subjects within the museum's remit. She is currently a curator for the new Second World War Galleries at IWM London.

Paul Cornish has worked at Imperial War Museums since 1989. He is IWM's firearms specialist, and the author of *Machine Guns and the Great War* (2009) and *The First World War Galleries* (2014), the latter published by IWM. He has also edited and contributed to a number of academic publications relating to the material culture of conflict. Between 2010 and 2014 he worked as Senior Curator on the First World War Galleries project, a role he is currently reprising as part of the team creating IWM's new Second World War Galleries.

Vikki Hawkins has been a curator at Imperial War Museums since 2016. She previously helped to deliver *Wounded: Conflict, Casualties and Care,* an exhibition at the Science Museum, London, which drew on First World War medical collections. In her current role creating IWM's new Second World War Galleries, Vikki has published and contributed to various conferences on the topic of displaying marginalized histories in museums, and is currently developing a research project on the material culture of sexual violence in conflict.

Front cover
A British soldier helps a woman in Caen after its liberation, July 1944. The French city was badly hit during the Normandy Campaign, with heavy civilian casualties.

Back cover
Troops of the 11th East African Division on the road to Kalewa, Burma, January 1945.

Frontispiece
US Marines unload supplies from landing craft at Iwo Jima, 1945 (see also page 214).